A *New York Times* Notable Book
An NPR Best Book of 2013
One of *New York Magazine*'s 10 Best Books of the Year
A *Chicago Tribune* Noteworthy Best Book of 2013
Boston Globe Top Nonfiction of 2013
A *Publishers Weekly* Best Book of 2013

Praise for

TO THE END OF JUNE

"Informative, poignant, passionate, and persuasive, *To The End of June* is almost certain . . . to generate a sense of urgency in readers to fix a broken system that has sometimes managed to fly beneath the radar." — *Huffington Post*

"Beam, a foster parent herself, delivers an engaging, narrative-driven investigation that centers on one of the system's most divisive questions: Does separating children from their birth parents do more harm than good?"
— **NPR.org**

"A triumph of narrative reporting and storytelling, as well as a thorough and nuanced analysis of an American institution deeply in need of reform . . . Beam gives [foster children] a much-needed voice and does what too many adults in the foster-care system can't, or won't: She advocates for them."
— *New York Times Book Review*

"With her many lenses on [foster care] . . . Beam invites the reader inside the system for sometimes uncomfortably close but always compassionate visits with parents, children and workers." — *Chicago Tribune*

"Beam offers historical background and keen analysis of the social, political, racial, and economic factors that drive foster-care policies ... A very moving, powerful look at a system charged with caring for nearly half a million children across the U.S." — *Booklist*, starred review

"An engrossing, well-researched examination of important social issues."
— *Kirkus Reviews*

"In this compassionate, rigorous book, Cris Beam describes the failures of foster care, often by way of the moments of light and hope that are inscribed in its brokenness. It is her largeness of heart, manifest on every page, that makes her arguments impossible to ignore, and that informs the deeply engaging stories she so eloquently narrates."
— Andrew Solomon, National Book Award–winning author of *The Noonday Demon* and *Far from the Tree*

"Packed with messy humanity, *To the End of June* is an urgent and necessary book. It would break your heart were it not for the recurring tales of good people trying to do the right thing, and an undercurrent of rage at what life has served up these kids. Cris Beam brings careful listening, unflinching poise, and her own experience as a foster mother to this account of how the state tries to step up when parents can't."
— Ted Conover, author of Pulitzer-finalist *Newjack* and *Coyotes*

"*To the End of June* is a clear-eyed and heartfelt look at foster care in America. It will astound you and appall you. Beam has written an extraordinary book about ordinary people trying to save kids' lives. She has cast a ray of light into a dark and hidden place."
— Tim Weiner, National Book Award–winning author of *Legacy of Ashes*

TO THE END OF JUNE

TO THE END
of JUNE

THE INTIMATE LIFE OF
AMERICAN FOSTER CARE

Cris Beam

Mariner Books Houghton Mifflin Harcourt Boston New York

First Mariner Books edition 2014

www.hmhco.com

Library of Congress Cataloging-in-Publication Data
Beam, Cris.
To the end of June : the intimate life of American foster care / Cris Beam.
pages cm
Includes bibliographical references.
ISBN 978-0-15-101412-5   ISBN 978-0-544-10344-3 (pbk.)
1. Foster home care — United States. I. Title.
HV881.B4193 2013
362.73'30973 — dc23   2013001331

Book design by Melissa Lotfy

Printed in the United States of America
DOC 10 9 8 7 6 5 4 3 2

I'm going to write a book about all the places I've lived in foster care — twenty-one homes. It's called *Until November,* 'cause that's when I'm going to be adopted. I never got what I was promised, though; that's why it's hard to believe.

—*Fatimah, age 16*

Now I've got to change the name of the book. It's going to be *To the End of June.*

I was planning on adopting in November but then they kept saying next month, next month. It happened at the end of June.

—*Fatimah Imani Green, age 17*

I don't care about being a writer no more. I used to want to be a journalist, but why, what's the point? What's the point now of anything? . . . Why do something where I can leave my mark on the world? That used to be important to me. But now, if I can just get some kind of job, take care of me, take care of my kid, then die, that's enough.

—*Fatimah Imani Green, age 19*

For the kids

Contents

Preface

IN MY MANHATTAN APARTMENT BUILDING, a mother leaves her two-year-old daughter, Alicia, asleep in her stroller just outside her front door, alone in the hallway for hours. For months, I've been tortured by the sight of this child. I live in a pretty safe building, so I'm not particularly afraid that Alicia will be kidnapped; I'm more concerned about what's happening *inside* their apartment to render this behavior acceptable. And I hate seeing the terror that streaks Alicia's face when she wakes up alone, surrounded by strangers gathering at the elevator.

Alicia's mom abandons Alicia to the hallway because she and her husband are hoarders. Their apartment is so crammed with junk that she can't squeeze a stroller filled with a sleeping baby through the door, and she'd rather Alicia continue her nap outside. I know this isn't a great way to grow up — the apartment is filthy and foul-smelling and most definitely a fire hazard — and my friends in child welfare say the hallway situation is a clear case of neglect. They say I need to call Child Protective Services immediately. And yet, I stall.

I know more than a lot of people do about foster care, from both research and personal experience, and I'm not sure that making that call would make Alicia's life any better. It could make it worse.

I know that there are more than 400,000 kids in foster care in America today. I know that foster children are twice as likely to develop Posttraumatic Stress Disorder than are veterans of war. I know that, in some states, they're more likely to be abused in foster care than they are at home. I know that kids stay in foster care for about two years on average nationwide, and three years in New York. More than a million adults are directly or indirectly employed to ensure their well-being, and $15 to $20 billion a year are poured into overseeing their health and management. And yet nobody — not the kids, not the foster or biological parents, not the social workers, the administrators, the politicians, the policy experts — thinks the system is working.

I wrote this book to find out why. We're a country of innovators, a country that claims in everything from television programming to presidential platforms to love its children, a country proud of its flawed judicial system. And yet none of these cultural themes resound in child welfare: there's little innovation, love, or justice in foster care.

It's a strange phenomenon, this foster care as *other*, as someone else's problem. Because foster care is intricately woven into so many facets of American society; it's an intimate partner to education and to poverty, to substance use and to mental health; it's tied to national issues like the deficit and unemployment and health care, and to our specific history with racism and class bias and power. A lawyer who has done litigation in foster care for decades once told me that foster kids are our country's canaries in the coal mine, and he's probably right: they're the most vulnerable members of society, and they reflect society's spikes in things like poverty and violence. If we were looking at foster care and foster kids, we could learn a lot. I wrote this book to look.

I also wrote this book to ask, albeit at a slant, a very personal question, and a very old one. I left my mother's house when I was fourteen years old, and I never saw her again. I was also never put into foster care — though, like Alicia, I probably should have been. I imagine the adults around my child self gazing in the other direction, the way we all do with Alicia.

Like most children, I didn't know exactly the way my family was different from other people's families, but I did have a sense that things weren't right. My father left when I was eight years old and my brother was three. That left my mother, a wrung-out mass of hysteria, to take care of us. At first, my mother was sure we would starve to death. I counted cans in the cupboard and rationed our food. Then she said prostitution was her only solution, and the men started staggering in. She gave me a deadbolt for my bedroom door in fourth grade. She began staying out late, sometimes all night; sometimes we had babysitters and sometimes we didn't. I remember being afraid.

My mother got a day job as well, and she said she loved us, but she also drifted into the corners of her own confusion, and we lost her far too often. She had headaches that would last for days, when she couldn't leave her room, and then she had so many men, with their work boots and their mustaches and their awful sweat smell, who took her away from us too. She often proffered vague suicidal threats when we visited my father. One Christmas she promised she'd be dead by New Year's.

Where was Child Protective Services during those years, from second to eighth grade, before I left my mother's house for good? I lived in a mostly white neighborhood of detached single-family tract homes, the last stop on the commuter rail line from San Francisco. It was a neighborhood of scrubby front lawns and strip malls, the kind of area where kids are molested or neglected as much as anyplace else; but still, I wonder about the neighbors, who may have noticed that my mother's car would go missing all night long. Did they think about making a call, or were they worried, like anyone, about the authorities nosing in their business? I didn't tell anyone about getting molested, but I wonder about the doctors who evaluated me for a mysterious illness that lit up my abdomen and wouldn't go away. I think about my teachers, who must have watched a girl who was manic about her stars and straight As suddenly failing classes in middle school. But perhaps I looked like dozens of other adolescents hitting bumps in a mediocre public school in a mediocre town.

I think about my father, too, who says he never knew how bad things were because we never told him, and of course: I had a fierce interest in protecting whatever glossy sheen I could maintain. I always knew somehow that we could lose my mother, and despite all the pain, I didn't want to. Above all, I didn't want it to be my fault.

I think about all the kids who are removed for far lesser crimes than my mother committed, and I worry that it was an accident of circumstance that freed me from foster care. People noticed, but because of who they were, or what I looked like, or where we lived, or a combination of all these factors, they didn't do anything about it. Race and class weave themselves through every tricky turn of foster care; they did in the early eighties when I was a kid, and they still do today.

Even still, had a call been placed back then, I wouldn't have been saved. My guilt would have compounded into a toxic knot for not covering her better, protecting her more. I left my mother's house without foster care intervention. But I've struggled, like every foster child I've ever met, between two opposing agonies: she didn't want me, and I'm the one who left. The guilt, still, is immeasurable.

So this is my question: How do the foster kids do it? How do they live with the guilt of leaving? How do they swallow the betrayal that still chokes my throat some thirty years on? It's been said that the economic impact of child welfare reaches upwards of $100 billion — in adult criminality, mental illness, homelessness, and so on — and this backsplash is traditionally pegged to the structural failings of a battered system. But I'm also curious about the a priori traumas, the kids' more primal psychic battering rendered by loss, then reinforced by a terrible system. I wrote this book to tease the two traumas — familial and societal — apart, if only just a bit.

My adult experience with foster care was similarly shrouded in a strange kind of secrecy. I became a foster parent when I was twenty-nine, somewhat by accident, and the ineptitude I witnessed in my small corner of child welfare was shocking. I had to find out whether somewhere we were doing better by our kids.

My journey began with a phone call from a probation officer in January 2001. It went like this:

"We have to put her into juvenile hall."

The probation officer was talking about a seventeen-year-old named Christina Quiñonez — the child who would become my daughter.

"There are no more beds in the group home, so that's where she'll have to go. It's only for a while."

I had been Christina's teacher in a Los Angeles public school for poor and disenfranchised teenagers, so this was not my first adult encounter with the foster care system, but it was the most stark and brutal. Los Angeles has one of the largest child welfare programs in the country, and a good number of the kids, like Christina, are officially categorized as "hard to place." Christina was transgender; she had lived in ten foster homes and run from several. Although she was happy at her latest group home, she was threatened at her school when some gangster students discovered she had been born male. She ran from the high school to protect herself, which was a strict violation of her home rules, and her bed was immediately given away to another child on the wait list. Her probation officer, her social worker, and her case manager, who were all professionals paid by the state, claimed she had to go to jail. There was simply nowhere else to put her.

"I'll take her," I said to Frankie, the probation officer, and suddenly we were polite strangers — cool and methodical, outlining the life of another human being. A moment before we had been fighting viciously: I was adamant she wouldn't go to juvenile hall. Seemingly relieved to get Christina's file off his desk and on to his next case, Frankie took down my name and address, filling me in as "guardian." He warned me that he wasn't sure this would work — after all, I wasn't a licensed foster parent and I had no biological ties to this child. He reminded me that juvenile hall, unlike legitimate foster homes for hard-to-place teenagers, always had plenty of beds.

Of course, I was scared of parenting, and scared of taking in a teenager who was bitter and sad and mad at the world. I was also scared by the bad reputation of "foster kids" and "child welfare." Nobody was a hero in that family story.

Frankie was right. A week after I became Christina's guardian, after we'd settled into a routine of sorts, setting up a bed and a dresser in the dining room, and explored school and job options and whipped up a new résumé and established house rules, Frankie told me I couldn't keep her. I'd be arrested if I tried. But good news: he'd found her a bed and it wasn't in juvenile hall. It was in a group home for adolescent sex offenders.

To become a licensed foster parent, I'd have to take a ten-week course — Christina said she wouldn't wait that long. So while Christina donned her fiercest makeup and bided her time at the sex offender home, I found a licensed foster parent who would take her in on the condition that I would keep her most weekends and many weekdays. This was off the books, and under the radar of the Department of Child and Family Services. Within a week, Christina was again living mainly with me. I called her my foster daughter; she called me her foster mom. Technically, we were lying, but to do the right thing by a child who'd been wronged by a system designed to protect her, we had to trick the system and go off on our own.

Before I started research for this book, most of my knowledge of child welfare came from working around it. But what I didn't know was why this particularly American institution was so particularly troubled. I didn't know how we could be spending billions on foster children in the United States and yet see half of them with chronic medical conditions, 80 percent with serious emotional problems, and then abandon nearly a quarter of them to homelessness by their twenty-first birthdays. I didn't know how we could be failing them so spectacularly.

Federal investigators recently spent three years looking into seven fundamental criteria for successful foster care in all fifty states. They examined the basics: things like kids being protected from abuse and neglect, being safely maintained at home whenever possible, and receiving adequate services for educational and physical health needs. No state met more than two of the seven criteria.

I spent five years looking at these questions for this book, primarily by looking at foster families who are deeply invested in the system's success — families who love their children and believe they can help — to more easily discover the flaws that foil anyone's best intentions. I live in New York, as do most of the families in this book; I've found it has neither the best, nor the worst, foster care system, so it provides one view into urban child welfare that can be projected onto other places.

And yet. Part of the problem with child welfare is that New York City is not like Chicago or Miami or Los Angeles or suburban Detroit in its child welfare designs or administration; they all grew from local cobbled-together religious and charity organizations, and they all now operate under different financial and philosophical restraints. Part of the problem with child welfare is that we're searching for a singular model that will meet all of the divergent needs of abused or neglected kids in all of their divergent places. Perhaps the only universal truth about each foster care program is this: every child within it is different.

No book could cover foster care, the institution, in this country — it's too varied, from place to place and theory to theory; any book that tried would be too shallow. So I have gone deep rather than broad, following a few families intensely for years. I was glad to discover some real hope in this work, in the form of both human resilience and creative new ideas crackling through child welfare, but by no means is this a comprehensive study or a litany of answers. I don't address several key branches of foster care — for instance, rural child welfare or the Indian Child Welfare Act and tribal laws — because they couldn't fit within the scope of one book. Certainly, there are thousands more narratives. This is an American story, and so I have an American's optimism: I believe we can do better.

• • •

Note: Every story in this book is true, culled from recorded interviews conducted from 2007 to 2012. I've used actual names except in the few cases where I've changed identifying characteristics to protect a source's privacy. These changes are indicated in the endnotes.

One

CATCH

Being a problem is a strange experience — peculiar even for one who has never been anything else.

—W.E.B. DuBois, *The Souls of Black Folk*

1

King Solomon's Baby

IT WAS AN UNUSUALLY WARM October in Brooklyn; the men had switched their puffy coats for crisp white tank tops, and the young mothers pried back the plastic casings on their strollers. All two thousand people from the Roosevelt housing projects seemed to be tumbling outdoors, leaning on cars or gathering at the bodegas, slanting their faces toward the sun to soak in the last bits of warmth before winter. You couldn't tell, on a clear morning like this, that the Roosevelt Houses still tipped the scales in the 81st Precinct with their homicide rates, that by nightfall the bodegas would fill with toothless addicts buying loosies for a quarter. A bright morning like this could make anybody grateful.

Slicing through the center of these projects is DeKalb Avenue, with its run of single-family homes and middle-class aspirations. But that fall, one of these houses stayed locked up tight against the sunshine. The ten kids, most of them teenagers, weren't allowed to go outdoors. In that house, in that family, outside spelled temptation, and besides, it was the Sabbath. So the kids, sequestered in their jewel-colored Nikes and their tight jeans, had to swallow their frustration and excess energy like a belly full of bees.

The house on DeKalb had a history. One hundred and twenty years before any Nike sneakers thumped up its three long staircases, and sixty years before the projects rose across the street, the place had been an evangelical "House of Rest." Such houses dotted the East Coast at the turn of the century to provide divine healing along with rest, teaching, and "spiritual quickening" for the sick or the wayward. In a way, the essence of the place had reemerged. In a way, beyond the stone lions that flanked the stoop and behind the beveled glass front door, a kind of holy crusade was revving up.

Bruce Green, a tall black man of forty with round cheeks and a quick smile, had bought the house on DeKalb in 1999. He grew up in the Roosevelt projects on his block, and most of his children are foster kids, raised on the same rough street diet he was — in Brooklyn, or Queens, or the Bronx. His wife, Allyson, is from Belize, and, although she may be more stridently religious than he is, they both wanted a large home to raise a large family, to protect their children against the many dangers of their city through the power of their God and their unwavering attention. What they didn't expect was that their children would come directly from the city itself, and that they'd be embroiled in several battles that would test their faith in just about everything.

The latest and largest battle was over a baby, born to a mother addicted to drugs and delivered to the Green family, after placements with a few other foster parents, when he was just over a year old. When I met baby Allen that Sunday some years ago, he was two and a half, and his biological father, also a former addict, was working with the courts to win him back. And at the core of this battle spun the core questions of foster care itself: Who decides the *correct* way to raise a child? Who makes the moves on the moral chessboard where a family's right to privacy opposes a child's right to protection from harm? And who should get to keep a child: the parents who nurse and tend him, or the parents who brought him into the world?

At the beginning, Allyson put the quandary in biblical terms. She told me the story of King Solomon.

In the story, two mothers are arguing over a single baby; both women believe the child to be hers. King Solomon procures a sword and offers to cut the baby in half so they can share. One mother agrees to the deal, but the second pleads: she'd rather have the baby alive and with the other woman than dead. Allyson is this second mother — she knows that if Allen were remanded to his birth father, destructive as this father may be, she'd rather have Allen physically and spiritually alive than eventually feeling imprisoned with her. Plus, she knows all of her foster children understand that if they leave, they can always come back. Allyson will always be "Mom." She hopes, in fact, that some of the other birth parents orbiting the Green household can make bigger strides and do right by their kids.

"I was blessed to have four children of my own, that I gave birth to," Allyson said, her thick Belizean accent pounding her harder consonants. Allyson is four years older than Bruce, and she's pretty; makeup rarely graces her chocolate skin, but her hair is straightened and highlighted and it falls in loose waves down the fitted blazers and silky blouses she wears, even on warm days. Next to Bruce's baggy jeans and T-shirts, Allyson's leather boots and stockings render her the sophisticate at first glance. But she's the one doing the dirty work: changing diapers and making dinner, wiping up the endless spills. "Then you have this other parent, who's been through hell and back — the dad, the mom, any one of them — say they want to turn their lives around. It would be very inappropriate of me when I have the right to raise my own children to not give him that fair chance. Why would I want to take away his one little thing when I've got four of my own?"

But that was at the beginning. That was back in the fall, when the case with Allen's dad was still theoretical and it looked as if the courts would lean in Allyson's favor.

Bruce and Allyson fell into foster care the way anyone falls into the traumas or miracles of their lives: by a mix of happenstance and hope. The year was 2000, and they already had three kids of their own at home — two little boys, Jaleel and Bruce Junior, and a daughter named Sekina who was just becoming a teenager. (Allyson's other son, born to a different father, was back in Belize.) Then one night, they got a phone call from the Administration for Children's Services (ACS) — the organization that handles child welfare for the five boroughs of New York. Bruce's sister's kids, then two and four, were being removed from their home; it wasn't safe for them to even stay the night. Could Bruce and Allyson take them? Of course, they said. Anyone would.

Bruce, who looks a little like Jay-Z with his bald head and soft jaw, stayed pretty private about the exact circumstances surrounding his sister's ordeal, but typically, this is the way a child is removed:

First, anyone who suspects abuse (by seeing marks, hearing shouts, noticing absence from school, and so on) can call a hotline. There are certain "mandated reporters" — doctors, police officers, teachers, daycare workers, and social workers, mainly — who are legally obligated to make these calls, but really, anyone can do it. The local city or county agency sends an investigator to the house to interview the parents and the kids, and to look around the rooms. A child abuse investigator can enter anyone's home at any time without a warrant.

Usually, the investigator just opens a file on the family and follows up on anything that seems suspicious or untoward on that first visit, but if the parents pose an immediate danger, he can take the kids then and there. This is what happened with Bruce's nephews.

Then the investigator has to find a place for the kids to go. He brings them back to the office, where a social worker starts making calls — usually to family members. In child welfare–speak, this is called "kinship care," and New York State law requires it as the first line of outreach, though this law is often ignored. Still, it's why the boys were placed with the Greens. If the child is older, say, a teenager, he might be able to indicate some adults with whom he could stay, *if* they're willing to foster him. This works in only some places, however; several states require that all foster parents be licensed via weeks of state-approved parenting classes before they can take in kids, even if they're related. Luckily for the Greens, ACS provides emergency licensing; Bruce and Allyson could shelter the boys first and take parenting classes later.

Once a child is settled for the night, his case gets passed from ACS to one of the roughly thirty foster care agencies that ACS contracts with, each with its own mission, style, budget, possibly a religious affiliation, and so on. At this point, ACS pretty much gets out of the way, and the foster agency handles the licensing, any troubles with the kid, connections with his birth parents, and so on. Which agency the child is assigned to is usually a matter of sheer luck, as they vary in aptitude as much as they do in approach. The kids too are subject to this roulette; if the ACS worker can't find a kinship match, the child is shuttled to whichever agency has an available family on its roster.

After Bruce and Allyson took the call and accepted the nephews, they were sent to an agency near their home for their licensing. Because Bruce's sister terminated her parental rights without a fight, they were able to adopt the older child. But the process took six years. The younger boy, who was severely autistic, ultimately had to be institutionalized. With four other kids in the house, Bruce and Allyson just didn't have the extra reserves to take care of him.

But still, they wanted more kids. Or rather, their daughter, Sekina, wanted a sister; the house was full of boys. When I first met Sekina, she was a bubbly and outgoing sixteen-year-old. She looked like a girl version of Bruce: same round cheeks and full lips, same large dark eyes that could spark with mischief or anger in turn. But Sekina's hair was what got her attention. When I met her, it was shoulder-length and streaked through with pink and neon purple, but I would see it red, blue, platinum, short, shaved, and razored through with her name curled around her skull.

Sekina started pestering Bruce and Allyson for a sister; now that they were licensed with an agency, she reasoned, they could just go back and ask for a baby girl. But Allyson was tired. She started longing for her life before motherhood, when she could go out with her friends on Friday nights, or take some space to herself. But with these desires, Allyson said, came illness.

The doctor called it depression. She called it her "mental battle": between what she *wanted* to do and what she was *supposed* to do. "I didn't want to be tied down with no children. I was crying all the time; I wanted to be free. So I get down on my knees and I pray, saying Lord help me. And after that is when the dreams come to me."

In Belize, Allyson was raised primarily by her grandmother, along with thirty-two brothers and sisters ("My father was a bit of a rolling stone," she admits), and her grandmother had dreams, too. Her grandmother's dreams were prophetic, or instructive, so Allyson learned from an early age to trust their messages.

Allyson's dreams were full of children, sitting on the floor with her grandmother. Her mother served them homemade apple juice. "I said, 'Ma, why are you giving them that? They don't want that stuff.' And my grandmother says to me, 'It's not what they want; it's what you have to give them.' And finally I got up and understood."

We were sitting in the living room, which, like most of the house's common areas, seemed designed more for quiet contemplation than for entertaining children. The couches are low and comfortable, the lights dim and soothing. In the bathroom, a tile mosaic covers the large domed ceiling, and candles circle the tub. Allyson interpreted the apples in her dream to be symbolic of appreciation and knowledge, the gifts you give a teacher. "I'm here to be a teacher to these children — the same thing that was given to me by my grandmother, I'm supposed to give back." Allyson told Bruce she wanted more children and the depression went away.

But what of her desire to be free, I asked, to live her own life? Allyson sighed and shook her head. "My will was to do what I wanted to do, but God's will — God's will was for me to do what I'm doing."

So Bruce and Allyson called the agency. Per Sekina's request, they told them they wanted to adopt a little girl. Or maybe two. Somewhere between the ages of six and ten, but definitely younger than Sekina.

"But they called us with a baby, sixteen months. A boy," Allyson remembered, saying that at first they wanted to decline. "But when they told us he had been in three different foster homes already, it hit something in me. I was like, 'Wait a minute, no. Bring him.'"

The baby was Allen. Sekina loved him right away; he was a baby after all. But then the agency kept calling. Their real emergencies were teenagers; couldn't the Greens take in a few more kids?

Unfortunately for Sekina, the calls coincided with more of Allyson's dreams. She dreamed of a woman saying, "This is my daughter; you have to take care of her." That daughter was the Greens' first teenager, Chanel, nearly two years older than Sekina. Then Allyson dreamed of a girl who looked like her niece, and a foster child named Fatimah showed up. And a white man, who was "spaced out" and followed Allyson everywhere. That was Russell, an autistic teenager. The dreams, and more kids, kept coming. Sekina never got her little sister; all the kids, save for Allen, were older than she was.

But Allyson couldn't resist her dreaming. "Because when I resisted it, that's when I got sick," she said. "And ultimately, it's not what you want, it's what you're supposed to do. This is what life is supposed to be. We're supposed to be of service."

So Sekina, in losing her place as the oldest child, became perhaps a little bit bossier, a little more specific about her position with her siblings. "I tell them all the time they're not just adopting parents, they're adopting a *family*, and if it weren't for me, if I didn't let them be here, they'd be out on the street," Sekina told me one afternoon early into that next spring. She was straightening her hair, heating up the comb on the stove. The pink and purple streaks were gone, and she had decided, for the moment, to go for a natural brown. One of Sekina's four foster sisters was sitting on the kitchen stool watching her, and she rolled her eyes. Sekina caught the look. "It's true. But I like to help people. That's why I want to be a pediatric nurse."

Sekina had a particularly proprietary hold over baby Allen, claiming to anyone who would listen that he was the only foster child she originally wanted. And Sekina, maybe even more than Bruce or Allyson, was terrified of losing him.

"I'll go crazy if Allen goes to his father's — did you hear about Allen's brother?" Sekina said, her eyes flashing as she ran the comb through her hair. "He's HIV positive — and he was in the system before he was even born! They called us and asked if we wanted him and my mother said yeah, but the thing is, unless Fatimah gets adopted or something, we already have too many people here."

Sekina was right: Allen did have a new baby brother, born to the same drug-addicted mother and a different father, neither of whom wanted him. The logical placement choice for this baby would be with the Greens, so Allen and his brother could grow up together. But there was the issue of space: even with four thousand square feet, the Greens were already at the legal maximum capacity with all of their foster kids. And there was the issue of Tom, Allen's biological father: if he got custody of Allen in a few months or years, he'd separate the boys, potentially adding more trauma to Allen's young life.

Sekina wasn't the only one on DeKalb who adored Allen; in a house full of teenage tension — especially a house with such strict rules about staying indoors — a toddler was a welcome distraction. That spring and summer, Allen could bumble around the warm house clad in only his diaper, reaching for anyone who would pick him up or keep him from bumping into the big glass table in the center of the living room. On nearly every surface there's a sculpture or painting or something equally appealing for a toddler to yank on; Allyson says decorating is her way to de-stress. A wooden elephant stalks the center of the table; a curlicued stand draped in gray cloth props up a painting of a lion; a gold Buddha perches atop the television screen. But Allen focused on people more than things. He was a quiet child, and trusting, sticking one of his feet into a conversation with a half-smile on his face and then running away, hoping someone would engage in a game of chase. If no one did, he'd scramble back, still without a sound, and climb into an open lap, settling his head into a chest or neck to suck his thumb. Everybody loved Allen, but he wasn't an easy baby at first.

"He used to cry a lot, and he was always angry — I've never seen a child who was so little with so much anger," Allyson said, remembering that the first week he was with her, he only wet his diapers and didn't soil them once. She thought he was constipated because of the poor diet in his last foster home. She still felt bad that a kid so young had been through so much change.

There are a lot of reasons that kids, even babies like Allen, end up shuttling from foster home to foster home before they get adopted or go back to their biological parents. In New York, the conflicts and the chaos start within twenty-four hours. After the child has been removed and placed with either relatives or strangers, the parents have the right to plead their case. The parents do this with ACS in a meeting called "family team conferencing." The biological family, the ACS caseworker, and a community advocate together determine what would make the home safe enough for the child to return. Does the stepfather need to move out? Could Grandma move in? Does the family need help with food stamps or vouchers to get heat and hot water? Does the mother need anger management or rehab? The team draws up a plan and they set a date, generally several months away, to present it to a judge. If the parents disagree with the plan, they can get their own lawyers, to fight for their side. After this come the court procedures, the promises, the reunifications, the battles, the multiple placements, and all the things that foster care is famously bad at, which is safely sailing a child through a temporary boarding while everybody waits for a fairy-tale ending.

In this time period, which can be months or many years, everybody gets a different social worker — the child, the biological parents, and the foster parents. In this time, more lawyers step in and draw up more plans: How often will the parent see the child; what will visitations be like? Where will visits be held; what are the milestones toward reunification? Throughout this, a judge, who in New York City sees about fifty family court cases every day, makes the binding decisions as to who must do what by when.

Meanwhile, the kid has been living in a real house, with real foster parents, placed at a moment's notice. If the foster family is a bad fit, if the kid doesn't like her new family, if they don't speak the same language, if there's abuse, if they live across town (and sometimes across state lines), if the foster parents practice a different religion, send the kid to new schools, have unfamiliar styles of discipline, or if the kid simply misses her biological parents, there can be conflict. Foster kids run away; foster parents terminate relationships. It's not unusual, while waiting for somebody to kiss the frog and the real parents to come home, for a foster child to live in ten or twenty different houses. Fatimah, Bruce and Allyson's sixteen-year-old daughter, had been in twenty-one homes since she was five years old — and before she was placed with the Greens.

In Allen's case, Tom wasn't around for the family team conferencing meeting with ACS when his son was removed. He was in an inpatient rehab facility. ACS removed Allen from his biological mother when she skipped out on her own drug treatment program, and Tom didn't find out about it until several days later. By then, Allen was living with his first foster mother. That woman, the story goes, found Allen too taxing and sent him back to the agency. The next mom wanted to go to Puerto Rico and couldn't take Allen with her, so back he went again. By the time Allen was placed with the Greens at sixteen months, he had lived with four different "mothers" and his future was still uncertain.

Tom had followed Allen through all of his placements; he saw his son during supervised visits at the agency. He graduated from rehab and started taking parenting classes. Allen turned two at the Greens', and then two and a half; he was talking more, smiling a lot, and running, running everywhere. And then a judge upgraded Tom's status: he could start bringing Allen back to his apartment for weekends.

When I asked Allyson how the weekend visits were going, she changed the subject. "The dad's white," she said, her face inscrutable. "You've seen Allen. He's darker than me."

I tried to push her; was she concerned that if Tom got custody Allen would lose some sense of his heritage? Did she, like many people, resist the notion of white parents raising black children? But I had entered icy waters and Allyson wouldn't budge.

"The dad will call here because Allen will be crying," was all Allyson would venture. She fussed with the snaps on Allen's brother Anthony's onesie; the HIV-positive newborn was, after all, allowed to come live with them, and he required much of her attention. "Allen will get on the phone and just say, 'Mama, Mama.'"

Sekina, as usual, was more blunt. "The dad doesn't feed him the right food. He gives him adult food — things he can't digest. He puts Allen in front of the TV all day. And when Allen comes back here, he's all upset. Of course — he's been here for a year. He's our baby."

Still, Allen and the Greens are an example of foster care working exactly as it should: a foster home is meant to be only a temporary holding place while parents get the support they need to get back to being parents again. The foster family should provide the kind of bonding and love that the Greens gave Allen and then, wrenching as it is, let the child go. The biological parents may be imperfect — they may feed the kids inappropriate foods or leave the TV on too long — but as long as there's no abuse, a child belongs with his blood. It's not the state's role to interfere with the way we raise our kids.

And apparently, a judge thought Tom was doing well enough. As Allen inched toward his third birthday, the courts claimed that Tom could indeed have custody, as soon as he'd accomplished a few more weekend visits. Allyson was stoic about it on the surface, but Bruce unmasked her.

"She's gonna cry like a baby when he leaves," Bruce said. He was eating pot stickers from the Chinese place down the street, shoveling them in quickly before one of the older kids could catch him with the takeout box and demand her share. Allyson shot him a look.

"He will too; he talks about it every day," Allyson said. Her prior easy acceptance of a King Solomon deal seemed to be slipping. "I don't believe that this parent has shown overwhelmingly that he is ready, not overwhelmingly. And this child requires a parent who shows overwhelmingly that he's ready. Because Allen's no ordinary child. He has his issues."

For instance, despite all his progress, Allen still hit the other children when he got enraged. Allyson doesn't allow hitting in the home; she had been working steadily with Allen to soothe him and had trained the other kids to react with only words. She wasn't sure Tom had the patience to continue this trajectory. Allen also needed constant attention and reassurance; he was slightly regressed for his age, though that too had been steadily improving. Attention abounds in a house of nine older children — less so, she said, in a small apartment with Tom and his adult roommates.

"The courts are saying that the father's taken his classes, he's met his minimum requirements, he's clean — no problem," Allyson said, forcing her tone to soften as she spoke of God's will and prayer for right action and surrender to whatever will be. She snuggled Allen's baby brother closer to her chest. "This is one of the reasons why a lot of people go straight for adoption, that they don't bother with foster care. It's because of the investment — you see your investment go down the drain in months."

The basic tenet of foster care, and its core complication, is that foster care is meant to be a temporary solution. It's a waiting room, tended by temporary parents, while the "real" parents scoot off to the back quarters to try to boost their skills or mend their ways, and then come back in and retrieve their children. Sometimes the parents just walk out the back door, and sometimes a judge orders them out, and then the temporary parents get a new title and can adopt the children. With other babies, in other waiting rooms, the cases aren't so clear. Sometimes, the birth parents won't, or can't, come back and the foster parents don't *want* to keep the baby — they're generally trained not to attach, and very often they don't. The babies, however, weren't privy to this contract and can suffer great losses when they're shuttled off to strangers. Logically, these babies should have been put up for adoption from the start, with any of the thousands of prospective parents in this country who are eager for newborns, but the conundrum is this: no one can tell from the outset which biological moms or dads will manage to emerge from the back rooms intact and able to retrieve their kids.

And this is where the experts weigh in. Some child advocates lean heavily on the side of social services, and keeping mom and baby together from the beginning. When a mom is homeless, drug-addicted, and mentally ill but expresses interest in keeping her child, they argue to shore up her treatment, medication, housing, and counseling. Others look upon this mother as a disaster waiting to happen — they advocate for a swift and permanent removal so the baby can be placed in an adoptive home and avoid foster care down the line. What happens, usually, is a mushy middle compromise. The mom (or dad, like Tom, but it's usually the mom) is provided services, and the baby is removed temporarily — and placed with foster parents who don't want to adopt. The kid ends up in purgatory — often for far too long — with no lifetime parent to attach to.

To counter this, social workers hedge their bets. When they hear about a particularly marginal birth mother, they try to place the newborn with foster parents who might be open to adoption. With moms who seem more capable, they call experienced foster parents who won't fall in love and can hand the child back after some months or years. But it's all guesswork and hope.

Sometimes, on the front end, cases seem more clear-cut. There are birth mothers who don't want their babies but who don't sign up with private adoption agencies either. These moms choose to sign away their rights and their children are put on a fast track to adoption, with a special type of foster parent called "foster-to-adopt." My good friend Steve Wilson is one of these parents — a parent who wanted a kid from the system.

Steve and I have been friends for more than fifteen years; he is unassuming, shy, and a book nerd like me, with an eye for the weird and offbeat. In the stuffy corporate offices where we once worked, Steve and I would find ourselves in the elevators alone and spontaneously dance a riotous jig, or swing each other around in a mock square dance, composing our faces and bodies to neutral just seconds before the elevator doors opened again onto a fresh group of suits, who eyed our red faces suspiciously. This game never ceased to amuse us, and I knew, one day, Steve would make a great dad. He was a kid at heart.

Steve moved to Austin with Erin, his partner of more than ten years, so she could take a magazine design job and they could buy a house and have some kids. They wanted to raise children who were already here, who needed parents, so they planned to adopt right from the start. They named their first son Wilson and gave him Erin's last name, and his adoption story went smoothly. Wilson's biological mom was a teenager who wasn't ready to care for a baby, and although she visited Wilson some in her first year, she signed over her parental rights without a hitch.

When Wilson had just turned four, Lutheran Social Services called Steve and Erin to tell them they had another baby available. Oliver was four months old, born to a teenage mother and a homeless father. In the several months that Steve and Erin would have to wait for the adoption to be processed, chances seemed slim that either parent would fight for, or receive, custody.

At first, Wilson raged, slammed doors, and threw his toys all over the place at the announcement of a brother; he didn't want to have to share a bedroom. And Oliver wasn't an easy baby. Born with drugs in his system, he cried a lot and couldn't sleep through the night. Wilson regressed some, stealing Oliver's bottles and pretending to be a baby too. But Steve is a stay-at-home dad, a professional writer who works from his own bedroom, and he could nurse these grievances and tend to Oliver's needs at all hours. He started waking up early to run with Oliver in a jog stroller, which was a way to get him to sleep, and then be home before Wilson woke up, to make him his breakfast and play with him. Slowly, the boys bonded.

Oliver is a round baby, with slightly crossed eyes, a mop of soft brown curls, and a drooly wide grin. He wants, and needs, to be held all the time, preferably belly to belly. When he's in his crib or high chair, he tracks Steve with his eyes and reaches for him with sticky fingers. All babies do this, but with foster babies you watch more, looking for signals of trauma, vestiges of unmet needs. Would Allen have always thrown ragey fits? Would Oliver have clung so much? the worried new parents ask. And they make up answers, trying to repair the world they're building.

Erin and Steve had Oliver for seven months; he started meeting milestones — crying less, clinging less. He was sitting up, then crawling. He watched Wilson with delighted, drooly glee, as Wilson marched around the house in capes and face paint, or stuck out his tongue, which was covered in chewed-up breakfast burrito from the taqueria down the street. At his low-key, hippie-ish school, Wilson was known as a troublemaker, but at home, Wilson was quickly becoming Oliver's hero.

I was happy for Steve, who called or wrote me e-mails about his growing family. At that time, I believed that Child Protective Services, in general, removed far too many children from far too many parents. These parents, if they were provided proper social services, could raise their own children; agencies should be in the business of supporting families rather than ripping them apart. I believed, based on my research with foster kids and my own experience, that separation from a family of origin is a wound that never heals. If the parents were so troubled that children had to be removed for a period, every effort should be made for a fast reunification. A biological parent's rights trump a foster parent's rights every time. Cases like Oliver's fell outside my rubric: Oliver's mom, Caitlin, had proved herself unfit early on, and she didn't want the child. Some good parents, Steve and Erin, swooped in for the rescue, to raise this unwanted baby in a house filled with books, and natural light, and a stay-at-home parent. So I was happy for Steve—he had taken a risk by choosing foster-to-adopt, and it seemed he was literally saving a life.

And then the agency started calling. Caitlin was getting better. Caitlin wanted Oliver back.

2

Eye of the Beholder

F OSTER CARE BEGINS and ends with an entirely subjective, contentious little word. *Abuse.* One must first define abuse to see it happening and start to turn the wheels of foster care. This is a problem: abuse, like love, is in the eye of the beholder.

The other conundrum is this: nestled next to abuse is the notion of *neglect.* Neglect may be harder to define because it's an absence of action, but it's harmful nonetheless. And neglect cases (of children's medical, educational, emotional, hygienic, you-name-it needs) actually make up three-quarters of the maltreatment cases in this country. In reality, abuse and neglect, in practice, are not things. They're people, harming littler people, for a reason. The reason may not be logical; the reason may be rooted in mental illness or addiction or learned behavior or accidental oversight, but there's usually a reason, and it's child welfare's job to consider it.

Take the case of baby Oliver. When Oliver was three months old, his mother, Caitlin, brought him to the doctor's office, where he was diagnosed with scabies. A month later, she brought him back for a follow-up appointment. Caitlin had not been administering the scabies medication; Oliver also had an ear infection, a temperature of 105.5, a cough, and congestion. He appeared dirty and dehydrated, and the milk in his bottle was curdled. Medical personnel called Child Protective Services.

Oliver's condition was deplorable, but did it meet a definition of abuse? Of neglect? Did it warrant taking a baby away from his mother at three months old? It's impossible to know without understanding *why* Caitlin was behaving the way she was. Were these signs of drug addiction, or inherent malice, or did they just signal a lack of support in a young mother's life?

Child Protective Services sent out an investigator and found that Caitlin was living with her boyfriend and his family in a trailer. Steve doesn't know what the investigator saw, but apparently it was enough to necessitate Oliver's immediate removal. Shortly thereafter, Caitlin signed away her parental rights. On a napkin.

There are no official, systematized rules about when a child in this country is to be removed from his home. At the federal level, the Child Abuse Prevention and Treatment Act requires each state to incorporate the prohibition of child abuse and neglect into its laws, with this as its minimum definition:

> Any recent act or failure to act on the part of a parent or caretaker, which results in death, serious physical or emotional harm, sexual abuse, or exploitation, or an act or failure to act which presents an imminent risk of serious harm.

The "imminent risk" is the loaded gun, and it's what child welfare investigators are looking for when they enter a home after a call reporting alleged abuse. If there are obvious signs of physical brutality on a child's body, say, bruises or open wounds, or malnourishment, the child is likely to be removed right away. The same if there's exposed wiring or drug paraphernalia lying about. But these cases are relatively rare. More likely, a parent might appear intoxicated, or rageful, or food might be spoiled in the refrigerator, or clothes in the drawers might be too small, or an apartment might be uncomfortably dirty, a toilet broken. Imminent risk? In whose eyes?

"It's a matter of fuzziness, and at ACS, it's even fuzzier. There's nothing written down," says Rudy Estrada, the deputy attorney-in-charge of the Juvenile Rights Practice of the Legal Aid Society in Brooklyn. For more than fifteen years, Estrada has been working to improve foster care services for kids in three different states, and from multiple approaches. He says that rather than black-and-white rules about when to remove a child, there are tools, and a mental checklist that all investigators use when entering a home.

"Part of the tool is to observe what's in the house, and go down the list, check, check," he said to me one afternoon at a coffee shop near ACS's main offices downtown. The federal office of child welfare has produced its own compilation of "signs of abuse," and state agencies pull from this list to develop their own in-house screening tools — the "checklist" Estrada described, covering a range of signs from changes in behavior to the appearance of neglect.

"The other part of the tool," Estrada said, "is what does your supervisor say, check, check. There's a dialectical model built in — the supervisor might say take the child, but the worker might say, no, the home's marginal but I think he should stay. And then we never take a child without first attempting to provide a help or service, so the other layer to this is the different intervention styles you might try. There's nothing formulaic about it."

The first people to decide a family's fate are called child protective specialists, or investigators — people like Spencer Cruz-Katz, who worked on the front lines as an investigator and caseworker in 1999. He was hired by an agency in the Bronx, near Yankee Stadium, right after he graduated from college with a degree in psychology. He had one interview and was offered the job right away for an annual salary of $21,000.

"I was thrown into it. There was no training, just a woman who drove around with me the first two weeks. Every day I'd just learn from the day before," Cruz-Katz explained, long after he'd quit and moved on to graduate school. Current caseworkers I spoke with were reluctant to give their names or speak on the record (ACS has a tightly managed media relations department and requires that all interviews be funneled and approved through its office), but their stories were similar to Cruz-Katz's. "I spent a lot of time driving and I spent a lot of time worrying about my safety. I was alone with the families that had histories of violence and drug abuse and I'd have to take their kids away. I'd be threatened, followed to my car. An uncle would stand next to me and say, 'I know what you did. I know your car.'"

Cruz-Katz played several roles in the year he worked for the agency. At one point, he was a case manager for sixteen foster families, in charge of making sure the foster parents were meeting their requirements, and removing the kids again when they weren't. "I'd have to send the kids back to the agency—mostly because they were refusing to go to school, but I also saw stained mattresses on the floor, drugs being brought into the homes, the bio children being threatened and bullied," he said, explaining that each time he'd have to decide whether the circumstances required a removal. "There was no handbook as to when to remove a child. If the agency was open, I would call my supervisor and ask."

Other times, Cruz-Katz was charged with driving these newly removed kids to visits with their biological parents, or to and from court. "I remember it wasn't the best of cars; my neighbor had just unloaded his car on me, and I'd be carting around five kids with everybody on laps," he said. "A lot of this comes down to the agency itself—they just didn't care. I do remember them giving me a car seat, though."

But they didn't train him how to use it. Cruz-Katz also had to do investigations, knocking on doors and interviewing family members and looking in drawers and refrigerators. If, by whatever judgment a twenty-two-year-old could cultivate, there was enough "imminent risk" to warrant driving away with the kids, then that's what he'd do. And sometimes, looking back, it seemed to Cruz-Katz that *he* was the one taking risks with the children—based on sheer inexperience.

"There was one crack-cocaine-addicted newborn—I took her out of her family home, and they were all yelling at me," Cruz-Katz said. He didn't explain what the family's circumstances were, but he said no police or supervisors came along for the investigation. "I had never been in contact with a child that young before. I didn't know how to hold her head, and I didn't know if she had to have her diaper changed or what to do if she did. I had to hope that I put her in the car seat correctly."

I spoke with a top executive at ACS about this problem, a person with several hundred employees under her command and therefore too much on the line to risk giving her real name. She said she found it deeply troubling that the people on the decision-making front lines, the people who choose to physically remove kids from their parents and their homes, are often just barely out of childhood themselves. These recent college graduates are often the only people who will accept the low pay and difficult demands of a caseworker job. They can make snap decisions, based on the black-and-white sense of justice that comes with the righteousness of youth rather than with the nuance and compassion that can come with age and experience. The commissioner herself was once one of these caseworkers.

"When I think back to the way I made decisions when I was twenty-two, it was horrible," she admitted, saying she moved one girl in her charge nine times in one year, always looking for a better fit. At ACS, the entry-level case managers now earn salaries in the $40,000 range; supervisors earn about ten grand more.

New York recently hired a new commissioner for ACS, and he says that the front-line investigators now have an average caseload of nine — a record low. Reduced job pressure means, ideally, that workers can make more careful, reasoned decisions about removals. The agency had also hired more detectives and consultants— experts in domestic violence and abuse — to advise the investigators when they were unsure about a case. Still, although every city manages child welfare somewhat differently, they all pay famously low wages for entry-level positions, so they generally resemble New York in that they hire the young and inexperienced to handle the most front-line work. Washington, DC's child services, however, required that its case managers have master's degrees a few years back. There, the benchmark figures for children's adoptions and reunifications with biological parents have gone up somewhat, though not enormously.

• • •

Abuse, slippery as it is to grasp and define now, is also a cultural idea that shifts with time. Whipping your child as a punishment was once perfectly acceptable; it isn't anymore. Spanking is borderline depending on whom you ask; who knows where we'll stand on spanking in thirty years?

Pan back further into our history and Puritan ideology sounds like modern emotional neglect. Even parental love was a carnal impulse once, and according to one Puritan observer, parents then should have kept a "due distance" from their children because "fondness and familiarity breeds and causeth contempt and irreverence." In the northern states in the eighteenth and early nineteenth centuries, poor or destitute white children were removed from their parents and forced to work as indentured servants to richer families. Children on the streets, whether they were homeless or their parents were busy at work, were routinely rounded up and tossed into almshouses or even jails. By the 1850s, a New York State investigation of county almshouses found that "common domestic animals are more humanely provided for" than the children who were "poorly fed, poorly clothed, and quite untaught." This, by today's standards, would be considered state-sanctioned, institutional abuse.

But the state was interfering because the *parents* of these children were seen as unfit. Being poor, in the nineteenth century, was largely perceived as a moral failure, and charities, both religious and city-operated, were growing to stem the degeneracy.

In general terms, there were three major periods of child abuse legislation in American history — and none, argue some historians, were prompted by an uptick in actual child abuse, but rather by changes in other social conditions. The first was in the mid-seventeenth century, when the Puritans of Massachusetts enacted the first laws anywhere against wife beating and "unnatural severity" toward children. These laws were intended to control what the Puritans believed was their divinely sanctioned community, to protect the group from God's punishment, and to set a religious example for the world. The second major legislation came in 1874 with the foundation of the New York Society for the Prevention of Cruelty to Children — which was launched after a child had been brutally beaten, daily, and a neighbor had complained. (That parent, ironically, was the girl's *foster* mother.) The name sounds familiar for a reason; there was an ASPCA and legislation protecting animals before there was a similar society for children, but the concept quickly spread. By 1910, there were 250 child protection associations nationwide. Still, some historians argue that the copycat organizations didn't emerge from a renewed devotion to children (the founders advocated flogging as punishment) but rather as a misdirected response to violent crime waves that had been hitting urban centers at the time. These associations were a way to monitor, and contain, pockets of violence and often control the children of immigrants.

The next big turn in child abuse legislation came about in 1962, when child abuse was, in the modern sense, "discovered." X-rays, a relatively new technology, allowed radiologists to recognize multiple, prior bone fractures in individual children, indicating intentional harm. A pediatrician named C. Henry Kempe and some colleagues compiled data on suspicious x-rays and then conducted a survey of emergency rooms where they saw further patterns of inflicted burns, brain damage, and other nonaccidental injuries. Kempe coined the term *battered child syndrome,* triggering a wave of articles and national discussion about the "epidemic" of child abuse. States started expanding their child protection laws to include a wider range of physical abuses, as well as neglect, and adapted an old English law to justify a social worker's right to remove a child from an unsafe home.

Perhaps the most significant change was that certain professionals — such as teachers, police, and doctors — were suddenly required by law to report suspected maltreatment. Before 1963, there wasn't a single law that mandated reporting "battered child syndrome"; by 1967 all fifty states had one on the books. Kempe's discovery also came about in the television era, which meant a much wider audience for the hype. All of this — along with some other shifts in law and policy — caused maltreatment reports to surge: from sixty thousand in 1974 to more than a million in 1980. The agencies had to figure out how to manage all those kids.

• • •

Just as it was in Kempe's time, the rate of removals today has less to do with the literal rate of physical abuse or neglect and more to do with a fickle public intermittently enraged by what they hear on the news. When kids die at the hands of their parents, headlines put child protection agencies under intense and sudden scrutiny. Investigators increase their removals, hoping to avoid another high-profile fatality. Child welfare administrators urge their workers to err on the side of safety, or "when in doubt, yank 'em out." They also call in teams of experts to evaluate systems, and then they change agency direction, philosophy, and leadership. The point is, it's all reactionary: transformation is driven by disaster, and innovation, generally, is incidental.

At New York's ACS, the biggest agency changes over the last twenty years have been in response to the tragic deaths of little girls.

Kids were dying under New York City's child welfare in the nineties at the rate of about two or three a month, but in 1995, one child's name rose above the rest. She was Elisa Izquierdo, a six-year-old beaten to death by her mother. Her murder was nationally publicized, and New York's then mayor, Rudy Giuliani, made a dramatic decision: he established child welfare as a freestanding agency reporting directly to him. The agency would get a new name, a new commissioner, and a new mission. It would be called the Administration for Children's Services.

The new ACS had a clear operating principle: "Any ambiguity regarding the safety of the child will be resolved in favor of removing the child from harm's way." It was legi-speak for "when in doubt, yank 'em out." And what resulted was known as the great "Foster Care Panic." In 1995, the old agency, called the Child Welfare Administration, removed eight thousand children from their parents in New York City; by 1998, ACS removals had increased by 50 percent — to twelve thousand. In 1997, when a mom left her ten-year-old and four-year-old alone for an hour and a half while she went grocery shopping, her kids were removed; she came home to an empty apartment and was arrested for endangerment. The same for a mother who let her child slip from sight when she was helping a friend move, and he wandered down the block alone. Another mother was essentially arrested for being poor; she lived alone with her son in an apartment with roaches and no running water. These were the years when many of the Greens' foster kids, now teenagers, were removed from their parents.

Ironically, while the policy of these "panic" years was meant to stem child fatalities, they actually rose: from twenty-four in 1996 to thirty-six in 1998. This may be because of caseload overload; when workers bring so many new kids into the system, they also have to cut corners, often overlooking vital details or failing to provide lifesaving services fast enough.

The fledgling administration did make some changes that ran counter to this philosophy, cementing its contemporary incarnation as a kind of split-personality agency. ACS was sued after Elisa Izquierdo's death, and a judge ruled that ACS be advised and monitored by an outside panel of experts. This panel recommended family reunification, fewer removals, and providing the parents support they'd need to keep their children — the precise opposite of the "yank 'em out" philosophy. From these recommendations, ACS implemented programs that *helped* the biological families. For one thing, they created the much-lauded "team conferencing" system for parents to have more of a voice: whenever a child was removed, parents and ACS would meet within seventy-two hours to decide where the kid should stay — before the case could be determined in family court. (This has since been shortened to twenty-four hours.) And so, after the initial three or four years of Foster Care Panic, the pendulum swung back in the opposite direction, and removals dropped.

The new agency also made efforts to keep kids in their original neighborhoods and to reduce time spent in care. The first ACS commissioner was followed by a second commissioner and finally by John B. Mattingly, who served on the original panel and was known for some progressive family reunification policies. And during their tenures, removals dropped further.

But then New York was hit with another high-profile murder, and the pendulum swung back. In January 2006, a little girl named Nixmary Brown was murdered by her stepfather for eating a cup of yogurt. ACS had known about this case and failed to intervene.

ACS was under fire once more. An independent investigation team was brought in to shore up the place; eight hundred new workers were hired. In the year of Nixmary's death alone, child abuse reports rose by 63 percent, and the files on neglect rose by 163 percent. They were yanking 'em out once again, spurred by the stigma of one big mistake.

While nationally, children die from abuse or neglect every single day, it seems that little girls around kindergarten age stir the most public outrage. The latest in New York was Marchella Pierce. Her mother was convicted of murder in May 2012, after a Brooklyn medical examiner testified that the four-year-old died weighing eighteen pounds, with acute drug poisoning, more than seventy injuries, and only a kernel of corn in her belly.

ACS had known about Marchella's family; worried neighbors had called, caseworkers had visited. When she died, the Brooklyn district attorney called for a grand jury to explore "evidence of alleged systemic failures" at the agency. And then, for the first time in the history of ACS, the caseworker and the supervisor originally assigned to Marchella's family were charged with a serious crime: criminally negligent homicide.

Ten months after Marchella's death, Commissioner Mattingly announced his resignation. The new commissioner is a former family court judge named Ronald Richter, and it's not clear, just yet, where his politics will fall. So far, he's gone on record saying he'd like to keep more teenagers at home, supporting the families with intensive home-based therapies. And his administration will be funding more in-home preventive services for medically fragile children like Marchella. But based on historical precedence, ACS could swing back toward family breakups, especially now that the caseworkers, who watched their colleagues get arrested, are likely scared. I spoke with the new commissioner about this at the ACS headquarters a few blocks from Ground Zero in Manhattan, and he said that investigators weren't leaving their jobs; retention was higher than ever. He talked about advocating for continued resources for them — like the detectives and consultants and supervisors hired to help them decide when to remove children. And he was supporting a bill that would make assaulting a caseworker a felony, which the governor signed into law later that summer. Still, I thought, as Richter praised his workers' savvy, something shifted with the Marchella Pierce case. ACS is responsible for sixty thousand investigations a year, and in any investigator's eyes, a hasty removal could be better than this disturbing new specter of jail.

The lawyer for Marchella Pierce's mother didn't debate whether or not she had abused her daughter. He blamed the death on ignorance and dysfunction: Marchella was born underweight and relied on a feeding tube, and the lawyer argued her mother didn't know she couldn't raise her the way she had raised her two healthy boys. Once again, abuse — even when it results in death — always has a reason.

The more progressive, or left-leaning, child welfare agencies and leaders tend to look for this reason and then help parents wherever they're struggling. Barbara Rittner, PhD, a dean and director of the PhD program at the University of Buffalo SUNY School of Social Work, thinks that, overall, agencies need to trust biological parents' better instincts. Dr. Rittner worked in child welfare for more than twenty years before turning her attention entirely to university work and has personally overseen somewhere near a thousand cases in three different states. In all of her years, working her way up from a case manager to a director overseeing 250 employees, Dr. Rittner terminated parental rights only four times.

One of Rittner's parental terminations was with a mother with schizophrenia who threatened to kill her daughters with a knife. A second had already killed one child and severely injured another. Another mother dropped her kids off at the child welfare office, had coffee with Dr. Rittner, and simply walked away; and the fourth just disappeared. Dr. Rittner believes most parents want to do right by their kids, and it's the state's job to help them do that. Removing children, she believes, is often damaging to the kids, and it's always demoralizing to the parents — often taking away whatever will they had to get better in the first place. When Rittner told a variation of this story to a room full of social workers at a conference in New York City, she received a huge round of applause.

For several years, Rittner had worked on a parental termination unit, and she said her decisions were fueled by experience: the biological families stayed connected whether she terminated rights or not. They found each other on Facebook; they reunited after high school graduations; and so on. Her approach, she said, was to motivate parents to be the parents they inherently *wanted* to be.

For me, Rittner's approach is too idealistic, as I've known people who don't love the children they have, or who are so broken themselves they can't access that love in this lifetime, no matter the resources you throw at them. For me, it's nearly impossible to judge a parent's ultimate potential by her words, or even her actions, because we can't truly peer inside the wreckage.

And yet, some are forced to judge. Which brings me to Oliver, my friend's baby. I don't know if Oliver should have been placed in foster care. I do know removals are based less on actual abuse and more on the experience of the individual investigator, and the culture of the agency, and what's been on the news this month or year. Also, Oliver technically wasn't earmarked for investigation because of suspected abuse, but rather *neglect:* his mom hadn't been giving him his medication or giving him healthy milk. Again, more than 75 percent of all child maltreatment cases in this country are neglect cases (as opposed to roughly 15 percent physical abuse, and 10 percent sexual abuse). Many child welfare reform advocates argue that *neglect* is just another word for poverty. Kids come into care because the food stamps ran out, or the parents were kicked off Medicaid, or somebody had to work and leave the baby with an older sibling.

If I read Oliver's story on paper, or saw his mother, Caitlin, in some courtroom, if Steve and Erin were generic and faceless foster parents and not my dear friends, I might agree with Dr. Rittner and be on Caitlin's side. Besides, I know the statistics: children do better with their (even marginal) birth parents than with foster parents. Drugs alone aren't usually a reason to remand a child, and Caitlin had been showing all the signs of getting better; I believe the state should support such progress.

• • •

And still. In August 2008, I found myself flying out to Austin to support an old friend who was facing the loss of a child. We sat in the living room, on the wide-planked wood floor with the sun streaming in on walls painted pale green and cornflower blue, and talked about Oliver's permanency hearing coming up in two weeks. At this hearing, a judge would decide his home. Oliver marched around with a toy shovel in his hand, oblivious. Steve watched him, and I watched Steve simply slump his shoulders and cry.

Steve, Erin, Oliver, and Wilson live in East Austin, in a neighborhood of bungalow-style cottages from the forties painted in wild shades of turquoise and pink. There's a taqueria on the corner, and Wilson's daycare, named Habibi's ("beloved" in Arabic) Hutch, is a few blocks away. It's the kind of place that sends kids home covered in mud or paint from a day of playing, and where Wilson is indulged in acting the superhero or in pretending that the juice he's drinking is really pee, so he can scream in delight and gross everybody out.

When Erin picked me up from the airport on a Friday night, it was nearly midnight, but she had to drive back to the local Moose Lodge where she and some friends were stenciling lettering and a moose's head onto the side of the building. Erin is a graphic designer with her own firm, but even with two kids and a full-time business, she has time to indulge her great sense of camp.

Early the next morning, Erin trooped off with Wilson to actually paint the lodge (Wilson loves paint), and Steve settled in with me to talk.

"The mom signed away her rights on a *napkin* — that should have been our first red flag," Steve said, handing me a cup of coffee. "Still, it was notarized, so we didn't worry about it too much."

We drank our coffee and the sun made dappled patterns on the bright living room rug. Steve continued. "Right after we got him, they warned us that sometimes the investigators can get a little idealistic about taking the kids away. Our social worker started saying, 'Hopefully this will work out, but sometimes it doesn't,'" Steve said, catching Oliver as he tumbled into his lap. He said that perhaps he and Erin were overconfident because of the way things had worked out with

Wilson, which is to say, without a hitch. They had found out about Wilson through a friend—a teenage girl was pregnant and looking for smart, sensitive parents to raise her child. She didn't want to go through an agency, and when she met Steve and Erin, she was thrilled. Although Child Protective Services had never seen a case where the parents made the agreements outside their jurisdiction, they approved the arrangement and stamped the papers. After Wilson was official, Steve and Erin understood the system in one way: they saw it as a functional kind of bureaucracy, the kind they could work with. And they saw themselves as helpful to society: as people who raised the kids whom others couldn't.

Steve said to me, that day on the floor, miserable and self-effacing, that maybe he had "a bit of a savior complex," but really he didn't want to add to the problem of overpopulation. He wanted to do the right thing; he had time and money and love to shower on a few kids abandoned to the system. He didn't bargain to stand between a mother and her child. That was never part of the plan.

On the day Steve was scheduled to drop Oliver off for a visit with Caitlin, he was promised one thing: he wouldn't have to meet her. Steve was to leave Oliver in a waiting room, where a social worker would be the intermediary. This is standard procedure in most places, as tension or arguments can break out between the various parents and in front of the children. Fighting is saved for the courtroom. But when Steve pulled into the child services parking lot, an old man in a tank top immediately marched up to the car.

"Did you ever read *Executioner's Song?* The guy reminded me of my mental image of Gary Gilmore. He was all grizzled and making faces at Oliver, saying, 'I'm the grandpa!'" Steve later found out this was Caitlin's boyfriend's father, who had lived with Oliver in his first few months. "It was kind of scary. I wasn't ready for that kind of contact."

As they walked into the building, Steve said, a pretty teenager with wide-set blue eyes and curly blond hair lunged at him and grabbed Oliver from his arms. This was Caitlin. An older woman was close behind, shouting, "Give the baby to me! He'd rather be with me!" and "Can you take a picture?"

Steve was overwhelmed and concerned by the chaos, and he didn't have a camera, which seemed to upset everybody. The social worker, who was supposed to coordinate the handoff, finally came out and told Steve to leave; she'd drive Oliver back in a few hours.

When Oliver got home, Steve said, he felt a tinge of worry: Caitlin and her in-laws had used up all four of the diapers he'd provided for the two-hour visit and not nearly enough of the baby formula. Aside from being tired, though, Oliver seemed fine.

The next week, after Steve made the two-hour drive to the welfare office, Caitlin didn't show. "I was so happy," Steve said. "She was screwing up, just like people said she would."

But then Caitlin made the next visit, and missed the next, and it was off and on like this for the next few months. There were excuses — it was raining, the family didn't have gas money, someone had a doctor's appointment, and so on. Usually they called, but sometimes they didn't, and Steve wasn't sure whether, to a judge, Caitlin's unreliability would look like unfit parenting or progress from her prior state.

At Oliver's next hearing, he found out. The judge upgraded Oliver's visits to overnight stays. When this happened, Steve said, both Caitlin and her boyfriend's mom, Jill, got nicer. They reintroduced themselves, Caitlin noticed the similarity in Steve's and Oliver's curly hair (claiming the two even looked a bit alike), and Jill started the hard sell on her maternal instincts.

"Jill talked to me for about an hour," Steve said, gently imitating her Texan drawl. "She said, 'I wanna tell you what I'm all about. I make my own baby food, I take my kids to Chuck E. Cheese and McDonald's 'cause you gotta treat 'em right.'"

Steve said, at the beginning, he tried to extend goodwill; he plainly had more education and money than Jill and Caitlin, but he also knew that wouldn't make him a better parent. Still, there was the complicated issue of love and letting go. Steve, Wilson, and Erin were already deeply attached to Oliver, and Oliver to them. And Steve didn't want to release Oliver into a family that would be dangerously irresponsible. His radar was up.

"Jill did say one thing that made me feel a little better," Steve said, handing Oliver a bottle. "She said, 'I know Caitlin's young — but if anything happens, if she tries to take that baby out of my house, I'm calling CPS and I'm calling you.'"

Just as Oliver was getting fussy and I was getting hungry and the morning sun was shining hotter through the window, Erin and Wilson bounded through the front door, Wilson covered in paint.

"I painted a moose!" Wilson said, and then, "Can we get tacos?"

Oliver threw his bottle to the floor at the sight of his brother and toddled toward him, arms outstretched and grinning madly. Wilson barely gave Oliver a glance and ran to the other room for some paper, suddenly struck with a new idea. "Mom! Will you draw me a truck? No dogs, no cars, and NO BUTTOCKS!"

Buttocks was Wilson's new favorite word, something he picked up at Habibi's Hutch. Most of Steve's and Erin's days were spent in the swirl and tumult of the thousand immediate feeding, sleeping, playing, and drawing needs of two small children — for the past several months, Steve had tried not to think too deeply about what it would feel like, or mean, to his family if Oliver had to leave for good. He and Erin had spoken to lawyers who said that they couldn't fight for custody anyway until Oliver had been with them for a full year; at that point, and only then, could they argue that so much emotional bonding had taken hold that it would be in Oliver's best interests to stay. When I visited, Oliver was still a few months shy. So Steve simply reported what he saw when Oliver came home from Caitlin's, or when she missed appointments, and he hoped, somehow, that everything would work out, whatever that meant. In a way, he relinquished control, but he also became a bit of a spy.

"It's awkward because I'm friendly with these people, but I'm also tattling on them," Steve said. Steve started meeting Caitlin and Jill at a restaurant parking lot midway between their two towns, and in the handoff learning more about their lives. He discovered Jill couldn't read, and that there was a pit bull in the house, for instance. He called a social worker to check on the dog, which was later kept on a leash. Caitlin told Steve she took Oliver to Golden Corral for his own chocolate cake, and Jill fed him tea and sugar water, which Steve didn't particularly love, but which wasn't particularly illegal either. Neither was the smell of cigarette smoke on Oliver's blankets, which Steve also reported. The car seat they were using, he felt, was too big for Oliver, but he wasn't really sure. Caitlin, he found out, was stabilizing a bit economically, as she had landed a job at McDonald's, and he took solace in the fact that under the "Goals for Child" section of Caitlin's file, she had written "college." But Jill confessed to him that Caitlin's moods were unpredictable. It was hard to get a complete picture, and Oliver couldn't talk.

"That's the hardest part of letting go," Steve said. "Because we have this vision of what we could give him — not to sound egotistical or whatever — but what kinds of schools he could go to, what kinds of opportunities he could have."

Steve struggled to find words. "But who's to say our lifestyle is any better than theirs really? Maybe they'll have a different parenting approach, like they'll talk to him in a more shrill voice or they'll be watching a lot more TV and there won't be too many books, but maybe he'll thrive in that environment in a way. He could become one of those disadvantaged kids who gets motivated to improve himself, instead of us just handing him everything." Steve paused. "Maybe he'll have a good, happy life."

He sounded as if he was convincing himself, his voice lilting and unsteady. Steve tried to picture Oliver growing up in the town where he'd been dropping him off; he'd looked at the teenagers there and imagined. "He may be some kid who wears NASCAR shirts and it might be a big deal if he graduates from high school. It's hard — you have this one vision of what can happen, and then he's going to have a totally different life. But then, it's like he'll be living, and I think he'll be nurtured and stuff."

One thing that did concern Steve was Caitlin's claim that Oliver was a "difficult baby." According to Steve, he wasn't. He needed to be held more than some children, but he wasn't an excessive crier, and he was engaged and friendly. Couple this with Caitlin's reported mood swings, and a case report that she once hit Oliver for grabbing the television remote, and Steve worried that she still wasn't emotionally equipped to handle the curiosity and constant demands of a growing child.

"If that mom thinks he's difficult now, just wait until he's suffering from the attachment problems that'll come when he loses Steve and Erin," my partner said when I got home from Texas and told her the story. My partner, Lo Charlap, PhD, is a psychologist and a professor of social work at NYU, and she teaches what therapists call "attachment." She says that the reason that Oliver regresses every time he gets home from seeing Caitlin (returning to the bottle and refusing solid food, clinging to Steve, getting anxious when Steve leaves the room, and so on) is that attachment is being disrupted. Attachment theory, in simple terms, goes like this: Ideally, in infancy, a child connects deeply with an adult who can intuit and then meet his needs and soothe his emotions. This is called a "secure attachment." As he grows, this child internalizes this adult who has taught him to manage his urges to scream or kick or rage, and he can begin to contain difficult internal states, rather than act them out. If attachment is ruptured, or never there to begin with, a child doesn't trust that there's anyone constant to soothe him, and there's no internalized, subconscious mom or dad to maintain impulse control. That's why, my partner says, nearly every kid in foster care is diagnosed with Attention Deficit Hyperactivity Disorder (ADHD) or even Oppositional Defiance Disorder (ODD)—they don't have impulse control, because they never had proper attachment. Unfortunately, the system tends to tackle the symptoms rather than the cause, by medicating the children for their hyperactivity or aggression, without addressing the underlying loss, which can take years to repair.

In the case of Oliver, my partner worried, he'd develop ADHD or ODD, and instead of facing a difficult baby, Caitlin would be facing a difficult kid and perhaps an impossible teenager. For his psychological development, my partner believed, Oliver should stay where he was — regardless of the better schools, or the pit bulls, the Habibi's Hutch versus the Golden Corral. And if he did go to Caitlin, both she and Oliver would need a lot of ongoing counseling to manage the mayhem that would come from breaking such an early and important attachment.

But still, I argued — a mother deserves a chance. Just because she screws up in the first year of her child's life, should she be banned from her own baby forever?

"Depends on whose side you're on: the mom's or the kid's," my partner said. "If she really loves her son, then she should leave him where he's already attached."

Child welfare, in general, has been soaking up attachment theory since it was first developed by John Bowlby and Mary Ainsworth in the fifties and sixties; it's why states shifted from keeping babies in orphanages to moving them into individual homes. It's the primary theory in the scientific papers on foster care's child-parent dynamics, and it's the reason experts leverage when they argue for fewer removals and fewer placements once in care. A child's bond with her parent, especially in her first few years, is almost unspeakably critical.

And yet, once a child has been removed and the damage to the attachment has already been done, it's pretty tough to argue that a new attachment to a foster or adoptive parent like Steve trumps any biological claim. Mostly, I've found, the experts don't try — they won't be as bald or assertive in their published papers as my partner was from the privacy of our living room. In one article for the *Juvenile and Family Court Journal,* the authors claimed family courts and judges were too often focused on young children's physical safety rather than their attachments. They described the case of a baby who had been in one loving pre-adoptive home for ten months, but because of some personal family problems, she was removed and placed in a second pre-adoptive home for four months. The first parents resolved their issues, and in the end, both sets of parents wanted the baby. The authors argued she should stay in the second home where she appeared to be thriving; a second rupture in attachment was just too big a risk to take.

The baby in this story was a composite of several cases the authors had overseen, so conveniently there was no biological parent to contend with. Still, the underlying message was to stick with the latest and best connection if, as my partner said, you were really rooting for the kid.

But I didn't know. I thought about all the kids I knew who mourned the separation from their biological parents and acted out all kinds of terrible things from that loss too. And I thought of Steve, hugging me goodbye at the airport, bracing himself to lose the baby he loved, who would clearly grow and flourish in his care. The court date for Oliver was two weeks away; I wished Steve luck and I meant it.

3

Timing Is Anything

BABY ALLEN'S BIOLOGICAL DAD, Tom, learned about parenting from his own family — and if Tom had been left to raise Allen by himself, there would likely have been a lot more physical aggression. I found this out from Tom himself one sultry summer day when I stopped by DeKalb to chat with Allyson. I was surprised to see him; last I'd heard, Tom was meeting the Greens for steely handoffs at child visitation meetings in a downtown Manhattan agency.

They'd recently realized they were living within blocks of one another, and ever since then, Allyson and Tom had been getting along great. If Tom ever wanted to see his kid, Allyson said, he could skip the agency mediation and just come on by.

We sat under a big umbrella on the porch above the carport, and Tom told me about the ways his views on corporal punishment diverged from Allyson's — but he was shifting.

"A couple of weeks ago, Chanel was putting the baby to sleep and Allen went right up to her and whacked her in the face," Tom said, referring to one of the Greens' older foster daughters. Allen had recently turned three. "Next thing I know he comes running out to me crying, saying, 'Nell hit me!' I was like, 'What did you do to Nell?'"

Tom is white, bald, and looks to be in his mid-forties, though he may be younger. He's tall and thin and has no front top teeth — a fact he tries to hide by tucking his upper lip over his gums when he talks or smiles. When he laughs, he covers his mouth with his hand. That afternoon on the porch, Tom was wearing glasses with one earpiece missing, and he leaned forward in his chair as he told his story, glancing every few seconds at Allyson, who was placidly staring at the table. "Turns out Nell had popped his hand after he hit her."

Allyson wasn't home for this episode, but when she did get back and Tom relayed the details, Tom said she was upset. "She said, 'No one hits the baby!' But I reminded her of a story that was in the paper. There was a child that hit some guy's girl and the guy choked the child. I don't want that happening to AJ," Tom said, referring to Allen by the name he prefers. "I'd rather Chanel, Sekina, Mrs. Green discipline him now — pop him in the hand, pop him in the butt, tell him not to do it. Because if he whacks the wrong person, he'll get hurt."

Allyson took a deep breath. "So I tell Tom that you're dealing with a child that has anger. Hitting him is not teaching him the proper technique for handling anger — because if he sees you do it, he thinks, 'OK, I'm angry, I hit you.'"

Tom didn't look convinced, but he nodded, slowly, in Allyson's direction. Both he and Allyson were punished as kids with whippings: Tom with a belt and Allyson with a switch. Still, Allyson said, "I was the oldest and I wasn't allowed to discipline my sisters by hitting them. You have to go to the adult and let the adult deal with it because you let a child discipline another child and it goes someplace else."

OK, Tom said, so what should he have done if Chanel had come to him claiming that Allen had just slapped her across the face?

"If you were mature enough, you would have said you'd speak to him," Allyson answered. "Let him understand that you're not supposed to hit, that there are other ways of handling things."

Tom and Allyson's relationship goes against traditional foster care philosophy and protocol. Everybody knows, this philosophy goes, that foster parents usually represent a barrier or even a threat to the biological parents, so the agencies have typically tried to keep the sets of caregivers separated — setting up meetings in neutral locations and through neutral third parties. Agencies worry that biological parents could either bully or charm the foster parents into allowing extra favors or visitations. Also, with shorter foster stays, agencies don't want the foster parents getting too emotionally invested in the kids' (or the kids' parents') lives, since the kids will be leaving. Historically, it has just seemed wiser to keep all the grownups from commingling.

But the biological parents are supposed to be learning the requisite parenting skills to earn their kids back. Theoretically, they could learn these skills by watching the foster parents with their children. So some agencies are encouraging biological parents and foster parents to interact — or to shadow one another and learn key behaviors. Ironically, it was John Mattingly — the previous ACS commissioner — who helped develop a program called Family-to-Family while he was at the Annie E. Casey Foundation, which encourages open communication between biological and foster families. In 2001, ACS required that all new foster parents be trained to mentor the biological parents of their kids. But this program didn't have a lot of traction, and besides, the scenario works only if the foster parents have significant aptitude themselves (many don't) or are attached to the kids in some way (they still often believe they shouldn't be). And it works only if envy or resentment doesn't burn the key players from the inside out.

This was, at the beginning, precisely the way Tom felt. When he first met Allyson, he had the classic parental response: "I used to say all kinds of things out of the side of my neck at this woman," he told me. "And she knew it."

"Yeah, like once, at the agency, when Allen was in one of his little moods and didn't go straight to him, Tom just looked at me and said, 'Is everything OK at the home?'" Allyson said, narrowing her brown eyes and pursing her lips. "I said what do you mean? I had to start saying scriptures to calm myself down."

Tom fiddled with his one-armed glasses and tried to defend his comment by claiming it wasn't personal; his son had just had bad experiences in foster care before. "The first foster mother that my son went to — she had him on a Monday and returned him on a Friday, and the next one went to Puerto Rico, and the one after that had a hard time handling him too," he said. Allyson didn't look as if she bought the story; she recognized that Tom didn't like her at first. Tom countered that he knew his son best: he'd slept with him nearly every night for the first year of his life. "At two months he was already turning over. I know he's a handful."

Despite their newfound friendship, Tom was still technically working to be independent from Allyson. The courts needed Tom to be clean, to hold a steady job, and to demonstrate parental loyalty before they'd release Allen into his care. The last requirement was easiest: Tom didn't miss visits or court dates, and the pain he felt about being separated from Allen was evident. But when we sat on the porch that afternoon, Tom didn't have a job anymore; he couldn't, because he'd relapsed and was back in a rehab program every day, morning through afternoon.

The first person Tom told about using again was Allyson — even though he knew that would mean he'd lose points with the courts, along with the privilege of unsupervised time with Allen. Allyson did what Tom expected her to: she called the agency, and Tom was ordered right back into treatment. Later, Allyson confided that Tom himself was a bit like one of her kids — he liked to come by the house and play video games with the teenagers and eat meals with everyone on Sunday nights. He may have been lonely, struggling with his addiction in an apartment full of adult male roommates down the block; he missed his son; he liked Allyson's maternal care, and her approval.

"I got my cousin staying with me at the house, and I got a gift certificate — so I was looking to buy a steam cooker or a deep fryer," Tom told Allyson proudly. "I got the steam cooker. I steam my chicken, I steam my fish. That's all I've been eating, chicken and fish."

Allyson nodded her assent, and Tom grinned, covering his mouth with his fist. He knew Allyson wouldn't serve pork in the house because she considered it unclean, and she rarely cooked red meat, so Tom recently forswore those foods too. He'd been changing his diet, he said, to be more like hers. This way Allen might not be too confused, he thought, when he made the move. "Look what she's done to my son." He laughed. "He'll eat bran cereal without the sugar. You can put a bowl of strawberries over here and a bowl of candy over there, and he'll take the strawberries."

Just then, Allen ran out onto the porch and into his father's lap. "I want candy!" he said, his fine, narrow features blooming in a toothy grin. Allyson reached into her purse and called out to her son Jaleel, to see if he would walk Allen to the store for a treat.

"How about we read?" Tom asked. "Go get your book."

In an instant, Allen was back with a dinosaur book, and twelve-year-old Jaleel appeared on the porch, grumbling about walking to the corner in this heat. Tom was pointing to the picture book, and Allen looked torn: candy, or a book with his dad? He opted for the candy. Jaleel marched off, obediently holding his younger brother's hand.

One of the things Allyson worried about, she said, was that if Tom got custody of Allen, he'd have another relapse. Not because Tom would hurt his son — she knew he was gentle and loving — but because if Tom relapsed again, Allen would be removed and the chances of Allen landing with the Greens' agency and thus back with the Greens would be slim at best. "Tom could have Allen for a while and then get Allen put back into the foster care system," Allyson fretted out loud. "He'd be put with a different agency and then just get lost."

We didn't have much time to talk through this scenario; Allen came bounding up the steps, clutching both candy and a temporary Spider-Man tattoo. He wanted Tom to help him stick it on. Tom told him to go inside and get a sponge. When Allen came back out, he had a picture to show me: it was a photograph of him, Tom, Bruce, and Allyson together in the living room. As Tom pressed Spider-Man onto his forearm, I asked Allen to identify the people.

"It's Allen!" he said. "And Mommy."

"AJ, who's that?" Tom asked, pointing to himself.

"Daddy," Allen answered.

"And who's that?" I asked, pointing at Bruce. I felt a little mean, asking the question right in front of Tom, and wondered how he'd react. But Tom just sat there, beaming at his son. Allen, though, seemed unsure. He glanced quickly at Tom, and then down at his new tattoo.

"Daddy," he said quietly. Allen had two daddies.

If Tom had lived in different times or different places, his chances of regaining his parental rights would have varied tremendously. In the sixties, for instance, they may never have been taken away. In the eighties, he may have been assigned all kinds of in-home services and been allowed to keep Allen with him, under some supervision. In the early nineties, Allen may have been removed, but Tom would have had a lot more time to make the rounds of promises and mistakes. Now, there's a deadline looming over Tom's head: under federal rules, a child cannot stay in foster care for more than fifteen out of twenty-two months; he must be either formally adopted or returned to his biological home. The day we talked on the porch, when Tom was in recovery from his latest relapse, Allen was nearing that deadline.

This legislation is called the Adoption and Safe Families Act (ASFA), which had bipartisan support and was signed into law in 1997 by President Bill Clinton. ASFA was developed to counter what's called foster care "drift" — the years-long delay that children in foster homes had been suffering, waiting for the courts to determine whether their parents were fit enough to take them back. So ASFA mandated that the parents could no longer stall: if they weren't stabilized and ready for parenthood again after fifteen months, the courts would terminate parental rights, and the child would be put up for adoption.

The results of ASFA are difficult to ascertain, largely because several states already had pro-adoption legislation on the books, and ASFA didn't adequately fund studies to tease out what, specifically, its mandates had accomplished. Still, a reliable national foster care count showed the number of adoptions from foster care growing from 25,693 in 1995 to 52,468 in 2004. (Growth has leveled off since then.)

But this doesn't mean that *all* kids who are in foster care will be adopted — and because ASFA encourages terminating parental rights so quickly, it means that more children are left without *anyone* — essentially orphans, with living parents. In the last few years, there have been about seventy thousand cases of parental termination annually, but only fifty thousand adoptions. ASFA critics hit this one hard; while ASFA's timeline makes some parents scurry to improve their situations, it allows less responsible parents to get off too easily. Overall, only about a quarter of the kids who entered the system in the nineties or after ASFA was passed will be adopted eventually.

Fifteen months is just too short for many parents, critics claim, especially if they're struggling with drug addiction. Numbers are hard to gauge, but two-thirds of the nine hundred thousand cases of child abuse or neglect are reportedly affected by substance abuse. (This number may well be too low, as a large national survey showed that child welfare workers missed 61 percent of documented substance abuse among investigated parents.) While ASFA was being debated, some members of Congress talked about the need for services for substance-affected parents, but they largely dropped the topic, asking instead for more research. Still, one of ASFA's three allowable exceptions for terminating parental rights is this: that the parents haven't been offered adequate services. (The other two exceptions are when the child is being cared for by a relative, and when termination wouldn't be in the best interests of the child.) Many times, caseworkers argue that the parents should stay connected to their children simply because these caseworkers haven't found any treatment for the parents. This can be both good and bad: children of drug-addicted parents may not become "orphans" — but then they may endure the foster care drift.

Because ASFA mandates what's called "concurrency planning," which means social workers must find kids a permanent adoptive family while also working on biological family reunification, a war can be played out directly through the child. Foster parents willing to adopt are the logical placement choice, should parental rights indeed be cut; this was likely the reason Allen was placed with the Greens. If Tom can't prove to the courts that he's able to parent his son, Allen can just stay forever with Allyson and Bruce and avoid yet another big adjustment to another adoptive family. But in a different kind of home — say, one like Steve and Erin's — foster parents can have a vested interest in undermining any biological family preservation efforts. And preserving the biological family is precisely what foster care was meant to accomplish from the start.

ASFA was, in large part, a conservative reaction to more liberal legislation that had passed in 1980, which was itself in reaction to a more conservative trend before that. The pendulum seems to swing every several years — from a family-based model that says we should make every effort to keep the biological family together to a model of child safety. It's a matter of values and emphasis: one side says kids are better off with their parents and the state's job is to provide and regulate security; the other side says kids are better off safe and the state's job is to provide and regulate a new family. (The terms *conservative* and *liberal* and *left* and *right* are somewhat strange and ill-fitting, as lawmakers on both sides of the aisle vote for both types of child welfare legislation. But the more progressive child welfare activists and strategists tend to favor keeping kids with their biological families — hence the terms *left* and *liberal* for the family-leaning policies.)

The early years of state-mandated reporting and child removals were grim; new laws passed in the late sixties and early seventies directed states to remove children, so state authorities squared their shoulders, steeled their jaws, and started marching in. The pendulum already swung left as the decade progressed. Maybe children didn't need to be removed from their parents quite so often, the thinking went, especially if they didn't have somewhere safer to go. In 1980, Congress passed the Adoption Assistance and Child Welfare Act (AACWA), which forced states to exchange their costly foster care replacements for preventive and family reunification programs. It was a paradigm shift fueled by thinkers like Anna Freud and Joseph Goldstein, who believed that kids are injured by uncertainty and disruption; that they are, except in the most extreme cases, better off coming home. Funding moved toward child abuse prevention, parenting skills training, and familial support. Programs called "intensive family preservation services" became popular, wherein caseworkers with lighter caseloads would work daily with at-risk families, to build their skills and their bonds.

But not all kids could stay at home; the eighties ushered in something nobody had predicted that infinitely swelled the foster care rolls, despite AACWA's mandates: crack cocaine. Between 1986 and 1989, the number of New York's foster children almost doubled. But because of AACWA, these kids were, by and large, neither going home nor landing in a permanent placement. Nationally, hundreds of thousands of children ended up hovering in a purgatory state: their biological homes weren't safe enough to return to, but they weren't eligible for adoption either, because AACWA mandated that parental rights be terminated as a last resort. So kids waited for years and years and years for their parents to get better — to pass drug tests or violence management classes, or to get out of jail, or to simply meet the backlogged bureaucratic requirements from an agency that had too many cases to handle.

So that's when the pendulum swung right again, and much of AACWA was essentially reversed in 1997 — with ASFA. Clinton's goal with ASFA was to double the number of foster children adopted annually to fifty-four thousand within five years. To do this, states would receive financial incentives: $4,000 for each so-called normal foster adoption, and $6,000 for each "special needs" adoption. Even within this landscape of changing legislation, not everyone sees a pendulum swing, with pro-adoption folks on one side and pro-biological families on the other. The laws do change every several years, but the changes are influenced by everything from scientific discoveries to psychological trends to surges or dips in the child welfare rolls. And many key stakeholders in foster care don't lobby for dramatic sea changes, but rather improvisational tweaks. For instance, with ASFA, some feel the adoption incentives unfairly disadvantage the biological families and argue that the same money should be awarded to agencies that successfully reunify families. Others have lobbied for more intense, but shorter, in-home support services for all but the direst (seriously violent or sexually abusive) family situations. If circumstances don't improve within a matter of months, they say, *then* the child should be removed, providing further motivation for parental progress. Many people in child welfare say we break up too many families, many say the kids stay too long in care, many advocate putting more money or emphasis into this program or that, but nobody's suggesting we ditch the system altogether, abandoning it for something entirely new.

Marcia Robinson Lowry, a lawyer who fought a famous battle for the rights of foster children, the Shirley Wilder case in New York, thinks the basic tenets of foster care laws have remained decent through all the shifts in public policy. Lowry says child welfare's spotty report card has to do with a simple lack of incentive. People at all levels of the system, she claims, will do as little work as they can do because there's no *reason* to do better. Because there's no real cultural value placed on the lives of foster children or their families, the people hired to work for their benefit don't strive to provide much value. So Lowry has built her life around making sure people in child welfare at least follow the laws as they're written.

After heading up the Children's Rights project of the American Civil Liberties Union (ACLU), where she fought for Shirley Wilder, Lowry went on to found a separate organization by the same name in 1995, and to launch lawsuits against *entire states* that were performing poorly — where high numbers of kids were dying in care and living in substandard conditions. She and her team have successfully sued the states of Mississippi, New Jersey, Tennessee, and others, as well as the District of Columbia; Fulton and DeKalb Counties in Georgia; and Milwaukee, Wisconsin. After a case is settled, Children's Rights sticks around to ensure that officials follow their mandates to appropriate more money to programs, audit agencies, hire more employees, and so on.

In her corner office on Fifth Avenue and 28th Street in Manhattan, Lowry told me there are good laws in place that tell us when to remand a child, and when not to. Everybody knows, she said, that it's best for a child to stay with his parents when at all possible. Everybody knows that a teenager should be with a family rather than in an institution. Everybody knows that providing good, old-fashioned social work services, like educational or financial resources to a mother, is preferable to taking away her kid. The law shows a clear preference for these things no matter what era we're in. The trouble is, these carefully crafted services take more time and effort for the system to provide than simply sticking a child into any old foster home or a teenager into an institution and getting his case file off your desk.

"The basic tenets of foster care are good," Lowry said. She's distinguished-looking, with a silver bob and a direct expression that indicates she's very busy, but she'll take all the time she needs to express precisely what she intends. "It's the implementation that isn't working — and that's what causes the slow destruction of a person, a kid, as he goes through the system."

For Lowry, what child welfare needs overall is more oversight — to make sure everyone is just following the rules. "There are no magic bullets," she said, answering a question I'd asked about some innovative new programs I'd read about. Her office walls are a sunny yellow, and all around are oversize black-and-white photos of the kids her organization has served — some smiling, some desperately grave. "There are nuances to programs and so on, but really we just need to implement the basic modes of social work: providing services, making individual decisions, following a case through."

For Lowry, a situation like Allen and Tom's would require a good social worker, doing what she's paid to do: provide Tom with rehabilitative services and then, if he relapses, do the extra legwork to find out where Allen was previously placed. But Tom and Allyson had been through their slice of the system too, and they didn't trust it. Tom listened to Allyson's fears, she said, about his potential relapse. He worried that Allen could get placed with some random family instead of the Greens. So by the end of that year, Tom became the generous parent in the King Solomon story. He decided to sacrifice the baby to a safer circumstance, rather than risk sacrificing him altogether.

"Tom came to his senses," Allyson told me over the phone several months after we all met on the porch. Her relief was palpable. "Tom has had this trust issue; he hasn't trusted people, but he started to trust us." While Allyson was watching Tom, she said, Tom was watching the family. "He's seen how we've been with Charles, that we adopted him but he still sees his mom, and that he could still see Allen if he was with us. He knows that the best thing is for Allen to stay with us. He's already talked to the court." Tom had agreed to sign over his rights and do an open adoption.

It was almost a year before I saw Tom again. He had continued to visit Allen and play video games with the other Green children and eat Sunday dinners with everybody, but our paths had never crossed. Allen continued to make progress with his anger and impulse control; Allyson said he never hit the other children anymore. He was also gentle with his baby brother, Anthony, whose HIV status had recently reversed without any drugs. Allyson called it a miracle.

In the carport, baby Anthony was practicing his walking. Allyson had made a barricade of plastic lawn furniture to keep him out of the driveway, and she gently scooped him up each time he tumbled. Allen, who was four, was stomping on an empty Capri Sun packet to propel the straw into the air.

I asked him what he called his game.

"Balloon Blaster!" Allen shouted, without missing a beat.

Once the straw landed on the dirty ground, Allyson told him he couldn't stick it back in his mouth to re-inflate the juice pack. Allen pouted.

"You'll have to throw it away," Allyson said.

Instead, Allen climbed to the top of a dirt mound in the corner of the carport, left there after some construction. He fell and scraped his hand, and started to cry, holding it out for Allyson to kiss.

"What happens to children who don't do what adults tell them?" Allyson admonished, delivering her boo-boo kiss.

"They fall down," Allen said miserably, examining his tiny scrape.

As Allen ran inside to find something new to play with, Allyson watched him admiringly. He was tall for his age, his limbs long and rubbery; his face was already losing the chub of babyhood and taking on the serious, almost adult lines so curious in children. "He's so creative; he can make something out of anything," she said.

Allen returned with a small blue bottle and a rubber band. "This is my Blue Shooter!" he shouted happily and scurried up the stairs next to Bruce, who was on the front stoop, to aim at the two concrete lions.

Tom, Bruce told me, had skipped out on the adoption hearing where he was supposed to formally turn over his rights to the Greens. The hearing had been canceled — but that hadn't stopped Tom from coming around the house. Bruce said he didn't harbor any bad feelings. He knew it was hard to sign that last paper.

"Tom's like a kid himself; he comes over, watches TV, has food, and gets to have family and community," Bruce said, adding that he and Allyson weren't worried about the botched hearing; if anything, it had reinforced their status as stable providers. This was September, and the next "final" court date had been arranged for November — with or without Tom, and long past the ASFA deadline.

"Daddy!" Allen shouted. And there Tom was, as though summoned by our discussion, grinning at the bottom of the stairs. He'd replaced the missing earpiece on his glasses. Tom nodded his hellos, and Allen jumped on his back to piggyback inside the house.

In steamy Bell County, Texas, Oliver's custody hearing had been slated for the middle of August. In the two weeks since I'd left Texas, Caitlin had missed both scheduled visits with her son. One time, she didn't have gas money, and another, she called Steve in the middle of the night saying her boyfriend, Rick, was in the hospital being treated for a potassium deficiency; she couldn't possibly make it the next morning. Surely, Steve reasoned, these blunders would count against her.

They did, but not enough to terminate her rights; the judge decided to give Caitlin one more chance. At the hearing, he scheduled another court date for October, six months shy of the ASFA cutoff, admonishing Caitlin with a warning: if she skipped even one more visitation, she would lose her son. Even for work? she asked. At that point, Caitlin was still living with Rick and his parents. Rick's mother testified that Rick had lost his job; Caitlin's shift at McDonald's represented the household's sole employment. The judge wasn't swayed; he told her plenty of good parents survived on welfare.

So at first, Caitlin made her visits. Caitlin didn't drive, but Rick got himself a car, thereby doubling Caitlin's chances of appearing (Rick's mother was her other chauffeur). But then, during one drop-off, while Steve was informing them of Oliver's switch from formula to milk, Rick's mom interrupted. She was hosting evacuees from the latest hurricane, she said proudly.

Steve immediately called Oliver's guardian ad litem, the person hired by the state to represent Oliver's interests; nobody was supposed to be in Caitlin's house without having a criminal background check. The guardian ad litem sent a social worker, who discovered Oliver didn't have a crib. The guardian ad litem also checked up on Caitlin's therapist, who was tracking her emotional health.

The therapist, who had originally recommended the overnight visits, had been observing Caitlin's interactions with Oliver since April and had issued a report for the court. In it, she claimed that Caitlin "did not know how to properly parent a child." This, Steve wrote to me, might finally do it; even the therapist found Caitlin unfit. Still, he said, "We're not getting our hopes up. The judge might extend again. This just represents how the system sits on its ass until the last second and plays with everybody's emotions on every side until it's all over."

The path to terminate a parent's rights may seem endless — and it often does take months or even years— and yet it's possibly the most critical, and certainly most contentious, stage of foster care work. *Parental termination* even sounds oxymoronic: parenthood is supposed to be the one job you can't quit. Experts rarely weigh in on individual cases when they aren't privy to all of the particulars, but it's at moments like these that they tend to have a lot of opinions. Mike Arsham, the executive director of the Child Welfare Organizing Project (CWOP) in New York, calls parental termination the "death penalty of child welfare." CWOP is an advocacy organization that helps biological parents work with the system to regain their kids and have more influence on agency decisions overall. CWOP and Arsham look deeply at the ways poverty, racism, and limited social resources inhibit parenting, and they argue passionately against parents taking the fall for society's failings. Other people, like Elizabeth Bartholet, a law professor and the faculty director of the Child Advocacy Program at Harvard Law School, who has worked with the NAACP and is a well-known voice in child welfare, sees things differently. In a book and several articles, Bartholet also links abuse or neglect to poverty and urges for better and more preventive services for moms like Caitlin, but she cautions against late-stage preservation efforts. She argues that adoption — after kids have endured abuse and neglect and then bonded with a new family — is better for those kids. She points to the potential for reabuse if they go back home and says there's an awareness outside of child welfare that "parenting is more about bonding than blood."

Some think that the family termination hearings can be biased. Family courts don't have juries or prolonged hearings; a single judge hears testimony from each side and makes his decision. And he makes it fast: in many jurisdictions all across the country, family courts — their dockets jammed with divorce, child custody, and child welfare cases — are the most crowded courts of all. So it's widely held that judges will follow whatever recommendations the child welfare agency makes; the agency, after all, compiles the data on the family and produces the reports. But it is the agency that targeted the parents in the first place and removed their kids; parents rarely feel the agency is on their side.

In the end, Steve was right: the judge did extend. At first for a week — and then for another three months, claiming Caitlin needed more psychological evaluation. The Texas Department of Family and Protective Services (DFPS) had been sending a therapist out to Caitlin once a week — to help her, but also, ultimately, to determine her aptitude as a parent.

The final hearing would be in January. Caitlin's visits with Oliver were downgraded from overnights to supervised one-hour appointments. Although the delay jangled Steve, it did bump his case into a kind of magical territory where, everyone said, he could finally get a lawyer and be allowed to take the stand. By January, Oliver would have been living with Steve and Erin for a full year, at which point they could argue that it was in Oliver's best interests to stay where he was bonded. Finally, Steve thought, he could step into view.

"Caitlin made some weird comments afterward that intimated she may just want to end the process, but that may be just wishful thinking on my part," Steve wrote to me a few days after the judge's extension. He recognized that the screws were tightening on her, and she was likely feeling the pressure.

Two weeks later, Caitlin was in the hospital. She had threatened suicide if she didn't get her son back. When she was released, she fought with her boyfriend, Rick, and moved out of the trailer. By early December, Caitlin was contacting her social worker, saying she wanted to see Oliver, but then missed her visit because she didn't have gas money. She made up with Rick and moved back in but still felt depressed. She then told her therapist that she wanted to sign her rights over to Rick's mom.

But by December, Rick's mom didn't want Oliver anymore; she didn't think he'd be safe in the trailer with Caitlin around. The therapist, too, wrote that she did not feel Oliver "would be safe in the home and is recommending termination." By the end of December, when Protective Services had to submit its final report for the hearing in January, they were reporting "concern about Oliver's safety if left alone with the mother." In the end, the DFPS recommended parental termination and "unrelated adoption."

For the final hearing, Steve and Erin prepared photo albums of Oliver playing with the cat, smiling in the sun, and wearing face paint alongside his brother, Wilson. They brought a bulging file documenting all interactions with Caitlin and her inadequacies and mistakes. They brought a lawyer. The DFPS report is eight pages long, and it details Caitlin's psychological deterioration, failure to keep appointments, and the incidents of hitting Oliver, for instance, when he grabbed the remote control. It describes the various interventions the department made. It says nothing specific about Steve or Erin or even Oliver — about their compatibility, the progress Oliver had made, the way Steve ran with him every morning, or Wilson drew him pictures. Steve and Erin are only briefly mentioned as "foster parents trained to take care of a child Oliver's age."

On the morning of January 13, when Steve was dressed in his best suit and ready, finally, to publicly plead his case, he never got the chance. Caitlin didn't show. The judge terminated her parental rights, on real paper rather than a napkin, and it was over. Oliver was theirs. Steve sat in the courtroom watching the next cases, about a woman with a kid acting up in daycare, and another mom in a prison jumpsuit and cuffs arguing for her rights, in a kind of daze.

I'm grateful, for Oliver's sake, that he will never know what judges and caseworkers and even family members have said about his biological mother being unfit to parent. When he's old enough to start asking questions, Steve and Erin can devise careful answers about her past. But kids who are old enough to remember their biological parents suffer differently. When you're being abused or neglected, that's one thing. When you're removed from the danger, and people start to talk, you have to split yourself in half.

I can't speak to living with strangers, but I do know about compartmentalization. When I lived with my mother, her kind of crazy was the only life I knew. I didn't know it was bad until I left, but once I did, I could no longer survive with that memory intact. I had to cauterize off entire interior landscapes, to become somebody new. I had to accept a new mother, with new mother clothes, new mother breath, new mother words — words that told me my old mother, my real mother, was unfit, my life before was unfit, I too was unfit. But it was when I left my mother's unfit home that I no longer could fit anywhere at all.

My mother gave up on me, the adult voices said, and I believed them. Even ten years later, or twenty, different adults have tried to designate proper roles: "*She* was the mom and *you* were the child," they say. "Your mother was too ill to care for you properly. Otherwise, she would have reached out to you after all these years." And I've believed those voices too. Except. Except for the part of me that remembers, the part that lives in the cauterized landscape, in the childhood that never knew to call itself abuse. That part also remembers a mom who brushed my hair and made me lunches. That part remembers loving her and remembers walking away. Yes, my mother gave up on me, but that small part knows I gave up too. And that part is very, very broken.

This is why I know it's different to talk about terminating a parent's rights when the kids are older. Older children remember. Older children have guilt. Older children are abused, older children need sanctuary and fostering and outside adoption, but older children, no matter how brutalizing or diminishing their home lives are, won't want to leave. And if they do, a part of them will always stay behind.

"If you have the choice of being abused by your mother or abused by a stranger, you'd choose your mother. It's abuse either way." This came from Arelis Rosario-Keane, a twenty-two-year-old college student and a veteran of the foster care system, referring to the likelihood of getting mistreated in care. (As an example, an Indiana study showed that children in group homes experienced ten times the rate of physical abuse and twenty-eight times the rate of sexual abuse of kids in the general population. A study of kids in Oregon and Washington State foster homes showed one-third being abused by an adult in the home.) Arelis now sees a therapist regularly and knows that all kinds of people develop deep psychic ties to their abusers. "Then again," she said, "I was being victimized back then."

Of all the foster kids I've talked with over the years, Arelis and her seven biological siblings have endured some of the worst, and perhaps most sadistic, abuse I've ever heard recounted. The Rosario kids I know have been starved, beaten, locked in closets, abandoned in shelters and hotels for weeks at a time, and yet they were repeatedly removed and then sent home again to live with the mother who abused them. Arelis speaks now from a position of relative safety; her mother's rights have been terminated, and she and several of her siblings have been adopted by a kind and fiercely intelligent woman named Mary Keane. Arelis admits, though, that before Mary came along, she would have told any social worker who visited that she wanted to be returned to her mother.

It can be difficult to tease apart signs of abuse from signs of a parent's external stressors in infants, but recognizing abuse in children who are old enough to talk is especially tricky. Older children will lie out of fear or a desire to protect their parents, or they won't know how to express the problems at home. For them, the problems are the only reality they know.

After cycling in and out of foster care several times, the six youngest Rosario kids were abandoned for good. The two oldest girls were already separated from the family: one had had a baby and run off with a boyfriend, and the other had been stranded in a shelter and picked up by ACS. That left Arelis, at fourteen, to care for her siblings, ages eleven, ten, eight, seven, and four, in their father's empty apartment; he was serving time. Before their mother left them there, she went grocery shopping and filled the cupboards with food. Unlike the other times she'd skipped out for weekends or took gambling trips to Atlantic City, she left the doorknob attached so the kids could come and go. At the beginning, Arelis said, they watched a lot of *Murphy Brown* since that was her favorite TV program and she had control over the remote. They figured their mom would come back eventually, but the weeks kept ticking by. Arelis said it "wasn't within my mind to grasp, 'Let's all go to school together,'" but some days she would walk the youngest ones to the library and read to them. It also wasn't within her grasp to call ACS — and none of them wanted to go back to that, largely because there were so many of them and the chances of them being placed in the same home were exceedingly slim. They'd been separated before, and Arelis said she felt tremendously worried and guilty. So when the food started running out, they stole from grocery stores. Pretty soon, the electricity was shut off. And then the water. They lasted for six months, until finally they called their older sister Aileen, who was in foster care, and she told them to call ACS.

Now all the Rosario kids were safely accounted for. Mary had taken in six of them — even Brenda, the oldest, was living upstairs with her eleven-year-old daughter, and Aileen lived down the block with her husband and two kids. The two youngest siblings had been fostered, and then adopted, by another family, and Arelis felt good about that and still saw them all the time. But now she looks back on all her suffering and wishes the parental termination could have happened faster. She didn't know any better, when she was little, than to keep wanting the mom who called her "Daughter of Satan." But she knows now, and she thinks the child welfare workers who removed her the first time around should have removed her for good.

I told Arelis about Dr. Rittner, the director of the social work school who was so reluctant to terminate parental rights. At the conference, Rittner said she terminated only two times in all her years of work (later she remembered a few more), but I recounted Rittner's public speech, and Arelis exploded. "For you to oversee a thousand cases and terminate only two, you're doing something wrong!" She slammed her hands on the table and gazed up at the ceiling in exasperation.

Coming from Arelis, this seemed a perfectly reasonable response. But I remember hearing Dr. Rittner tell the story. It was at a big conference at NYU, and the audience of social workers had responded positively to her theory that parents inherently want to do best by their children; I too had nodded right along.

"Did the people in the meeting call that lady out? Did they think she was doing her job?" Arelis, who generally speaks softly and with a slight lisp, raised her voice again and then had to get up for a cigarette. On her way out, she fumed, "Less than half the parents could get better if you gave them the right help. Did they have a former foster child there to speak for us?"

4

Drugs in the System

DOREEN SOTO IS A MOTHER and grandmother who now lives in a brand-new building in the South Bronx. I first met Doreen in 2007, when she was an inmate at Bayview Correctional Facility and a student in my precollege writing class. Doreen has a big body and an easy laugh, and she always sat at the back of the classroom, her left leg kicked out in front of her, resting from a recent surgery. Even in her state-issued forest-green pants and matching button-down shirt, Doreen had style. Her work boots were laced just so, her hair was shorn close to the scalp, and a gold pinkie ring glinted every time she raised her hand with an answer, which was often. Doreen grasped the complexity of the Baldwin we were reading on sight, perhaps because she had swallowed so many sharp paradoxes in her own life, or had to live with so much ambiguity.

"You gotta accept the system, *and* fight it, *and* be good with you," Doreen said, summing up *Notes of a Native Son*. She leaned back in her chair, crossing her arms across her three-hundred-pound frame, and smiled.

Doreen lost her daughter, Shameka, to the system when Shameka was eighteen months old. Shameka's now twenty-three, and her own daughter — Doreen's granddaughter — is in foster care. Drugs were the reason that ACS (then Special Services for Children) took Shameka away from Doreen. And drugs are behind Doreen's three long state bids in prison.

There's no way to talk about foster care without bringing up substance abuse; methodological approaches vary, but most studies show upwards of two-thirds of system-involved parents have some substance use problem — and others put the figure much higher. "Other than a case with one schizophrenic mother," Dr. Rittner said to me after her talk about terminating parental rights at the conference at NYU, "I don't think I knew anyone where alcohol and drugs weren't involved."

Despite all her arrests, her years in prison, her homelessness, the beatings and the prostitution and the drug sickness she's endured, Doreen says the worst day of her life was the day a cop and child welfare investigator came to her apartment to take her baby away.

"I was dopesick that morning, so I put Shameka on the bed, surrounded by pillows, and went out. The drug spot was around the corner," Doreen said. She noticed an older white woman loitering in her hallway. "Can I help you?" Doreen asked the woman. The woman just told her she was waiting for someone, so Doreen went to get her drugs.

"When I came back, I could hear the baby screaming, and the lady was still there. I was like, 'They didn't come yet?' She just said, 'No, they're on their way,' so I went inside my apartment," Doreen said. "Shameka had fallen behind the bed! So I'm comforting her, and trying to not let her fall asleep, because they say if you fall and hit your head you're not supposed to go to sleep. That's when the doorbell rang."

Doreen continued: "It was the lady. I was high. I hid the bag. I say, 'Can I help you?' And she says, 'No, unfortunately, I'm from BCW [Bureau of Child Welfare, the old name for ACS/Special Services] and you've been under a ninety-day surveillance.'" Doreen narrowed her eyes, hardened her tone. "I was like, 'Ninety-day surveillance of *what?*'"

The woman told her that BCW had received an anonymous phone

call that Doreen had been neglecting her child. "She said, 'Remember when you went out? And you came back and your baby was crying? I bear witness to that.'"

It was then that a policeman stepped in and told Doreen to start packing a bag for Shameka.

"I said, 'What do you mean pack a bag? Where are we going?' The woman answered, 'Well, we're going to take her.' And I said, 'You're not taking her without me!' But the woman told me I couldn't come, and she handed me her card. I thought, 'You're taking my baby, and all I get is a fucking card?'"

Doreen said she was sobbing as she packed Shameka's bag and, although the BCW woman was decent, the policeman's presence didn't make it any easier. "I knew that cop," Doreen said. "He was a crooked cop. He used to get paid off by the cocaine dealers on 164th and Amsterdam. He just kept saying, 'We can do this easy, or we can do this hard.' I wanted to say I knew who he was, but I said to myself, 'No, bitch, you don't want to end up in jail, because they're still gonna take your daughter.'"

The worst part was handing Shameka over. "She didn't want to go," Doreen said. "She was holding on to me, and screaming at the top of her lungs. But then the cop and the lady went out and I watched them go from the kitchen window. My daughter was screaming and looking at me; she was turning blue from crying so hard. I was sobbing and thinking, 'I'm no good, I'm no good.'"

That night, when Doreen went to get high, she was arrested for the first time in her life. She never lived with Shameka again.

Doreen thinks it was her own mother who made the call to child welfare. This can happen, but it's far more common for mothers like Doreen to be "caught" when they have to interact with some institution. Such as when they go into labor.

This is what happened to Robbyne Wiley — another African American woman in her forties — who had her baby taken from her in the hospital back in 1991. Robbyne had three children already, and she'd been warned when her last child, a daughter, was born positive for crack cocaine to stop using. But Robbyne didn't expect, the morning after delivering her fourth child, that her doctor would walk in empty-handed.

"I said, 'Can you bring me my baby?' And he said, 'Your baby's not here.' They just took my baby like that," Robbyne explained, her eyes growing round with the memory. "And I did not get him back until he was four years old."

The federal government requires that all fifty states have a system in place to notify Child Protective Services if a baby is born "positive tox," or drug-exposed. Twelve states and the District of Columbia define a positive tox delivery as child abuse or neglect (meaning a fetus can be abused in utero), and twenty-five states have laws that allow a woman to be incarcerated for such a crime — either at delivery or while still pregnant. A sad byproduct of this legislation is that moms in many parts of the country won't seek prenatal care, as a dirty urine test could land them in jail.

There's no universal testing for the newborns; in most places doctors simply decide who looks like a drug user and test subjectively. But black women have been reported to health authorities at delivery up to ten times more often than white women, even though studies show that drug use is relatively equal, for instance, between blacks and whites (9.5 percent and 8.2 percent, respectively), and that more pregnant white women use drugs than pregnant black women (113,000 versus 75,000).

Racial prejudice in drug testing is only one reason that there are proportionally more kids of color than white kids in foster care. Nationally, African American children represent 47 percent of the children in foster care placement, but they constitute only 19 percent of the total child population. White kids have an inverse situation: they constitute 61 percent of the children in this country but only 38 percent of the foster care kids.

Part of the current inequality in foster care comes from infinite reproductions of the drug-testing scenario in places where families of color are scrutinized by those mandated to report suspected neglect or abuse — places like schools, mental health settings, welfare offices, and hospitals. Studies have shown, for instance, that African American kids are more likely to be suspended or expelled or labeled "aggressive" in their schools than their white counterparts — and these actions trigger calls to Child Protective Services. African American youth are also more likely to be prescribed psychiatric medications for their aggressive behaviors, or to be labeled schizophrenic, and sent to lockdown correctional facilities, whereas white youth with the same violent behavior are more likely to be referred to outpatient clinics, without any marks on their record or risk of removal. (Fifteen percent of all kids in foster care were placed there because of delinquent behavior or status offenses, meaning acts prohibited by their status as minors.) Back at the hospital, doctors are more likely to report injuries in African American families as "abuse" and in white families as "accidents."

Still, this doesn't explain the reasons families of color are maintained in the system year after year after year. Reformers talk about this question a lot, and in broad terms, they fall into three camps. There are those who say that children of color are overrepresented because of a statistical pileup of family risk factors — like teen parenthood, substance abuse, domestic violence, incarceration, and poverty — all of which are stressors, all of which can lead to child maltreatment. Others argue that overrepresentation isn't so much about race as neighborhoods — which, for African Americans, can have disproportionately high levels of homelessness, unemployment, poverty, drug use, and street crime, both adding stress and making families more visible to police scrutiny. And the third group looks at systemic problems, blaming child protective leadership, government, workers' cultural insensitivity, and the system's legacy of institutionalized racism. In terms of where to direct reform efforts, each group would propose different solutions: fix the family, fix the community, or fix the system from the top down. The real answer is probably yes, yes, and yes.

Within these generalized descriptions, there are thousands of subtleties and examples of various other kinds of racism threading their way through child welfare. Most of it isn't intentional or centrally located in one "bad" child welfare director, or organization, or design flaw. It's akin to the criminal justice system, which is also disproportionately filled with people of color — and where, again, experts argue about the sources of disparity. Is the root problem there one of poverty, inequitable opportunities, institutionalized racism, or one giant pileup of minor discriminations? Again, the answer is yes, yes, yes, and yes.

Another way to look at race and foster care is to look at money, because this is one area where the numbers match. African Americans accounted for two-fifths of the 558,000 children in foster care in 2000, which is similar to the proportion of all poor children who are African American (40 percent). In other words, African American children are represented in child welfare in comparable proportion to their distribution in low-income families. And the National Incidence Study (NIS) for Child Abuse and Neglect, which gives the most comprehensive estimate of all cases, has unequivocally determined low income to be a strong risk factor for all forms of maltreatment.

In the eighties and nineties, the NIS studies consistently reported that African American parents do not abuse their children any more than white parents do. In fact, they found no significant differences in the incidences of abuse and neglect across any ethnic or racial lines. But then, in 2010, the NIS produced its most comprehensive report yet and something shifted: it found a 73 percent higher rate of black maltreatment over white. Chapin Hall Center for Children, a major progressive policy research center, released an issue brief on both these findings and cosponsored a conference with Harvard University on race and child welfare. Although the brief addressed the potential of racism in foster care, the authors mainly attributed the disproportionality in maltreatment to the disproportionality in poverty among blacks and whites. It's time, they said, to stop trying to reduce the numbers of African Americans in care because we presume there's a bias and instead focus on the *reasons* the numbers are so much higher and direct help toward the families that need it. If poverty and its attendant burdens — depression, anxiety, drug use, heightened community violence, paucity of support systems, and so on — can sow the seeds for child abuse, then child welfare needs to go back to prevention. But this is a tall order for one sprawling and splintered administration, which has always been reactionary: it treats symptoms, not disease. The solution, as it has always been, is bigger than foster care, bigger than abuse; the real solution will be rooted in society as a whole.

This kind of perspective shift, on a smaller scale, has been a rallying cry for drug-using mothers too; rather than just calling in foster care and removing a baby at delivery, we could pan back and treat the addiction. We could see addiction as a health issue, rather than a crime.

This would be an important change, because drug testing largely spotlights the substances that harm adults — not the ones that harm the infants. Alcohol, for instance, is not illegal and it won't turn up in a drug test, but it is one of the most dangerous substances for a fetus. The so-called crack babies, on the other hand, have grown up — and the dire predictions about them proved false. A review in the *Journal of the American Medical Association* of thirty-six studies that looked at physical growth, cognition, language and motor skills, behavior, attention, affect, and neurophysiology found *no connection* between prenatal exposure to cocaine and a decrease in functioning.

Dr. Barry M. Lester at Brown University is a principal investigator for the largest longitudinal study on cocaine-exposed babies (thousands of these babies are now in their late teens), and he's working with the National Institute on Drug Abuse on a similar study looking at babies and meth. At a conference in 2009, Dr. Lester said that they'd tracked around 450 babies (half meth-exposed and half drug-free) for the previous three years, and so far no substantial differences had emerged. In fact, meth-exposed infants exhibit many of the same characteristics as cocaine-exposed babies, Lester said: at birth, these babies can have some difficulty feeding, then they seem to even out symptom-wise for a couple of years. I spoke with Dr. Lester a few years after the conference, when the kids in the meth study had hit five years old. By this time, just like the kids in the cocaine study, the kids started showing poor inhibitory control, which means that they acted out more and didn't always know how to stop themselves.

"We see this when they go to school, probably because there are more demands put on them there, and because their failure in behavior control becomes more obvious," Dr. Lester said. And he contextualized the findings further. "Yes, there are drug effects, but they aren't of the magnitude everyone thought they would be; they're much more subtle — on the order of ADHD."

Lester's studies subtract for factors like poverty and foster care, so that only prenatal drug exposure is considered. This means he can add back in, for instance, a child's experience with child welfare to see how that affects the developing brain. "Out-of-home placement is one of the factors that seems to ride along with drug exposure, in terms of affecting the prefrontal cortex and poor inhibitory control. It's sort of a double whammy," he said. That's why he doesn't think we should be legislating automatic removals in the delivery room. "We're seeing an escalation in the legislation getting more punitive with meth. We already learned this with all the research on cocaine — that addiction is a mental health disorder. There's plenty of evidence that it's treatable. There's also plenty of evidence that mothers who use can be adequate parents. Of course, some are not adequate parents, but then there are also mothers who don't use who are not adequate parents either."

One final troubling statistic is that the newborn drug tests are *wrong* on average more than 25 percent of the time. A study by the U.S. Substance Abuse and Mental Health Services Administration and the American Association for Clinical Chemistry found that initial urine screenings can produce false positives. Even tests on a baby's first stool (long considered the gold standard in drug testing) can be wrong up to 70 percent of the time.

I'm not suggesting that doctors shouldn't be looking for signs of use of drugs like meth or cocaine in the hospital. But the American College of Obstetricians and Gynecologists, even as a moderate and mainstream voice in the medical establishment, has come out against newborn drug testing. It endangers critical trust between a mother and her obstetrician, the College claims, and mandated reporting can conflict with the therapeutic obligation. Patients have the right to informed consent and bodily integrity and shouldn't be tested for anything against their will or knowledge. And as for the business of states penalizing women for their behavior during pregnancy: it's a slippery slope, as all sorts of things (drug use, poor nutrition, prescription medication, depression) can affect a baby's health too. Punitive policies discourage prenatal care, the lack of which also harms children —

the very thing the drug laws were designed to prevent. Addiction, they say finally, is a disease and not a moral failing.

Robbyne and Doreen lived in a city, and an era, when using drugs could get your children removed but wouldn't necessarily land you in jail. Now, in twenty-five states, it's a crime to expose children — not just the fetus — to illegal drug activity, such as narcotics possession, sales, or manufacture. For example, it's a felony to possess any controlled substance in Idaho, Louisiana, Alabama, and Ohio in the presence of a child. Also, crystal meth has eclipsed crack cocaine as the most highly legislated drug, and fourteen states have singled out the manufacture or even possession of methamphetamines around children as a particular felony.

The trouble with this is what happens to the children in such cases: the children go into foster care because the parents go to jail, and the parents don't receive treatment for what many still consider to be a health issue, rather than a criminal issue. Drug treatment in prison is notoriously worse than what parents can receive on the outside. And if they're afraid they'll be locked up and have their children taken away, parents aren't likely to ask for help early on.

In states where drug use isn't criminalized as child abuse, many child welfare agencies are connecting with drug rehabilitation programs and referring or court-ordering parents into rehab. Studies have shown that parents who are given treatment earlier, in settings they can easily access, are more likely to be reunited with their children than parents who don't receive treatment. And women who keep their kids complete treatment at a higher rate.

In one way, this is obvious: better drug treatment yields better parenting. If you're a mom who's using, you probably know you need help — and many mothers want it. Some don't, or won't, or can't, accept treatment for reasons that range as wide and as deep as the range of human frailties: there's mental illness, there's ego, there's community and loyalty and loss in the network of drugs, and there's the protection drugs afford, the scabbing over of one's own early traumas and scars. But if you live in a state where you're going to be charged with child abuse for your addiction, or you know your kids will be taken away if you show up at a treatment site, you're stuck regardless.

You have to try to get sober alone (which has disastrously low success rates) or continue raising your kids while using drugs on the side.

For this sole reason, Robbyne is grateful that her children were removed; even after her son was taken at birth, she couldn't get clean on her own. Once the children were gone, though, she continued to use for some months, and then missed them terribly. Unlike Doreen, who had landed a prison sentence, Robbyne could enter rehab and regain her kids.

For six months, Robbyne lived in a residential drug treatment program. She faced down her depression, memories of sexual abuse in childhood, and the trauma of a car accident—all of which she felt contributed to her addiction.

After Robbyne graduated from the treatment program, she fought to get her children back, but with the delays in child welfare and family court systems, it took another two years for her oldest two to come home. Caiseem, the baby, wasn't returned until the following year. Robbyne, sober and determined, visited her kids at the agency regularly while they were in care; once, she saw a foster mom slug Bacardi straight from the bottle as she dropped them off. Robbyne demanded a new placement. Her daughter complained of sexual abuse; Robbyne called an emergency meeting on that case, and her kids filtered through several homes. It was torture to watch her kids leave with strangers she felt were dangerous.

And at that time, Robbyne said, there weren't the kinds of programs and support available to parents that there are now. "I can honestly say that I needed that time to get me together," Robbyne told me, leaning forward on the cane she still uses to walk. Robbyne is short, a good three inches shy of five feet, and the day we met she wore a pink sweater and big gold hoop earrings with another gold circle on a chain around her neck. Much about Robbyne connotes roundness—her jewelry, her body type, her cheeks that plump upward when she smiles. Her manner is soft and open, and her many Facebook pictures show her grandchildren piling on her lap or snuggling in her neck. She's a young grandmother, her hair still dark and her skin still young, and she looks blissful in the role. "But if I'd had support groups and parenting groups or people to come into my home and help me and not be afraid they were going to take my kids if I said something—" Robbyne choked up and looked down at her hands. "If there was more support, I could have done it with the children at home. But the way things were back then, there was no option but removal."

Robbyne says there are better programs now, and she works for CWOP, the nonprofit organization that didn't exist when her kids were taken. CWOP provides biological parents who have kids in care with support groups, parent training, and advocacy. CWOP also created the first parents' advisory group to the commissioner of ACS, so that for the first time ever, biological parents had some say in the system. ACS now has a division devoted entirely to preventive services— though the budget has been cut, then reinstated, always on less stable funding grounds than direct foster care— so when a child's situation is determined to be somewhat risky but not bad enough to warrant removal, ACS caseworkers can suggest, and even fund, certain protocols. They can identify the treatment programs or support groups Robbyne had wished for, and then follow up sometime later, so the kids can stay at home. But many parents are hard-wired to panic at the mere mention of ACS, and much of Robbyne's job is devoted to re-education.

"There are moms out there who are too afraid to get help because they're too scared of ACS: they think ACS is out to get them," she said. "A lot of parents are unaware of how much the system has changed. I have to tell them—it really has changed."

Or this is the idea. Of course, kids are still removed all the time, and determining a child's risk and a parent's commitment to improvement is entirely subjective, dependent on a caseworker's personal experience and perception. In the case of drugs, even Robbyne knows there's a lot of gray area. Some parents, she says, can't or won't get better. "But most parents just need help when drugs overpower them, and I want them to know they don't have to be as afraid as before. People are listening to us now."

Because drugs and alcohol are such potent plot points in the saga of child welfare, people often give them more stage time than they deserve. Even when drugs aren't the obvious problem in a family's life, judges and lawyers assume that they are.

Brooklyn's Family Courthouse is a boxy building the color of stone on the corner of Jay and Myrtle in downtown Brooklyn. Inside, the five family court judges can oversee upwards of fifty cases a day; like the caseworkers and lawyers who represent the kids and parents, the judges are overworked and don't have time to mull over nuance. They've seen what works and doesn't in many families, and they often apply quick formulas to complicated family groups that result in a lifetime of positive bonds, or fractures and separations. And these formulas often revolve around drugs.

On one wintry November Tuesday, I spent the day with Lawrence Robinson, a lawyer with the Brooklyn Family Defense Project, which provides attorneys and legal counsel to about half of the several thousand cases that come through Brooklyn's family court each year. Lawrence has since left the job, but at the time he had a rotating caseload of around a hundred clients, and when he was in court, he could attend five or six trials a day. He worked every weekend and kept extra suits and ties in his office, for the times he spent the night. He earned $51,000 a year.

On the day we spent together, Lawrence had five trials on his calendar. Two were with a "good" judge, two were with a "bad" one, and one case was being settled out of court, because everyone was amenable to the case plan, and both sides needed to simply agree on the details. With so few judges, Lawrence explained, each one developed a reputation; some are known for siding with ACS and keeping kids in foster care or terminating parental rights (these are the bad ones in his eyes), and others are more likely to try to keep biological families together.

Relatively speaking, very few parents are ever brought to trial for crimes committed against their children. For one thing, there's the widespread sentiment that losing their kids, even temporarily, is punishment in itself. And then there's the practical reality of criminal court: for a person to be convicted, his crime must first be proved. Child abuse is considered a crime against the state rather than against the child, so a state attorney's office decides which parents to prosecute based on which cases they think could succeed. Mostly, these cases don't stand up well; there's often too little evidence, and child witnesses are notoriously challenged on their credibility. Also, a child has to testify against her parent, which can be traumatizing, and the parent, like any citizen, has the right to self-defense — which can lead to brutal cross-examinations. Often criminal prosecutors don't want to put these kids through any more hell.

This means that nearly all child abuse and neglect cases are settled in family court (and even after a criminal case a child's placement is determined there too). In family court, protocol and precedence rule the day. For instance, Lawrence says, judges often automatically order parents to undergo drug testing as soon as they show up in front of his bench — regardless of the circumstances that brought them there.

At one of Lawrence's afternoon cases, a family investigation had been launched because of a phone call from a toddler's grandparents. These grandparents didn't like their daughter's live-in boyfriend, so, with the hope of getting him thrown out, they called protective services. The courtroom for this case felt like a bad wedding, with the aisle dividing the two parties in the beige windowless room. The mother, her lawyers, and a few of her friends sat on the benches on one side of the court, and the grandparents, the ACS lawyers, and witnesses sat grim-faced and rigid on the other. Before we had even entered the room, the lawyers threw barbs at one another.

"You sure you don't want to just drop this case?" the lawyer for ACS, a man in a rumpled suit clutching a pile of folders, said to Lawrence.

"You sure you don't? My client *did* leave her child with a sober adult," Lawrence shot back.

"I'm sure he wasn't sober when she left," the ACS lawyer said.

"You don't know that," Lawrence retorted sharply, and entered the courtroom.

When ACS responded to the grandparents' call and went to investigate the apartment, I learned during the trial, only the boyfriend was home. The door was unlocked, and the boyfriend was passed out on the bed, with the baby sleeping next to him. The cop who was with the ACS investigator was on the witness stand.

"How many beer bottles did you see in the room?" the ACS lawyer asked the cop.

"I don't know, there were some," the cop answered.

"Did you see any on the floor?"

"Maybe." The cop looked up to the ceiling, as if searching his memory.

"Did you see any on the windowsill?"

"Yes, maybe two."

"OK," the lawyer said. "So there were four or five beer bottles in the room with the baby."

"Yes," the cop answered, still looking a little unsure.

The case that day was actually a follow-up to the first hearing, held shortly after the investigation, when the child was removed from the home. At that time, it was determined that the boyfriend was unsafe, and he was ordered to move out. The mother, who had no prior convictions, displayed all of her child's medical records, and had never been accused of abuse or neglect by anyone aside from her parents, was required to take a drug test as a matter of course. She tested positive for marijuana.

The mother, Lupe, was pretty, with rosy cheeks and lip gloss, chubby in her maternity jeans and her peach cable-knit sweater. Unlike some of the other parents Lawrence represents, Lupe met Lawrence at his office half an hour before the trial to talk about strategy and provide him with even more medical records to prove her maternal diligence. She had followed the instructions from the last hearing to the letter: she had thrown the boyfriend out and not seen him again, she had attended drug treatment and graduated, and her urine test was now clean. She claimed the grandparents' call to ACS was based on an old family feud, and she rarely smoked pot — only with friends sometimes to relax, and never in front of the baby. She was a good mom, she said, and she was desperate to get her child back.

Still, the details of the trial focused on the long-gone boyfriend.

"Did your boyfriend tell you how many beers he would drink?" the ACS lawyer asked Lupe when she took the stand.

"Did he tell you if he preferred marijuana?"

"Did he tell you how many beers he drank when he smoked marijuana?"

"Did he tell you what his drink of choice was?"

"Did he tell you what his drink of choice was and if he would drink that when he smoked marijuana?"

"Did he drink his drink of choice along with beer when he smoked marijuana?"

The questions felt endless. This mother was no longer involved with the person in question, and I was confused: why wasn't ACS trying to reunite mother and child when clearly this mother had jumped through all her hoops and then some? I thought about friends of mine who had also smoked pot here and there while raising children. The difference was, my friends' parents didn't think to use Child Protective Services as a weapon in their personal family battles. And my friends didn't get caught.

Was it ACS's job to fight against this mother, on the chance that this child could be harmed, and Lawrence's job to fight for her because he was paid to do so, and the judge's job to see the whole picture and make the right decision? But judges see fifty cases a day — how whole could their picture possibly be?

This judge was a "good" one in Lawrence's eyes, and he ordered the baby back into Lupe's care, as long as she continued to take her drug tests and come up clean. Lupe's eyes welled, and she turned to hug her friend. Her parents walked stiffly from the courtroom.

5

Catch as Catch Can

FOR PEOPLE LOOKING TO adopt kids out of foster care, *drug-addicted* can be a very good set of words. They were for Shawn Wilson (no relation to Steve), who, along with his partner, Martin, was hoping to adopt a baby they would later name Noble through Episcopal Social Services of New York. Shawn and Martin picked Noble up when he was six days old, after Episcopal told them about the mother. Shawn was ecstatic.

"They told me she was a homeless woman who had been living on the streets, who had been doing drugs, with a history of mental illness, and I was like, 'Yes, yes, yes! Thank you, God! She's not going to be able to get him back!'"

Shawn hadn't always felt this way. Like most people who consider adoption, he originally imagined a young, healthy birth mother for his child. "My vision of the perfect mom was this: she's sixteen, she's on her way to college, because she wants to be a doctor, but she accidentally got pregnant," Shawn said, laughing lightly at the memory. Shawn is a strikingly handsome African American man in his mid-thirties, with a narrow face and a shiny shaved head. He can seem both elegant and silly at once somehow, as if he belongs behind a university podium, but also on the playground rumpusing around with a bunch of kids. "She takes all her vitamins, and all I have to do is talk to her mom and dad and it'll be just like *Juno*!"

It wasn't like *Juno;* Shawn and Martin ultimately chose a path that he now wishes more parents would consider — New York City alone processes about sixty newborns a year who need adoptive parents. Noble, like many of these babies, was born with cocaine in his system, but so far Shawn says there haven't been any real problems. I met Noble when he was two, and he was an outgoing and friendly child, running around with a shirt on his head that he called his hair and eating pizza from both fists. As far as developmental milestones go, Noble may be slightly behind, but Shawn says he isn't concerned.

"I use those milestones as a loose guideline as to what I should expect from Noble," Shawn said, emphasizing the *loose.* "Your kid's gonna walk. Your kid's gonna talk. We've been doing that for millions of years! I disagree with a lot of that milestone stuff too — because it talks very little about empathy, sympathy. What about a milestone when your kid can have empathy for another kid, or not lash out? Those are the kind of milestones I want to create."

Noble's first clear words were *thank you.* The only vestige of trauma from his time in utero, Shawn thinks, might be the way that he eats. As with the pizza, Noble always has to pack his food into both fists, then suck just a little bit out and close the fist up tight again. "Someone who's doing a lot of crack is not eating a lot," Shawn theorized. "So when something came down the pipeline, Noble was eating as much as he could — holding, saving. He spent months not knowing when the next food was coming, so now, so what if he has food in each hand? Eventually he'll know he doesn't have to do this."

I first met Shawn and Noble Wilson at the Lesbian, Gay, Bisexual & Transgender Community Center in downtown Manhattan, at a recruitment event for prospective foster parents. Noble made a great poster child as he sat on Shawn's lap at the front of the room and Shawn took questions; he was cute and snuggly, gazing up at Shawn and then grinning out at the audience of the fifty or so adults. Stationed around the perimeter of the room were about a dozen tables manned by the employees of ACS's various foster agencies; the tables were cluttered with brochures and bowls of candy, free pens and clipboards to sign up for more information. They looked like tables for credit card offers, or cable TV.

For most of the agency workers, this was their first time recruiting at a community center or at anything gay; more commonly they looked for fresh foster parents at churches or welfare offices. But they were all excited to be expanding their reach, as foster agencies are always fairly desperate for new, and better, parents. Nationwide, there's a shortfall. Some states — such as Pennsylvania and Oklahoma — have roughly twice as many foster kids as they do available parents.

What the agencies offer the prospective parents, generally, is confusing: there are benefits, but the drawbacks are built right in, which may be a reason for the shortage in supply. So it may be time to rethink the way we recruit foster and adoptive parents and teach them about what they're in for. This is the junction where there's so much need, and where so much goes so terribly wrong.

To become a foster parent in most parts of the country, you have to take some state-sponsored parenting classes, have a social worker visit your home and verify that you have the requisite space and a bed, and undergo a criminal background check. Then you get the benefits.

Front and center is the money (hence the recruiting in welfare offices), but it isn't enough. Current monthly pay rates range from $229 in Nebraska to $869 in Washington, DC, with a national average of $568 for a sixteen-year-old kid. This falls far short of the estimated real cost of $790. Still, the money's a draw for some parents, as nationwide, foster parents seem to be more likely than not to live close to or below the poverty line. But money's also sort of embarrassing to talk about; after all, there's something anathema, something maybe even biologically repulsive, about the idea of getting *paid* to love another human being.

So then there's the love benefit to becoming a foster parent, but that's a mixed message too. Simply stated, you can get a kid (there are plenty available) and you can love him, and he might love you back. But don't get too attached. If you want to adopt the child, be warned: the birth parents could reappear. And if you're only fostering, keep your front door open and your heart locked tight, because these kids come and go.

Which leaves the last argument for signing up, and perhaps the weakest. It's the reason foster care agencies recruit in churches. You become a foster parent because it's the right thing to do. When I'm feeling especially nihilistic, I think this argument fails because it clashes with our deeply grooved notions of ownership and industry; we don't want children if they can't be *ours,* and we expect to be rewarded, in the end, for our hard work. Other times I think no child will truly believe she's part of a family if she knows, at heart, she's a charity case.

So Shawn thinks that ACS, and agencies like it across the country, should change their approach. He thinks they should launch an aggressive PR campaign to teach the general public that babies like Noble are available for adoption. Because people just don't know.

Shawn said, "People always see Noble, and they ask me, 'Where's he from?'" Noble is African American and he doesn't look much like either of his dads; Martin's white and Shawn is all lean lines to Noble's round face and almost rounder eyes. "When I say St. Vincent's, up the street, they say, 'I never knew you could get a wonderful, healthy, cute, social kid through the city.'"

At the beginning, Shawn didn't know that either. He had been with his partner, Martin, for more than a decade when they started talking about kids, but he had wanted them long before that. "When I found out boys couldn't have babies — I was probably four years old — I got so angry at God," Shawn said, his face breaking into a grin. "I got angry at God!"

Shawn was making me coffee one rainy October morning in his floor-through loft in Manhattan's Chelsea neighborhood — an open space with a white leather couch, high ceilings, and big windows facing Sixth Avenue. Toy train tracks, a plastic horse, and a tricycle evidenced Noble's hold on the living room, and the couch, while austere, was a bit sticky with juice. Noble was at nursery school and Martin, who's in real estate, was at work. Noble is named after Noble Frisby, an African American doctor in Shawn's hometown of Greenville, Mississippi, who delivered Shawn in his private clinic. Shawn is a documentary filmmaker and often works from home. "I always knew I wanted kids. I realized it was not necessary for me to pass on my DNA but to pass on what my mother gave me: the nurturing, the patience, the love."

Shawn grew up with an older sister and his mother, who never went to school past the eighth grade and died when Shawn was nineteen. Her picture hangs above Noble's bed, a glamorous formal portrait in black and white, her head tilted, her smile wide and wistful. "I describe her as a boat with wheels. She was ahead of her time," Shawn said, explaining that his mother's intuition and kindness were her strengths, and that intuition is the way that God speaks through him and guides his parenting today. He speaks of God often. "What my mother gave me — it would be a sin if it went to the grave with me."

At first Shawn's partner, Martin, wanted to do surrogacy. This is, Shawn feels, the upper-class option for gay male families: the community knows it costs $80,000 or $100,000 to have a doctor inseminate a donor egg with your sperm, and to employ a surrogate to carry the baby to term. Of course, Shawn concedes, we live in an era when gay rights are traded at the state level like poker chips, and having your own genetic child is a way to ensure he won't be snatched away in an anti-gay political sweep. But surrogacy also signals money, distinction, and, Shawn believes, narcissism.

"I would have been able to love any kid, but because of where I come from, it was hard for me to wrap my brain around creating another life when there are so many already here who need exactly the same thing," Shawn said, explaining that over some months, he was able to chip away at what he called Marty's "brick façade" of wanting to be seen as an upper-class gay person. He also had to work through his partner's fears that an adopted grandchild would not be as loved as, say, his brother's biological children. "I commend him because he came through all that. But then initially the last place I wanted to get my kid was through foster care."

This was Shawn's own "brick façade." He believed, as many do, that a newborn from foster care would be damaged, traumatized, and unreachable. "At the time I thought a foster kid would never amount to anything because of what his circumstances were — his parents druggies, no prenatal care. He won't have the capacity to be a smart kid."

Shawn laughs now at his ignorance and his own prior elitism. He didn't want surrogacy, but he did want private adoption. This is when he started imagining the *Juno* scenario, with the teenage mom who took all her vitamins. "I was like, 'Pooh-pooh on all those vanity-stricken egotistical gay guys who need to spend $100,000! I'm spending $20,000 for this beautiful WASP-y baby from Connecticut.'"

When Shawn and Marty met with an adoption attorney, though, Shawn was put off. They had to place an ad in a newspaper for prospective moms, get an 800 number to speak with potential mothers without traceability, and build a book about themselves describing every minute detail of their histories and their plans as parents. "It felt like a shopping mall, like mothers were going to go into a Barnes and Noble, see our book, and say, 'OK, you.'"

The home study was the clincher. A fairly standard procedure, a home study is the process wherein a social worker examines and certifies your home as suitable for a potential child. It's the exact same process foster parents go through, and when Shawn learned this, something clicked.

"I had been talking to my friend Bruce, who was a foster parent in Georgia. I was seeing all these newborns coming in and out of his house, and he didn't keep them because 'Oh, they cried too much,' or 'Those boys were too much work.'" Shawn said he was relieved when Bruce finally decided he didn't really want to be a dad, but Bruce did provide Shawn a critical window into the system. "He said, 'Shawn, these newborns have been healthy. And the adoption is free.'"

Shawn and Marty decided to check out Episcopal Social Services, simply because it was the agency closest to their home. "We were so welcomed as a couple, I guess because their need was greater," Shawn said. "It was so different from 'Make a book, put an ad in the paper, get an 800 number.' They were saying, 'Thank God you've arrived! We get twenty babies a month we gotta place!'"

I've talked with both friends and strangers from a wide range of backgrounds who carried the same prejudices and misconceptions as Shawn originally did: if you wanted to adopt a baby, they thought, you'd never look to foster care. Some didn't know babies were available, and some assumed the "good" ones (meaning healthy) were probably already gone.

But this isn't true. Plenty of pregnant women use foster care as a kind of adoption agency for their babies; they just don't think of it that way. If they don't plan ahead or aren't functioning at a level to be able to surrender their newborn to a private adoption organization, they can still give birth and walk away. Safe haven laws mean anybody can abandon a baby at a hospital or police or fire station without question. All of these babies are handed over to the state. They become foster babies first, and then, if the mom doesn't reappear after some months (usually around a year), they're available for adoption. This means that if you want to adopt a baby through foster care, you have to tolerate your status as a foster-to-adopt parent — and you have to take the same training classes (ranging from zero required hours to twenty hours annually depending on your state) that any foster parent does.

For Shawn, these classes were particularly frustrating, because the lessons weren't tailored to adoption at all. They were geared toward the general foster parent population, who would be contending with, or even working toward, a biological family reunification.

"We started taking classes every Monday for four months," Shawn said, claiming he was very clear with Episcopal that he only wanted to adopt — not to foster a child who would ultimately leave. "They were fine with that, but — and they always said *but* — foster care is about fostering a child until the family is ready to reunite. So in the classes I was in a rainstorm with the fanciest raingear on, letting it all roll off."

Episcopal told Shawn and Marty that of the sixty newborns that the city received each year, only 10 percent would be returned to their parents. The odds were good, but Shawn said because the class focused solely on the 10 percent who would be sent back, they scared potential parents away from adopting the other 90 percent.

So Shawn thinks the classes and the emphasis in foster care overall should shift into a more clearly defined two-prong system. "They should say, 'We foster to get the kids who should be, back home; and the ones who shouldn't, we adopt,'" he said, echoing the core concept of ASFA legislation. "But in the training, their job is to scare the living daylights out of you, to give you the worst-case scenario. I never in my ten weeks of training heard a best-case scenario."

The trouble with two prongs is this: they twist up together. Although thousands of children are available for adoption, and hundreds of agencies do concurrent foster and adoption planning, the biological parents themselves — their abilities, desires, promises, and fallibilities — change all the time. Yes, there are the moms who walk away from the delivery room and never look back, but there are also the Robbyne Wileys, who had their babies removed against their will, and who fight every day to get them home. And then there are the moms like Oliver's mom, Caitlin, who change their minds. Agencies can't predict the birth parents' actions, and they don't want to promise something they can't deliver.

But maybe there's a middle ground. Maybe foster care agencies could do more recruiting among the parents who are looking to adopt privately or overseas and say, "Hey, we've got kids right here." They could manage the odds, being even more careful to tease out the birth parents who don't want to, or can't, take care of their kids. And frame the argument in a new way: from the adoptive parent's perspective there's a risk, and from the biological parent's perspective there's a chance — but if a mom takes her baby back, you've provided a young person with a vital foundation. It sounds terrible, but if you lose that baby, you could try again. It sounds terrible, but that sounds a lot like pregnancy. Or like love.

Luckily, Shawn and Noble were among the 90 percent. Noble's biological mom left him at the hospital, and she didn't have any plans to try to retrieve him. But she did call the agency one day, when Noble was two months old — long before the adoption could be finalized.

"The social worker called and said, 'Can you bring Noble to the agency at such-and-such time? His mom wants to meet him,'" Shawn said to me. "I was so nervous, but my intuition said, 'They're not going to jerk you around. The experience of you losing him is not meant for you.'"

Shawn planned to simply drop Noble off for the prescribed two-hour visit, but he ended up staying the entire time. "I go in, and there's this big woman, who limps on one side of her body, like she's had a stroke. She didn't recognize Noble, so I said, 'Would you like to hold him?'" Shawn replayed the scene for me, imitating the gesture of handing over a bundle of baby. His eyes were wide, and his face was open, as though he were coaxing a child. "I felt empathy toward her, and I didn't expect to."

Shawn had to encourage the woman to cuddle her son, to kiss him — not because she didn't want to, but because she was clearly unfamiliar with infants. "One of the first things she asked was 'Does he like salads?'" Shawn laughed. "I told her he was too little now but I'm sure he will, and she said she wondered because as soon as she found out she was pregnant, she started eating a lot of salads."

Noble's mom realized she was pregnant when she checked herself into a hospital one day not feeling well. She was already five months along and had been using crack the entire pregnancy. She delivered Noble two months later.

"She talked mostly about the tragedies in her life, all the adversity she encountered. I learned some important things, though — like she said, 'When I see that man again,' meaning Noble's dad, 'I'ma punch him in the stomach!' And she punched really high. So I thought, 'OK, he's tall.'" Shawn leans forward slightly when he speaks, and his voice has the cadence of a happy, sped-up lullaby. "Noble's going to be tall!"

Shawn also learned that Noble had two brothers, sixteen and seventeen years old, who were living with their grandmother. Shawn later met this grandmother at a court date, along with an aunt. The family thanked Shawn for keeping Noble and said that when everything was all signed and sealed, they hoped they could visit him.

"I was like, awesome! I want Noble to hang out with his older brothers." At the end, Shawn was glad he'd met Noble's mom. "That was the thing; all the demonizing I had done — living on the street, drugs — dissipated. Gone. I walked away thinking she probably wouldn't get it together to get Noble back, but she loves him, and that's the greatest thing of all for me to be able to tell him."

Shawn's story runs in sharp contrast to that of his childhood friend Bruce, the one who introduced Shawn to the notion of foster care in the first place. Just as birth parents can change their minds about keeping their kids, foster and adoptive parents can too — and no agency policy can entirely safeguard against human fallibility. Bruce also initially wanted to adopt children, but unlike Shawn, once he was paired up with a few boys who matched his criteria, he sent them back. In all, more than thirty child placements failed in Bruce's home. Bruce blames the state, but then, the state kept sending him more kids.

Bruce lives in Cobb County, Georgia, but he met with me at a coffee shop on one of his visits to New York. He was a friendly, outgoing guy, with a soft southern accent, a shiny bald head, and a closely shaved goatee. He is the youngest of six children, he said; he grew up in a midsize Mississippi town, around a lot of kids, and he always expected to have some of his own. But he went the corporate route, becoming a human resources director at a large company. When he hit thirty-five, he realized he had the big house and all the fancy material goods, but he was still single and childless. Because of this, his siblings presumed he'd be the one to care for their aging parents. "I started thinking about what will happen if I'm sixty-five or seventy, God willing I live that long, and I don't have any kids of my own to step in that role and help facilitate that process for me."

This is why Bruce started thinking about adoption. And it happened to converge with the foster care presentations at his church, which focused on the children's needs — and what the church members could provide. Bruce started to pray about it. "God told me, 'I didn't place you in this huge home to be consumed with yourself and all your toys. To whom much is given, much is required.'"

So Bruce got licensed as a foster parent, with the intention to adopt. The first two boys were simply a shock to Bruce's system: their first overnight visit was at Christmastime, and Bruce wore himself out doling out presents and driving to the movies and the ice rink. Unfortunately, the boys' social worker told them Bruce wanted to adopt them, but Bruce drove them back to the group home after Christmas and never saw them again. The next big chance was a baby, very much like Shawn's son, Noble: he was a newborn, and Bruce named him Carrington. After ten months, Bruce and Carrington had bonded deeply and the county called with an ultimatum: the mother's rights had been terminated, and if Bruce wanted to keep him, he would have to adopt. Otherwise, the county wanted the baby back, as Carrington was still young enough to place in a real adoptive home.

"Here again was the pressure to make a decision," Bruce said. Because Carrington was under a year old, he wasn't considered "special needs," so, if Bruce adopted him, he wouldn't receive any assistance from the state. He would have to raise him entirely on his own. "If this had happened three months later, I would have continued to get fifteen bucks a day and Medicaid until he was eighteen years old. But in this case, everything would have stopped. Here's your baby. Congratulations. Nothing else from the state of Georgia."

Bruce said members of his church offered to pay for Carrington's health insurance; they would collect, they would help out. But he refused. "I am not a charity case. This child was the state of Georgia's. If they wanted me to have this kid, they should be able to do something to help me." The state couldn't, or wouldn't, and so, Bruce said, "I just ended up severing all ties with him."

And the state kept sending Bruce kids; there's always a shortage of college-educated, financially stable foster parents. There's always a shortage of dads, especially African American dads. And technically, Bruce was providing the only things required of foster parents: food, shelter, and medical and educational attention. But while Bruce could have adopted many of the thirty-plus children who cycled through his home in under four years, none ever seemed quite right.

Bruce pegs most of his troubles with his placements on the state of Georgia, though there were problems with the kids too. He's sent back babies after twenty-four hours because they cried all night, and he's sent back children who were too wild or destructive. "If I have a kid in my home who's destroying my home and not respecting my rules, I just can't do it. I have a huge wall of plasma TVs or whatever, and

DFS [Division of Family and Children Services] is not going to replace them, so I can't have this kid in my house," he explained.

I asked Bruce about retraumatization. He knew that many of the kids who came to him had been badly abused and were acting out to test him and their new surroundings. I suggested that sending them back to the county would only harm them further, or deepen their sense of being unwanted.

"There may be some truth to that," Bruce said. "But the other side of it, for me, as a single parent trying to keep my sanity, is this: if I lose it, I'm no good to myself or to the child, and I have to do what's best for myself and my home. And if DFS is not going to give me the resources to facilitate that, then it's your problem."

Bruce has heard about services like wraparound care, where a child might get tutoring or daycare or therapy — all kinds of services in addition to what the foster parent can provide. But so far, Bruce says, he's seen none of it. When he takes in a hard kid, all the hardship falls on him. "If I have to leave my office because a troubled child that I've placed in the school district nearest my home is now cutting up in school, at least DFS could go pick him up, provide some resources. But no, I'm the one that gets the call," Bruce said. He's struggled with the fact that he's sent so many kids back, but, he said, "My truth is, if you're not going to help me, then it's not my place to put myself in peril. It's your problem — it's your problem."

In a way, Bruce's confusion about who bears the responsibility for an abused child's problems makes a kind of historical sense. Bruce, and other foster parents like him, may not know the history of child welfare precisely, but they do often know that government aid has been used to both help and control various segments of the population at various points in history. This legacy is a heavy one, and understandably it can engender the contradictory feelings of both suspicion and entitlement. With foster care, it's no wonder everybody's pointing fingers in different directions.

Foster care is actually the fascinating, if sad, culmination of *three* separate lines of social policy — toward poverty, racial difference, and child abuse — finally braiding together in the middle and end of the twentieth century. Each one of these historical lines helped form our current notion of the proper family — and the improper family that should get broken up, their children sent to foster parents like Bruce in Georgia or Bruce in Brooklyn. Because the "improper" families are so disproportionately poor and black or Hispanic, there's an understandable — if often unspoken — friction inherent in aligning in any way with the institution that "destroys families," even as a foster or adoptive parent. It's just uncomfortable all around.

But that's partly because the history — along all three lines of social policy — is so damning. As it is with a single dysfunctional family, there may be no way for the country to wipe the slate clean and start over. There will always be the shadow.

When this country was in its infancy, poor, indigent, or otherwise incapable families were cared for by their local community governments, and it was the white families who garnered such assistance; they were the perceived community members and were funded via taxes. The assistance was called "outdoor relief," and it came in the form of grocery orders, fuel, doctor fees, and small amounts of cash, delivered directly to the family home. By the turn into the nineteenth century, state aid shifted to almshouses, and the white poor were increasingly taken away from their communities rather than helped from within. As the nineteenth century progressed, a breed of "child savers" cropped up — emboldened with the mission of "rescuing" the children of impoverished families. (At this point in history, no one was considering the biological parents' feelings or experiences.) Child savers were private citizens, mostly middle- and upper-class white women, who created orphanages and worked with churches and synagogues to find other families with whom these poor children could live, thus creating the first foster homes. African Americans didn't receive any state aid and had to create their own institutions (there was a Colored Orphans Asylum in New York as early as 1836).

Wealthier white families, generally, were spared the scrutiny of authorities; as long as they weren't indigent, families were seen as precious and untouchable units wherein the man was head of household and could do what he liked with his wife and kids. (There was even a "Stubborn Child Statute" in Massachusetts that allowed a father to execute a son for misbehaving.) After all, in the mid-1800s and as late as

1880, children could contribute nearly half of a household's income in a two-parent family. Kids would sell flowers or matches, or scavenge for wood or coal, or even work in factories.

The children of the urban poor were removed at times for physical violence, and at others simply because their parents had unrecognizable parenting styles. This was a time of major immigration, and foreign parents were often mistrusted; kids could be removed for their own "protection" from strange, un-American ways. For instance, at the time when Italian immigration was increasing, garlic was considered a powerful aphrodisiac. Mothers who cooked with it were deemed unfit, as they neglected their daughters' decency. Many child welfare associations, like the one in New York, were private, but some had police authority to remove children from their homes at will. New York State, in fact, outlawed any inspection of these associations, reasons for child removal, or the kids' treatment (usually in religious-run institutions or orphanages) once removed. Biological parents, including those who cooked with garlic, had few rights.

Immigration laws of 1924 curbed the flow of newcomers into Ellis Island and changed the face of the urban poor. African Americans were moving north after the war and filling the cities, and these families became the focus of child welfare, post–World War I. In rural communities, a large family was desirable and culturally expected, as more hands could handle more crops, bring home pay from more jobs, and so on. But as these families migrated to the cities, they were viewed with suspicion, especially by the middle classes, where fewer children were the norm. Having too many "dependents" was reckless — a view that bleeds through foster care rhetoric today.

Controlling this recklessness came mostly in the form of institutionalization; the orphan trains that had been moving thousands of (mostly white) urban kids out of New York City and off to country homes died out by 1929, and "caring agencies" had cropped up in New York and elsewhere to place children in orphanages. But these caring agencies were private, and mostly religious, institutions — and they were thus free to discriminate widely. In 1923, for instance, a census report shows 1,070 child-caring agencies in thirty-one northern states; 711 of these were for white children, 60 were for black kids, and the rest were for others or a mix of the two. Children of color were being removed from their families, but there weren't enough places to put them, and the kids were crammed into overcrowded, dangerous, and unsanitary institutions.

Along a separate track, in 1911, welfare as we know it was first established in Illinois. Originally called Mothers' Pension Programs, this public aid was set up primarily for white widows to be able to raise their children in "suitable homes"; to qualify for such money was deemed a sign of respectability, requiring, for instance, home inspections and character evaluations from neighbors and clergy. By 1935, every state except Georgia and South Carolina had a pension program, or what came to be known as a "mothers' aid law." In 1931, the Department of Labor conducted the only survey on the demographics of "mothers' aid" recipients: 96 percent were white, 3 percent were black, and 1 percent were of "other racial extraction." Mostly, states didn't employ mothers' aid programs in areas with large African American populations, and the subjectively imposed "suitable homes" statute allowed states to discriminate widely. Although many families had their kids removed because of their poverty, some poor parents, namely, single white mothers, were allowed to keep their children at home and were given the help to do so.

In 1930, the White House held a conference at which the director of research at the National Urban League described systematized discrimination in subsidized programs. Aside from the mothers' pension programs, he said, infant and newborn care was mostly for whites. And despite the fact that more black mothers worked than whites, daycare provisions were provided by and large for white children. Legislators finally recognized the need for parity with the famous Social Security Act of 1935 and the AFDC (Aid for Families with Dependent Children) program, wherein states were to receive matching funds from the federal government to provide relief for needy families. While superficially an equal-opportunity program, AFDC eligibility was again subjectively determined. Each state could "impose such . . . eligibility requirements — as to means, moral character, etc. — as it [saw] fit." Aside from restricting access based on a "suitable home" or "moral character," during the late thirties and forties, southern states determined that "blacks could get by with less" and would cut their funding off during cotton-picking season. Even in Washington, DC, social workers had a two-tiered welfare system — one amount for blacks, another for whites.

This is where racism and foster care begin to wind together. Poverty is and always has been the one constant in child welfare: the poorer you are, the more likely it is your child will be taken into custody. But in early times, poor white kids were the only kids marked for provisions; they were the ones whose families got outdoor relief; they were the kids, by and large, who were sent on orphan trains, or placed in almshouses, terrible as these options were. But as the country systematically made African Americans poorer, we were about to widen the lens on the children viewed as needy or abused.

During the civil rights movement, activists began demanding access to the public monies they'd been paying into with their taxes but had been steadily denied to them. In 1961, the secretary of Health, Education, and Welfare (now Health and Human Services) changed the "suitable home" rule. If states wanted matching funds from the federal government, he said, they could no longer discriminate. The Civil Rights Act of 1964 strengthened this decision, and racist eligibility practices in welfare administration were effectively dismantled.

And with that, welfare offices surged with applications and buckled under pressure to comply with new federal regulations. The public perception of public assistance began to shift from that of a noble and needy mother to that of a welfare queen with too many kids, another idea that threads through foster care rhetoric today.

As the public face of welfare changed from white to black, so did the face of foster care. At precisely the time blacks qualified for welfare, child abuse was "discovered" by Kempe and his x-ray data. It was a perfect storm: for the past century, state-sanctioned foster care had been about "rescuing" (albeit mostly white) poor children from their parents, but now black families, with their access to the AFDC money, were the recognized poor. African American families were prime suspects for child maltreatment and their children the targets for foster care.

The federal government, as it rose to meet the public outcry against "battered child syndrome," embodied this stereotype with its funding mechanism. It opened a new line of foster care funding to states directly through AFDC, or welfare. In 1969, every state had to enroll; to receive the federal dollars for their foster kids, they had to prove each child was poor enough to receive welfare, thus cementing the notion that the poor (and often black) parents were the child abusers. There are federal monies available for abused kids from wealthier families, but the same funding system operates still, and the bulk of any agency's budget is for AFDC-eligible children. We fund the treatment for the abuse where we believe it's happening, and we find the abuse where the funding is.

And that's pretty much where we are today. Since the sixties, foster care has undergone surges in size (such as with the crack epidemic in the eighties) and contractions (after Clinton's 1997 Adoption and Safe Families Act). And it has gone through loose swings in overall philosophies — from those that favor biological family preservation to those that favor removing children at the first whiff of harm — but this is a system plagued with a history of deep racism and classism and the state-sanctioned separation of family members. We've been building a city for children on a sinking foundation.

Shawn Wilson's friend Bruce isn't alone in his litany of failed placements. In fact, most matches do fail: about 70 percent of all foster children in this country who have been in care more than two years have been moved three or more times. This sobering statistic may be due to child welfare's history and the sinking foundation, and it may be due to all kinds of poor management and low funding and scrambled priorities and on and on. Regardless, for the child, it's a statistic with deep and lasting ramifications: each move means another ruptured attachment, another break in trust, another experience of being unwanted or unloved.

• • •

The former deputy director of the New York State Psychiatric Institute is also a former foster child. Her name is Francine Cournos, and she says it's normal for kids to behave the way they did at Bruce's. It's normal for them to act as if they don't care about what you're giving them, to act as if they don't want to connect, because basically they can't. This is what we should be training foster parents to understand in their ten weeks of classes.

I first met Cournos at Columbia University, where she was giving a talk about her life in care and a memoir she wrote called *City of One*.

"Trauma forecloses grief," Francine Cournos said to the audience, mostly composed of social work students. She told us that she was devastated by her mother's death but not traumatized. The trauma came from her placement in foster care. "Trauma shuts you down, so you can't grieve. Nobody thinks of children in foster care as bereaved, but they are."

Now Francine is a doctor and professor of psychiatry at Columbia, and she's a small white woman in her sixties with short white hair and wire-rimmed glasses. She spent nine years in psychotherapy twice a week followed by eighteen years in psychoanalysis, four days a week, to access the grief about her mother; before that, she said, she didn't feel much of anything at all.

Or rather, she could feel the suffering of her life, in parts, but she couldn't feel joy. "After I was placed into foster care, I could no longer connect to anybody new. I was so numbed out and I would say that was probably the single most disabling symptom because you're numbed to pleasure more than you are to pain," she said to me later, from her office at 168th Street and Riverside in New York. We met during a blizzard, and the world outside Francine's window was an impenetrable white. Inside, two couches faced one another over a glass table that held a bowl of candies: Tootsie Pops, Jolly Ranchers, Mary Janes. One wall showcased an oversize rug; the other was crowded with books. Francine pulled an electric teakettle from under her desk and offered me tea. "There's something about betrayal that makes you feel more traumatized — that you trusted somebody to behave in a certain way and they behaved in the very opposite way. And that is, I think, more devastating than somebody dying."

Francine and I sipped our tea and watched the blizzard. She continued, "If your spouse dies you don't say, 'Here's a new husband' the next day. But in foster care, that's the expectation: you know, 'I'm your new mom so love me.'" In her case, an uncle contacted child welfare after Francine's father, and then mother, died, because he himself didn't have any extra beds. A foster mom in Long Island accepted both Francine and her sister, but it was rocky for years: the foster mom loved Francine and expected Francine to love her back. Francine couldn't betray her mother's memory like that, and she never understood why her own uncle didn't step up; for him, she would have slept on the floor. Before they met Mary Keane, the Rosario kids felt the same cold chill toward foster parents — as they too had biological family all over New York who didn't come through. These foster parents were strangers; why would the kids soften up enough to love, or even form an alliance, if their own blood had cut them free? I once met a foster girl with "Matthew 27:46" tattooed on the inside of her arm. I had to look it up. It comes from the moment Jesus is nailed to the cross, and he cries out to his father, "Why have you forsaken me?"

Cournos thinks we need to train the parents to expect and withstand this outlook from foster kids. It's hard work, so we need to offer better incentives. Caregivers and foster parents face a paradox after a child has been taken from a primary parent. On one hand, kids need attachment to develop properly, but on the other, after they've just lost a parent, they're not ready. "Right up front we need a more therapeutic foster care model in which parents are trained to understand that when kids come to them they're going to be distrustful, cut off, and too traumatized to make an attachment."

In most places, children go into traditional foster care first, where they live with a foster parent who has undergone the requisite training classes. If the kids "fail out" of this (and that's the language), they move on to therapeutic care, with parents who have had more training and are paid more money. Cournos thinks most kids should be placed in therapeutic foster care right away. Or, in other words, change the model: rather than waiting for the child to exhibit psychological or behavior problems, we should be investing money in training and paying the foster parents to help the kids manage their grief.

"If you're earning $18 a day, and you're on call for twenty-four hours, you're getting less than a dollar an hour to be responsible for a child. That's not a lot of money," Cournos said, adding that, traditionally, child welfare has been primarily concerned that foster parents meet a child's physical needs for food and shelter. "But physical survival without psychological survival doesn't help a whole lot."

I asked her about the oft-quoted notion that foster parents "do it for the money." If agencies increased the paychecks to help foster parents do more attaching (or rather, to wait patiently for the kids to attach), could we end up with even worse parent applicants? People should be foster parents because they're called to do it, because there's a need, because they have big hearts — but not for something as base and mercenary as cash. The money's just there to cover expenses, the argument goes, and if we offered foster parents a penny more, venality would trump humanity.

Cournos admitted that some people might, in fact, come forward only for the higher pay. But we need to shift the cultural attitude toward foster parents and treat them with more dignity. Part of this, she says, is providing a respectable wage.

Bruce Green, who has brought several foster kids into his home on DeKalb in addition to baby Allen, doesn't see anything wrong with treating foster parenting as a job. "You have people who have been foster parenting for years, and there's no health insurance, no life insurance, and if they stop, there's no retirement," he said. Bruce riled at the notion that giving parents more money and benefits would yield a more selfish crop of applicants. "There *should* be incentives to being a foster parent; there should be deals with cable, lights, and water. Being a foster parent should be something that's earned."

And more money, maybe even more than expanded agency recruitment, will draw a broader pool of foster parent applicants. "Right now," Cournos said, "we can't find enough good foster parents for all the kids. And is it worth it to continue putting them with bad foster parents?"

Cournos's ideas — of providing foster parents with more money and training, and children with more continuity and respect — seem to be backed up by a recent study. Its authors compared an enhanced foster care system run by the Casey Family Programs in Oregon and Washington with standard public foster care in those states. The Casey program is endowed by a large grant, and the children involved are allotted about 60 percent more in funding than the kids in standard care. This means that the caseworkers are paid more and have more education and lighter caseloads than their counterparts in regular child welfare. Because the caseworkers at Casey manage half the number of children that the state employees do, they can better ensure that kids stay in one place and also provide more support services when home life gets rocky.

At the time of this study, the Casey foster parents were paid $100 more per month than the regular foster parents. Caseworkers provided access to other financial resources, as well as to tutoring, mental health care, and summer camps. There was far lower caseworker and parent turnover in the Casey group than there was in the state, so the kids generally had more stable attachments. They were also offered postsecondary job training and college scholarships, which the state foster kids were not.

The nearly five hundred kids in the study had entered foster care as adolescents between 1989 and 1998 and were evaluated in the early 2000s. The Casey kids, now adults, had experienced less than half the rate of depression and substance use, and about 70 percent the rate of anxiety. They also endured significantly fewer ulcers and cardiometabolic disorders. The authors, who were headed up by a team at Harvard, claimed this was the first study ever to look at the long-term effects of enhanced, or more thoroughly funded and supported, foster care.

Who's to say where the seeds of positive influence were planted in these kids? Was it in the more stable parenting, or in the therapy they received? Perhaps the promise of college, and the tutoring. Perhaps having a consistent and available caseworker made a difference. In any case, "front-loading the system," as Francine calls it — or allotting more money and services for all children as soon as they enter care — is a valid and oft-considered idea.

When you ask the foster kids themselves what they want, they tend to focus on the parents. The kids I've talked to have generally wished their foster parents were more compassionate toward their moods and frustrations, and they all hated getting sent back to the agency. Mary Keane, the adoptive mom of Arelis and the other Rosario kids, runs foster parent training and recruitment classes all over New York City. At one of the recruitment nights, she had gathered up a few older foster kids to talk about what they wanted from their parents.

"Basically, I just want someone to understand me, and support me," one of the girls said plainly from the front of the room. The girl had dirty blond hair, with streaks of purple washed through, and she smiled patiently at the roomful of adults, perched at the edge of their chairs. The adults were more specific about their desires.

"I'm looking for a chorus," one older woman in the audience said eagerly. "I'm a singer in my church, and I'd love to have a houseful of children to sing with me."

A man in his forties, who was looking forward to becoming a single dad, said, "All I'm looking for is respect."

Mary told him it was likely he wouldn't get that, at least not at first. "They're not going to meet the parents' needs — to be appreciated or anything else. Not until they're grown," Mary told me later. She was speaking specifically about teenagers, famous for their obduracy whether they're in care or not. Foster teens can be particularly rough, I thought, so I asked her: Why on earth would anybody sign up for this?

"Altruism," Mary said, and suddenly we were back to foster care argument number three: you become a foster parent because it's the right thing to do. Mary has been a foster and adoptive parent for over ten years, and she's taken in more than twenty-five teenagers and young adults. She has never sent one of them back. She said she parented all of her kids only because she felt the pull to "make a difference in the world."

"Parents should do it because the kids need. Otherwise they're going to be disappointed," Mary said. More money, more training, all of these things would be a boost, but foster parenting, by definition, means personal sacrifice. "You do it because you want to help a kid, and because you enjoy seeing them grow. The gratitude for what you've done might come later. Like after five years of hell."

Two

HOLD

The price one pays for pursuing any profession, or calling, is an intimate knowledge of its ugly side.

— James Baldwin, "The Black Boy Looks at the White Boy"

6

Surge Control

WHEN SHE WAS THIRTEEN years old, a child named Lei was removed from her apartment in New York City's Chinatown and placed with a Dominican family in Brooklyn who spoke little English. Lei lived with the family until she was eighteen, by which point she could swear a mean streak of Spanish curse words, if nothing else. The foster mom never learned any English or Chinese to communicate with Lei, but she had provided her with the bottom bunk in a bedroom full of other girls, she had fed her, and each month she had handed over the clothing allowance provided by the state. Lei wasn't loved (or even talked to), but she also wasn't abused, so her foster home was fine. No reason for Lei to look for something better, because she could have gotten worse.

There are so many crises in foster care — the original abuse, the shock and alarm when a child is removed, the courtroom fights, kids rebelling, bio parents panicking, foster parents molesting, relapses, rehabs, reabuse — that basic, low-level functioning begins to seem exemplary. These are the mediocre flatlands of child welfare, where if it's not a crisis it's not a problem.

Despite ASFA legislation, which requires that foster children either be adopted or go back to their parents within fifteen months, the average foster child in this country has been in care for a little over two years, though this has come down some. In New York, it can be even longer: more than a third of the kids have been in care for three or more years, and a major investigation of ACS kids who had been in foster care for more than two years showed that their average stay was nearly five and a half years.

Lei, with her five-year run with the family who couldn't talk to her, was entirely average. So was her status as a teenager: about a third of all foster kids nationwide are teens. And where the system swells, it also tends to falter; it doesn't manage the numbers, or the needs, of its older children very well. But where Lei broke with the averages and the reduced expectations of her placement and the system was this: Lei went to college.

"You just have to meet this girl," Lei's caseworker, Tolightha Smalls, had gushed to me. In her ten years as a caseworker for adolescents, Ms. Smalls had known only two kids who left for a college or university; many hadn't graduated from high school. Nationally, somewhere between 3 and 11 percent of former foster kids go on to get their BAs (depending on what adult age group you poll) compared to 28 percent of the general population.

So I went to meet Lei at a Starbucks, on the edge of Chinatown, where she often went to hang out with her friends. Lei was twenty-two by then, had short, boyish hair, and was wearing green army pants and a plain T-shirt. Somehow I recognized her right away when I walked in; she looked young, and a little tough, and entirely comfortable sitting alone.

The first thing Lei did was pull out a photo album from her high school years. Most of the pages were empty, and the handful of pictures were of her friends — some were from school, but most were from church, where Lei hung out on weekends for the youth groups. Lei had only one picture of her foster family, and she dutifully pointed out each child, and the mom, as though she were naming employees at a job she once held a long time ago. Said Lei, "When I left her house, the mom never bothered to call. I felt like, 'Screw you, man. I'm ready for my life.' I felt like she did it for the money. What can I feel?"

Like many kids I've talked to over the years, Lei asked me to change her name; foster care is a major reputation stain. But unlike the others who tried to hide the stigma from their friends, Lei was looking to protect her biological family. "My friends knew I was a foster kid; I was always open about it," she said. Between sentences, Lei sneered a fierce "mmm-hmmm," like a tic. "I feel like if I can't deal with my past, then I can't go any further in life, mmm-hmmm."

Lei lived in China until she was eleven, when her parents sent her and her brother to New York to stay with an aunt and grandmother and the aunt's daughter. At that point, Lei didn't know any English. Both her aunt and grandmother had been destabilized by their own moves to New York; her aunt was angry and violent, and her grandmother was deeply depressed and occasionally paranoid. Lei described her new home, simply, as "the shithole."

Lei survived the shithole for two years, but when the aunt kicked the kids out of the house and into the street and the grandmother attempted suicide, ACS was called in for an emergency removal. Lei's brother was a legal adult by then, but as Lei and her cousin were zipped away in a cop car, she said, "I felt relief. My grandma was mentally abusing me; she always told me I was bad, and that someone was after me."

I would learn that Lei approached many of her struggles philosophically, rather than with a quick bolt of action. The signature quote at the bottom of every e-mail Lei sent read, "Knowledge without humanity is ignorance." Lei tried to understand her complicated family, which spanned two continents, with humanity and empathy.

This isn't to say Lei wasn't angry with her lot; she was. She sucked her teeth and raised her eyebrows with contempt when I asked her about the foster agency she was placed with for eight years, which was closed in 2005, primarily for accepting hundreds of thousands of government dollars for supposed programs it never ran. "Miracle Makers? To tell you the truth, they were crap. They didn't do anything to prepare us," Lei said, with her Chinese accent, but the intonation of a Dominican girl on any tough street in New York — a vestige of her time in care.

"I took advantage of everything Miracle Makers had to offer, mmm-hmmm, and Ms. Smalls and my law guardian were awesome," Lei said. (A law guardian, like a guardian ad litem, represents the child.) It was her social worker, who believed in her, and her law guardian, who funneled her cash for the SAT tests and college applications, who paved her road to college. "They were the only two people I invited to my graduation from college."

Lei not only went to college and graduated in four years, but she went to an Ivy League school, where the acceptance rate is around 25 percent. Could that accomplishment be traced back to a few good agency hires? Was it because Lei lived in one, albeit substandard, foster placement for her entire time in care and didn't suffer the trauma of transferring from home to home to home? Or was it something simply about Lei's tenacity or courage, inherent and ineffable, and hers alone from birth?

"The reason I was able to survive all this was because of my childhood, mmm-hmmm," Lei said, explaining that her parents sent her to the United States in the hope of better education and opportunities for her. Back in China, Lei's mother ran a tailoring business, and Lei learned to be friendly and outgoing from her. Lei's father, she said, protected and adored her and even babied her somewhat. They both encouraged her in school. "We came from a pretty good family, and I had a childhood, a stable childhood, up until eleven."

Lei cried the first few nights in the shelter, before ACS found her a home, but she did it secretly. "I called my brother and said, 'I'll be all right. Tell Mom not to worry about me.' Before I came here, I was a daddy's girl. But after that, I learned to be tough."

And while the toughness got Lei through five years in a home with strangers, the isolation was tempered by the knowledge that foster care wasn't her fault. "I never felt like I had been abandoned. I was angry — like 'Why me?' — but I understood why my mom had to make that tough decision, and we were always in contact over the phone. I never felt like a child nobody wanted," Lei said.

Lei's cousin, who was exactly her age and placed in the same Dominican family, didn't fare as well. "My cousin still has a very hard time telling people she was in foster care because it was her mom, and for me, it was my aunt. My cousin has very low self-esteem because of it, mmm-hmmm," Lei said. After leaving the family, the two lived together in a foster apartment for a few years while Lei went to college and her cousin simply aged out, the way most foster kids do. "I saw a future, because I know why my mom sent me and my brother to this country. Because of this, I felt like I was destined to go to college."

And this may be the critical difference between Lei and other kids in child welfare: Lei didn't carry the crucial, crushing belief that foster care was her fault.

Dr. Eliana Gil has worked in child abuse and prevention for nearly forty years. She's the author of more than a dozen books on the subject, for both professionals and lay audiences, including *Outgrowing the Pain: A Book for and About Adults Abused as Children*. She currently directs the Gil Center for Healing and Play in Fairfax, Virginia, where she and her team observe and assess children for signs of abuse and make referrals to child welfare. For her doctoral dissertation, Eliana interviewed one hundred kids in foster care, asking them why they thought they were there. Ninety percent said it was because of something they did.

This was in 1973, but Eliana says kids are no different today: she's seen hundreds, and mostly they believe that they're to blame for ending up in child welfare. It's part of the wiring of childhood: they know themselves as the axis around which events and mishaps and parents and everything else will spin.

And the teenagers get an extra boost to their self-loathing because once they're placed in care, nobody seems to want them. They're unlike the babies, who are the most likely to attract adoptive interest, or the young kids, who signify innocence or easy compliance in foster parents' minds. Forty-nine percent of all teenagers have to be placed in institutions or group homes (as opposed to just 7 percent of children between one and five), largely because there aren't enough families who will take them.

Teenagers represent the largest segment of child welfare for several reasons. First, they're the hardest to adopt out, so they often have only two means of escape: return home or grow too old for the system entirely. Second, they can enter foster care through a traditional abuse scenario in their family of origin, but their parents can also *put* teenagers in foster care, if they decide they're just too unmanageable to deal with. Finally, juvenile delinquents are often made wards of the state and thus piled onto the foster care rolls too. Add it all together, and more than a quarter of all foster kids nationwide are fifteen or older.

We know the ways the system fails this population, in part, by tracking what happens to them right after they "age out," or graduate, from foster care. By age nineteen, 30 percent of the boys have been incarcerated, and the girls are already 2.5 times more likely than their nonfostered peers to have been pregnant. Within four years, 51 percent are unemployed. Within an average of six years, the median income for former foster kids who have landed work is only $8,000 per year. Ultimately, according to some figures, 30 percent of the homeless in America were once in foster care.

"Find me someone in one of these houses who wants a teenager," Bruce Green said to me one day as we were driving around his Brooklyn neighborhood. He waved his arm out of the minivan in the general direction of a bunch of large apartment buildings. "They're sexually motivated, they're rebellious, they're outspoken, very lazy, dirty, self-centered, and when something goes down, it goes down BIG." Here Bruce paused, seemingly reflecting on his own frustration. "Compound that with the possibility of theft and destruction. Teenagers have no respect for the property they didn't pay for."

Bruce has a good sense of humor. He calls me Chris Rock and he laughs when he catches any of his teenage foster kids with hard-core music on their headphones. "Whaddya want us to play, Dad? Alicia Keys?" they whine. "That'd be fine," he answers with a smile, snapping the headphones away.

Bruce and Allyson Green are polar opposites of what Lei experienced in foster care; the Greens didn't expect to wind up with a house full of teenagers, but once they got them, they rallied. The house on

DeKalb was more than a roof and walls: it was a permanent home for a growing family. And once the teenagers came, it was a growing family with a mission.

Their agency, Edwin Gould, kept calling and, perhaps because the Greens just kept accepting the kids, sent them six teenagers in the course of a year. One of the teenagers was autistic and previously violent; several were being treated for depression, trauma, and mental illness; others had learning disabilities and developmental delays, truancy records. All, Bruce said, were "special needs"; all were "hard to place."

Caseworkers, famously overstressed and underresourced, try to match up parental interests, cultures, and their preferred child type with the kids in their caseloads, but often their caseloads look like disgruntled kids in a high school lunchroom. And because adolescents are the hardest to place, the Greens must have looked like a feast for the starving: they had a teenager of their own; they had kinship-fostered, and then adopted, a family member; they'd fostered a troubled toddler; they had an enormous home with eight bedrooms; and two parents — a mom and a dad — were engaged with the kids. Bruce told me that of the 450 homes licensed with Edwin Gould at that time, only four had dads.

Both Bruce and Allyson were horrified by the stories their new foster children told them about the multiple placements they'd endured. In some cases, the foster kids weren't given enough to eat or were fed from different cupboards from the rest of the family. In others, they were verbally or even physically abused.

"Sometimes where they go is as bad as where they came from," Allyson said sadly as she and Bruce talked with me in their living room. The kids were all hiding out in their bedrooms because we were in front of the biggest television and the kitchen was occupied by a math tutor and one of the teenagers. "The foster parents need to be more educated — not just this little mock training that they do. The agency is so busy looking for somewhere to put the child that they don't really evaluate a lot of these foster homes."

In truth, we don't know much about foster parent demographics nationwide; most information is anecdotal rather than cumulative or comprehensive. The largest study was a sample of a little more than 1 percent of all foster parents — and it found that they were more likely to be older, have less education, and live below the poverty line than caregivers in the general population. They were also half as likely to provide stimulating environments for their kids.

Bruce said a lot of foster parents he knew didn't properly supervise their kids. "These children have had freedom since they were twelve or fourteen, roaming the streets until four in the morning." And this is why he shifted his vision from wanting younger children and became excited about helping the teenagers. Bruce knew what happened to young adults with too many distractions and too little discipline; every day cop cars pulled up at the projects across the street. When he fostered teenagers, he could stem the tide just a bit.

"I tell you, I think they love the environment here," Bruce said, explaining that all the foster kids first resisted, but then relaxed into the rules of the Green household. The basic rules were these: every child had to come home directly after school; no going out on weekend nights (even for the teenagers over eighteen); and on Saturdays, after chores, the kids could have free time, as long as they were in the door by 8:00 p.m.

Generally, Bruce had to play bad cop to Allyson's good: she gave them the nurturing and religious instruction, and Bruce took away their television privileges when they didn't come home right after school. But they both explained why the rules were important. "We had a family meeting on Sunday and the kids were under the impression that the rules were about right now," Bruce said, smoothing his hand across the top of his shaved head. "But it's not about right now. Ultimately, there are a million and one rules outside of here that if you don't follow, you'll lose your job. If you don't follow them, you'll go to jail. Ten years from now, what you're going to have are these past experiences to help you."

Allyson liked taking teenagers in particular because each one reminded her of an aspect of herself. "I used to lie, for example — say I'm going to the library, but where am I? With my boyfriend. It's the same behavior these children come back and do," she said, revving up for storytelling, her Belizean accent coming on thick. Allyson herself was raised almost entirely by her grandmother, so she handled her kids with the same love and firm determination — a mix of spiritual grace and resolute work ethic — that her grandmother showed her. "You see a lot of you. That is why you cannot judge them. I just have to be understanding and teach them. I look deep into myself — to be patient and nurturing. I say, 'I see what you're doing and where you're going with this. This is not the right way, but eventually you're going to get it.'"

The family didn't earn enough to get by on the $500 and change they received each month per foster child, so Bruce worked nights as an electrician for the train company, for $80,000 a year. In the daytime, he was carting around and parenting the kids. He didn't get much sleep. Then again, neither did Allyson, who was responsible for cooking and cleaning and parenting too. At night, she shared her bed with any number of children who ended up climbing in.

And the agency didn't help. Once they've sent a child, both Bruce and Allyson claim, they pretty much wash their hands of him. "All the goods and services we tracked down for our children ourselves," Allyson said, ticking off that each child was enrolled in a charter school; most had after-school enrichment activities; many went to therapy; many had tutoring; and much of this was free or provided through the state. "Nobody held our hands through any of this stuff."

Bruce was busy trying to get the agency to make even small changes — such as providing the family with portrait vouchers at Sears whenever a new child came into the home, to make her feel more welcome. The Greens have pictures of all of their kids framed on the living room wall. "Given what they pay facilities to house the children," Bruce said (and it can cost five times more to keep a child in a group home facility than in a family home like his), "I would say the city owes at least that much."

One day, I went with Bruce and Allyson and their biological son Jaleel to something their agency did provide: a Saturday afternoon class on family emergency preparedness. But what was supposed to be a quick lecture ended up being a long, de facto support group for foster moms. They complained about what was most difficult in their lives: the teenagers.

When we walked into the conference room at Edwin Gould, Bruce was the only man in attendance. I was the only white person. Everybody else was an African American woman, and they were mostly older, parenting their foster children alone. They fit the demographic of the families in their neighborhood (single moms of color) but not that of foster families nationally, where there aren't enough minority foster families to meet the disproportionate number of minority children in care.

The fluorescent lights audibly buzzed as a middle-aged woman in a headscarf and jeans called the meeting to order, apologizing that the firefighter who was supposed to explain emergency procedures for foster families hadn't arrived yet, but there were still orders of business to discuss. An older woman in a flowered blazer and fishing hat leaned back to listen, and another one took a call on her cell phone. Foster care meetings are one place where people won't turn off their phones; there can always be a crisis at home.

"OK, so there are a whole lot of things being put in place with this I.O.C.," the leader started in. Bruce leaned over and whispered that she was a parent advocate, meaning someone who lost her kids to foster care but eventually got them back. She advocates for biological parents in the system but also does crossover trainings, like this one, to help foster parents understand what it's like on the other side. "One new rule is, you have to honor the ten days. You can't just drop a kid off at the agency anymore with a garbage bag all filled up with clothes."

I.O.C. stands for "Improved Outcomes for Children," and it was part of a new set of standards and rules that the city's then-new commissioner of ACS, John B. Mattingly, established in March 2007. His idea was to streamline operations somewhat, to incorporate consensus building from the bottom up with the "family team conferencing" (essentially giving biological parents more of a say), and to make sure kids get moved around less. And part of this meant foster families couldn't just dump their wards as easily as they used to. They had to wait ten days.

"I understand when it's not a match," the parent advocate said, responding to the wave of murmurs rising up in the conference room. People were asking about the most difficult pairings — what's a parent to do when a teenager continually breaks curfew, skips school, swears at you, is all-around *nasty?* "To be honest, if you don't want my child in your home, I don't want my child in your home, and at the end of the day, they're still mine. But for now, you've got to honor the ten-day rule."

This meant that rather than loading up the trunk with a child's music, socks, photos, and T-shirts and leaving him at the curb of the agency (and most kids I know have experienced this), the parents had to make a warning call. They had to tell their social worker of their plans to "terminate" and then sit on it for ten days, during which time (the thinking went) the family may be able to work it out.

Of course, the foster moms willing to give up a Saturday for training at Edwin Gould were among the more dedicated on the rosters, and still they were worried. In lieu of the firefighter, they vented about their own emergencies. One woman in sweats and gold jewelry said the social workers were never available when she called, and if she ever did get through, they talked to her "like you're lower than they are." Others nodded in agreement.

Another mother in a white T-shirt and a headband was concerned and angry about the turn her foster daughter was taking. "Our relationship as mother and daughter has been going quite a distance," the woman said. There were several children in the room, some foster, some biological, all under twelve years old. They were well behaved and listening to the story, or picking at the breakfast the agency provided. "Everything's been fine, until lately; her attitude's been changing. She lost three cell phones. She's been coming home later. And now" — the mother paused for dramatic effect — "she tells me she's gay!"

Several women in the room gasped. One covered her mouth and threw back her head. Another said, "Oh, no!" and another whispered,

"Oh, Lord." Everybody looked distraught, and the foster mom nodded miserably, her eyes wide.

The parent advocate lifted a hand to quiet the room. Her hoop earrings bobbed as she shook her head solemnly. "Remember," she said. "This could happen with a biological child."

The implication, of course, was that you can't take a biological child back to the agency with a bag of clothes. Stitched into every foster care arrangement, as every foster kid over ten will tell you, is that he can be shipped out, ten-day notice or no. It's a threat foster parents use, sometimes, as a punishment.

"They don't equip foster parents with enough knowledge to deal with these children," Bruce told me later, in the car. (The firefighter had never shown up.) Allyson lamented the parenting classes she and Bruce were forced to take, taught by caseworkers asking rote questions from photocopied packets. The questions proposed anecdotal scenarios that Allyson found ridiculous, she said, such as: "If your child was burned by cigarettes in his former home and he saw cigarettes while in your care, what would you do?"

"It was all simple common sense, common knowledge," Allyson said. Instead of hiring case managers to run the trainings, or parent advocates for the supplemental meetings, she wished they had psychologists. "A lot of these children have mental illnesses, and we need doctors telling us how to structure their lives to best deal with the diseases."

But foster parents don't get much training, and they have to come up with their own structure on the fly. Bruce and Allyson's system was one that may seem very strict from the outside, but it was one that worked to manage all their children's disparate temperaments and background experiences equally. It was fair: there were no curfews because everybody (biological children included) had to be home straight after school. It wasn't punitive, because the rules were formed around good morals rather than as responses to bad behavior. And it wasn't too lonely: even if all the kids were stuck inside, there were always ten of them stuck together.

And there was a loophole. If the kids could find some positive, extracurricular activity, like a job or a sport or an extra class, they could get it approved by Allyson and come home later. The loophole had a double-edged benefit: the kids felt more freedom *and* they were doing something good for themselves. Kids buy a juice for the flavor; moms buy it for the vitamins. So this is what they did.

Both Sekina, the biological daughter with the crazy hair, and Chanel, the first teenage foster daughter to arrive at the Greens', had jobs after school. Tonya, the second foster daughter, went to therapy a few times a week and sometimes to tutoring. Fatimah, the third, played sports and ran on her track team every day and often on the weekends. Russell, the fourth foster child, was autistic and didn't like breaking his routine or leaving the house very much, so the rules weren't a problem for him. Jaleel, a biological son, was a nationally ranked chess player and stayed out for chess clubs and training and sometimes got to travel for tournaments.

Allyson monitored all of the kids' whereabouts to the minute, and when I first met the family, it seemed to be working like a well-oiled machine. These kids who had once been "roaming the streets until four in the morning" were now attending charter schools, rounding out their extracurriculars for college applications, and going to bed by ten.

The trouble hit only when a new foster teenager came in, wearing the hard face of rebellion and the ineffable scent of freedom and the streets that the other kids used to know. The new kid had to be molded to the Greens' way, and this was a tough transition for everybody.

"The last one we got, she's been in foster care since she was five years old, and she has so much pain. She argues with everybody; she argues with Russell, she argues with the baby," Allyson said to me that day we were talking in the living room. I met this argumentative girl later, about three months into her tenure on DeKalb. Her name was Dominique Welcome; the other kids teased her about her name because they said she was the least welcoming person in the house. Dominique was seventeen years old, and on the day I met her, she was particularly miserable because she had just broken a particularly big rule. She was in serious trouble.

"If somebody's eating, it's gotta be Dominique," Bruce said, by way of introduction, as he and I walked downstairs to the kitchen. A teenage girl was slumped over a cup-o-noodles at the kitchen counter, and she lifted her head to glare at him. Dominique had straightened hair that she'd tried to collect in a tiny bun, but it was sticking out in wiry spikes all around her head. Her protruding top teeth made her mouth look defiant even when it was closed. Her almond-shaped eyes, I realized, could be pretty, but they were glittering with a steely hatred.

Allyson was already dressed up in a knee-length maroon coat and high-heeled boots and was mixing kasha and organic yogurt at the counter. She smiled gently at Dominique and reminded her that she had therapy later that morning. We would all pick her up. Dominique groaned.

Out of earshot, Bruce and Allyson explained to me what had happened. Dominique had been getting better, they said; she'd been following the rules and trying to get along with everyone. When she hit her three-month mark, she asked for a special favor. Her very best friend was having a birthday party on a Friday night at the movies, and she wanted to go. Against their better instincts, the Greens relented — as long as Dominique was home by ten. She walked in the door at 1:30 in the morning. Dominique was never going to be let out again.

When we went to pick Dominique up from therapy, she was ready to talk. She'd tamed her hair, put on makeup, and seemed interested in having someone new around — meaning me — to listen to her point of view.

"I always like my opinion to sound different from other people's, so I'll say the opposite of what you're saying no matter what," Dominique said, leaning in toward me conspiratorially. We were sitting together in the back seat of the minivan.

Bruce cut in. "You like to be the devil's advocate."

Dominique narrowed her eyes at him and made sure he could see her in the rearview mirror. "No," she said brattily. "I'm talking about something else. For example, you might say Kanye West is the corniest rapper, and I might agree with you, but once you say it, I'll tell you I love him."

Bruce threw up his hands and Dominique spoke more quietly, so he couldn't hear. She said her attitude comes from her anger, of which she has a lot. "Every time I trust someone or love them, they leave. So I can't trust," she whispered. "That's why I'm angry."

Dominique was removed from her biological mother's house at five, already physically and mentally scarred from the iron her brother had burned her with and from the crack she said her mother had smoked throughout her pregnancy. She then went through a few long-term placements that ended in rejection and loss.

Allyson worked to temper her children's past traumas and their attendant misconduct through religious guidance. Every Sunday, in lieu of church, she held a long Bible study for all the kids at home. She called it her class, and that day, after Dominique's therapy, she gathered everyone together.

"I practice forgiveness so that I may be forgiven. I will serve joyfully and peacefully, for it is the will of Allah," Allyson said, reading from the notebook she prepared throughout each week — jotting down stories, quotes, and parables that she organized into themes focused around whatever household trouble had been brewing. While Allyson and her lessons are unequivocally Christian, she'll sprinkle in a few "Allahs" for broader appeal; foster kids in New York have often been exposed to a range of religions. These lessons are usually thinly veiled, say the kids; this week's directive was aimed at Dominique, and the focus was on obeying one's mother and father. "Whatever goodness I expect of others, I will be that goodness."

Allyson stood behind the kitchen counter; Dominique, Fatimah, and Chanel perched directly in front of her on barstools. Beyond them, around the dining room table, were the biological kids — Jaleel, Bruce Junior, and Sekina — and the adopted nephew Charles, along with the foster kids Russell and Tonya. Only Allen, being so young, was exempt. Sometimes these lessons lasted an hour; sometimes, the kids said, they could go on all afternoon. Today, Allyson was starting with Creation; it could be a long one.

She described the Garden of Eden, saying that God simply spoke life into all the plants and animals, but he took extra time with the humans. She said he breathed their thoughts into them, so, "We can learn what?"

"Right from wrong," the kids all answered in chorus. They'd heard this before.

"Who'd like to be in a garden right now?" she asked.

"I wish I was on a cruise to the Bahamas," Dominique mumbled, her head in her hands. She knew this was about her, and she looked miserable.

Allyson took the bait. "Well, when you get something, you don't just inherit it," Allyson said, careful not to look directly at Dominique. She didn't want to embarrass her.

"So God says to Adam and Eve, 'You can have everything in this garden' — like we say to you, 'You can have everything in this house,'" Allyson said, still standing in her high-heeled boots and shifting her weight. "Except he told them, 'Don't eat from the tree of knowledge.' It's like your mother and father saying, 'You can have everything but you have to come straight home.'" Like her grandmother in Belize, Allyson had a throng of children at her feet, soaking in her stories and morals. "Your friends might say, 'Don't go home — lie to your parents — they won't know.'"

Dominique peeked up at Allyson with one eye. The other kids seemed to be listening closely. Allyson continued. "God said to Adam and Eve, 'Don't eat from the tree of knowledge,' but they did. And what happened? They had an increase of pain. You have consequences." Allyson lowered her voice. "If you have consequences from the Creator, why shouldn't you have consequences when you are placed in the home of a mother and father who are placed in authority over you?"

The Greens' trinity of religious instruction, strict rules, and family unity had a slow but steady impact on the longer-term foster kids. As an example, Bruce pointed out Chanel, their first, and now oldest, foster daughter.

"Now, if you'da met Chanel a year ago, if she'd seen a stranger sitting in the house, she'd have cut her eyes at you. Isn't that right, Chanel?" Bruce said, after Allyson's Bible class.

"Mmm-hmmm," Chanel answered, cutting her eyes at me. Chanel was eighteen — a pretty, quiet girl with a face as inscrutable as stone.

"But now," Bruce continued, "Chanel's doing well in school, and she has more trust."

"And they're going to adopt me," Chanel said, over her shoulder and to no one in particular, as she left the kitchen and headed outside to sit on the stoop with her sisters.

Whether the kids truly felt more trust than they had before I couldn't yet tell, but they called Allyson and Bruce Mom and Dad, and they all wanted to stay. Fatimah, who had been with the Greens almost as long as Chanel, was also hoping they'd adopt her.

After the Bible lesson, as the younger kids were eating pizza and drinking juice, Fatimah and I also headed outside to talk. She told me she was writing a book called *Until November,* since that was the month the Greens would be formalizing her adoption. The book would be about her years in care, and the twenty-one homes she'd lived in, but it would have a happy ending: it was September then and the court date for her adoption was only two months away.

Fatimah was about five foot five, compact and muscular from running on her high school track team. Her style was fairly plain, just jeans and a T-shirt; her only adornment was a gold SpongeBob charm on a chain at her neck. Fatimah loved SpongeBob. She talked so fast sometimes it was hard to understand her, as if her mouth couldn't catch up with her mind, and she had a lisp. This was new, she said as we settled in on the top step — a holdover from the five months she didn't speak after a particularly traumatizing experience — which she told me about but asked me not to repeat — in one of the foster homes. When she finally started talking again, her voice was entirely different — more high-pitched and fast, with a stress on her *s*'s and *l*'s.

"Wanna see my grades?" Fatimah suddenly asked, and bounded inside. In the house, in the foyer and stairwell, hung framed drawings by Fatimah's birth mother. One was of a man playing the trumpet, and one was of a feminine face surrounded by feathers, and both were quite good.

Fatimah's mom struggled with alcohol and drugs, and she had signed away her parental rights when Fatimah was five. Still, she strung Fatimah along with occasional promises. Throughout her childhood, Fatimah said she remembered various foster parents dropping her off at the agency for visits with her mom. The agency was in downtown Brooklyn, with a view of the subway through its window. "I'd watch the trains and think, 'She's probably on this one.' I'd watch all these trains go by and she'd never come." Fatimah was sixteen on the day we talked, and the disappointment with her mother had calcified into a kind of resignation. "I never got what I was promised," she told me, adding that she rarely visited her mom anymore even though she lived close by. "That's why it's hard to believe I'm really gonna be adopted."

Fatimah had returned to the stoop, clutching her grades. I looked at the photocopied sheet, while Fatimah beamed and picked at her cuticles. All As from her charter school, except for a B in history. With Fatimah, topics tend to jump all over the place, and she told me that when she first arrived at the Greens', she had been dating but she'd stopped thinking about outside relationships entirely.

"I'm not going there right now," she said. "You see what it's like — this is a Christian house."

So she closed that part of herself down. She was used to it, she said, having to sacrifice one part of herself for another, and right now, having a stable home — which she'd never experienced — and parents who wanted her eclipsed any other needs. She wanted desperately to go to college, so she said she kept her mind focused entirely on school. She played with the SpongeBob charm. "I can't really think about that in this kind of house."

Just then, Dominique pushed past us to talk to Bruce, who was also now sitting on the lower steps of the stoop. She asked him if she could sit for a while in the backyard. When he turned in the other direction, she promptly marched off toward the corner store. I braced myself for a brawl.

When Dominique got back, Bruce was distracted and talking to his other daughters, so she quietly slipped past them and came to sit with me. Dominique is tall and curvy and prone to wearing bright colors. She speaks with a slight stutter, which is intensified when she's excited or upset, and her face can transform in an instant from delight to rage. "They do things that are very weird," Dominique said, about Allyson and Bruce. In her most recent foster home, she had no curfew at all — and, she said, the Greens don't seem to understand that she spent seventeen years of her life living in a particular way, and children just can't turn on a dime. For instance, the other day, her best friend, Diamond, was over at the house. The other Green children don't generally ask to bring friends over, because like many kids in the system, they don't like to admit they're in foster care. But Dominique doesn't care. "It's like Diamond's been in my life for four years, but you recently came into mine, and you're trying to exert control? They try too hard to be parents. It's fine with their own children, but not with me."

I asked her if she thought she'd stay, if she wanted to stay, and she said she will, and she does. But if it's so difficult, I persisted, why would she want to? To this she had no answer; she was frustrated with her new family, but she wanted to continue living with them.

It's just that with so many people in the house all the time, she said, she gets overwhelmed. Sometimes she needed to get out, to clear her head and think things through. It's not to break a rule, but to break away from the noise. She looked at the trees across the street and said, "When I have my space, I find myself."

Suddenly Bruce interrupted. Bounding up the steps from the street, he demanded, "How do you get along with your biological father?"

Dominique's face went dark. "We're not talking to you."

Bruce was unfazed. "I know your dad was stricter than I am." He squatted so he was nearly eye to eye with Dominique. "You have problems with male authority figures."

At this, Dominique's voice went shrill. "See! This is what you always do! You always interrupt! That's being disrespectful!"

In my own head, I conceded that Dominique had a point. But Bruce wasn't finished. "What do you call what *you* do? Coming in at 1:30 in the morning — and then now — saying you're just going to the back-yard — and when I go to look for you you're not there?" Bruce's tone was intense — not exactly angry, but at her level. "This is how you're always starting arguments."

Dominique threw up her hands in disgust and looked at the sky. A gurgly sound escaped her throat, and then she sucked her teeth. "Well, I don't argue with people I don't love."

Bruce jumped up from the step, a look of glee widening across his face. He bounded down the stairs and out into the street. The other sisters, Fatimah, Chanel, and Tonya, who had been gossiping together on the bottom step, exchanged embarrassed glances. Bruce was ec-static.

"She loves me, she loves me — Dominique said she loves me!" Bruce was shouting and doing a kind of football touchdown dance in the middle of the street. A passing car had to stop and wait for him to fin-ish. "It's only been three months, and she says she loves me!"

"No I didn't!" Dominique shouted back. "I said I only fight with people I love. I didn't say I love *you*."

"Same thing!" Bruce retorted, skipping around. Some teenage boys from the projects across the street were leaning against a tree and watching the scene unfold. But this was Bruce's territory; he grew up here, and everyone knew him. "You argue with people you love, and you argue with me. So you love me. I been telling you I love you every day, and finally you said it back."

At this, Bruce moved out of the way so the car could pass, and he started a little singsong dance at the curb. The girls all shielded their eyes with embarrassment, as though they could block him out with their hands. "My daughter loves me, my daughter loves me, my daughter says she loves me!"

Despite herself, Dominique let out a laugh. "You so crazy," she said.

"I may be crazy," Bruce answered, "but I love my Dominique."

7

Chutes and Ladders and Chutes

Tⁿ HE ROAD TO FULL assimilation in a new family is a treach-
erous one; the "I love you" confession was a good step for Dominique, but I knew she'd probably continue to struggle. Allyson explained it to me like this: "They can say I love you but they don't know
how to love you wholly because they're scared of losing you. They
build walls within themselves and you've got to try to chop at the lay-
ers."

Bruce thinks the walls he's seen in his kids come not so much from
the abuse in their original homes but from all the placements they've
endured afterward. "A lot of times these children go into homes where
they never get to understand what happened to them emotionally and
then they're gone into another home," he said. "So I don't know what
your issues are, you don't know what your issues are, but you can't act
them out — and nobody's taking the time to put it all together."

The Greens' second foster daughter, Tonya, is a good example of
what happens to a child when she rebounds through multiple foster
homes. Tonya didn't (or couldn't) "act out" the trauma she was experi-
encing directly, but signs of her suffering seeped out, and intensified,

with each new placement. And Bruce was right. Tonya couldn't begin to identify or integrate all the pieces.

Tonya appears tougher than Dominique at the outset because she's quieter. She's pretty in a kind of straightforward, unprissy way; she's thick in the thighs and slim in the face, with a square chin and small white teeth, bright against her dark skin. She straightens her shoulder-length hair but doesn't get manicures; her hands are marked with the scars from her many fights with boys and girls alike. Although her laughter comes easily, it's a hard laugh and her eyes stay flat and far away, whether from disinterest or distrust, I can't tell.

Tonya was removed from her home when she was five and someone caught on to her mother's cocaine habit. She doesn't remember much about the first foster house except that she started wetting the bed, and she and her brother, William, had to leave after a week — probably, she said, because of the soiled sheets. Next, they went into an apartment with a family that spoke Spanish, and nobody could communicate at all. Tonya continued the bed-wetting, and after two weeks they were driven to a third family in the projects, with "a nice lady." One day, this lady drove the kids to the foster agency, and Tonya's mom was there, to take them home. By this point, Tonya said, she was just like "OK, whatever," her six-year-old skin thickened and her mind cool and detached, more prepared for the next unanticipated hurdle.

Bed-wetting in a six- or seven-year-old can be a sign of trauma, or a stressful change in environment. (The literature suggests child abuse, a death in the family, or the birth of a new sibling.) In the span of a few months, Tonya had moved four times, acquired and lost several siblings, and then landed back at home again. The bed-wetting subsided, but she started skipping school. Because of this, after a year or so, Tonya and her brother were back in the system again.

"We went to a lady's house who used to beat us," Tonya said, her eyes intermittently flicking to some cartoons on TV. She said she didn't want to tell anyone about the abuse; she just wanted to stay in one place long enough for her mom to get her back like the last time around. But then, on a Christmas visit, her mom saw marks. "She was like, 'What's them scratches on your face?' And that night, they just took us out of that house — we didn't even get our clothes or nothing. They just took us to another home."

The new place was worse. The family was fostering an older boy, Tonya said, who used to bring her to the basement and molest her. She was eight or nine by then and knew how to keep mum. But in a kind of quiet rebellion or attempt to reach out, she started stealing from her classmates, just little things: pencils and trinkets. "I had developed sticky fingers. I don't know. I just wanted to be friends with people." But she didn't know how.

Throughout this time, Tonya's mother was visiting the kids and promising she'd get them back. But once again, Tonya and her brother were moved to a new place, at night, in a van, like stolen merchandise themselves. Every night in every city, children are buckled into vans or police cars (like criminals), as wards of the state (like criminals), and driven to strangers' houses and told to behave. Children explain this to themselves in a myriad of ways: often, because they're children, it's because of something they did. ("I wet the bed, I was stealing at school.") Often, the reality is bureaucratic (the foster home was meant to be only temporary, the foster parents needed different licensing). And almost always, the kids get no real explanation.

In Tonya's case, the move meant a new family with a new teenage boy — this one with a fighting fetish. He forced Tonya and another little girl in the home to beat each other up, while he watched — rooting for one or the other, in turns. In school, the sticky-fingers behavior escalated to hallway fights, mirroring what was happening in the foster home. It was Tonya's fifth school in as many years, and she "didn't like to be picked on." Still, Tonya said the foster mom wasn't so bad; she took Tonya to a hair salon for Easter and bought her new Air Jordans, and once, when she caught the teenager picking on the younger kids, she hit him and said, "You will leave my kids alone!" Tonya smiled at the memory. "I felt like I was wanted because she said 'my kids.' She was including us, and it felt like we were a part of something — but then we had to leave her."

This time, Tonya knew the reason: the foster mom hadn't been taking the kids to therapy and got docked for noncompliance. Back to the van — and to a home in Mount Vernon — a city just north of the

Bronx that Tonya said felt like the country, with "mad houses, and a room that was banging, with a canopy and shit." It was so foreign, and so isolating, Tonya said, that she and her brother used to tear up the place just to see if they could.

They could, and they stayed — for four years. Until Tonya's mom found a new boyfriend and was pregnant again — and thus appeared stable enough for the authorities to return her children home. Tonya was in seventh grade and fistfighting on a regular basis, because she liked it, because she was good at it, because it helped her articulate aggression indirectly and in ways that wouldn't really matter, at least for a while.

Tonya's six-year foster care "drift" began the year Clinton's ASFA was passed, with its supposed fifteen-month cutoff for kids like her. So why didn't she get adopted or go back home earlier? Tonya doesn't know, and the case managers who do are notoriously tight-lipped regarding client privacy. Likely, her mother showed continued signs of improvement, and the drift slowed to a drag, with both the hope that the mom would get better and the fear that nobody would adopt a preteen with a record of violence.

As Tonya and I got closer, she confessed that she had an escape valve from the tight restrictions in the Green household that the other kids didn't. The escape was through her mom, who lived in the Bronx and still had visitation rights.

"I live a double life, basically," Tonya said casually to me one afternoon when we were alone in the living room. She was watching TV again — this time, the Disney remake of *The Parent Trap*, a movie about rich girls duping their parents and masterminding an idealized family for themselves. Tonya viewed her mom less as a parental figure and more as a respite; when she went for weekend visits, she could party as much as she wanted to. Her mom was often not even home at all. "My mom allows me to do whatever I want — it's like going on a crazy road trip. And then I come back to reality, listen to rules."

Freedom was something Tonya had a lot of in the four years before she came to the Greens, when she was living with her biological mom.

"At first my mom was really strict, but then she started drinking and she got looser." Tonya didn't mind the liberty that came with alcohol, but her mom got meaner too. "She used to call me all types of bitches for no reason. And she'd say, 'You know what? I'm getting tired of seeing you all. Go outside or something.' So I did. It would be like eleven o'clock at night."

ACS removed Tonya again and sent her to the Greens. Now, Tonya said, she was just using her mom's apartment as a crash pad — an easy place to party on the weekends. The Friday before we talked, in fact, her mom had entered another inpatient detox program, so that coming weekend Tonya would have the place entirely to herself. Because she was technically allowed these weekend parental visits, the Greens would never know about it.

Did she think her mom would actually get sober? "No," Tonya said, laughing. "She just complies with the program because she's so damn smart she can fool all these people into believing she's doing what she's got to do. That's why we're allowed these weekend visits."

Tonya was two months shy of eighteen when we talked, so if she wanted to, she could drop out of foster care on her birthday and live at her mother's place full-time. But, she said, she wouldn't do it — mainly because her mother can't give her what she needs or wants, which is money. That she can get directly from the agency. New York City extends foster care until twenty-one, and Tonya planned to go the distance.

"You get $80 a month allowance, plus $20 more once you hit sixteen, and $5 more for every year after that. So I get $105 a month. Plus I'm a team mentor, which means I talk to kids at night if they need to talk," she said, and that pays too. What if nobody calls? "I just say they did and put it on my time sheet. The hours add up — no questions asked."

Tonya used people — the Greens, her mother, her teachers and shrinks — in a careful game of cover-up and self-advancement. As a metaphor for her survival instincts, she turned again to money. "It's me before you," she said, poking carefully with a Q-tip at an infection in her ear that she refused to get checked out. Tonya hated going to doctors. "Like if I have a dollar and you ask me for ninety cents, I'm going to say no. You can have a dime and go ask a fool for ninety cents, because they're a fool. You give a person the majority of you, and what do you have left?"

Tonya was going to work the system, and everybody in it, to her advantage. Tonya wasn't like Chanel or Fatimah, who wanted to get adopted; she was smarter than all that. Besides, she told me, she heard you got a laptop computer from the agency if you were still a foster kid on your eighteenth birthday.

Tonya's tumble through multiple foster homes was typical, as was her attempt to control her environment by working as many angles as she could. Foster parents like Bruce Wright in Georgia may complain that system kids act crazy and tear up his plasma TVs, and kids like Tonya may in fact steal things, get in fights, and trash their nice new rooms with the canopy beds. But the reason behind this behavior isn't crazy at all: it's a predictable response to their unpredictable past.

When a child has been screamed at, or hit, or sexually molested, she processes the trauma as a sequence of cause and effect; she'll look for ways to modify her behavior so the adult won't do it again. But because abuse is random, chaotic, and out of the child's control, kids can also learn to *provoke* the adults around them in an effort to direct outcomes. If you're going to be abused anyway, the maltreated brain reasons, you might as well decide *when*.

A kid in a foster home may be accustomed to chaos or anger or screaming, and the trauma of relocation can make him especially desperate for familiarity. So he'll push to make the "nice" home familiar, to make the new parents mad and to get the hitting or the screaming out of the way, and to place himself, the child, back in control.

Mary Keane, the foster and adoptive mom to all the Rosario teenagers, told me the story of an eight-year-old boy at her agency who was famous for getting thrown out of foster families. Wherever he went, he looked for the one issue that would make his new parents crazy; he'd find their particular hot button and then press. Hard.

"He was always looking for the limit. If he figured out one foster mom hated cursing, he'd start cursing. If another one said, 'You can do anything, but don't steal,' then he'd steal," Mary said.

This makes sense to me, even for kids who haven't experienced foster care or any real trauma. My two-year-old niece can sense that my laptop computer is off-limits, so this is the toy she most wants to bang against the radiator. Teenagers from conservative families flaunt new tattoos; rich kids wear rags; the preacher's son sells dope behind the 7-Eleven. We've all pushed and poked and tested at some time to say, "Will you love me anyway?"

Foster kids usually believe they caused their biological family to tumble from orbit, so of course they could dislodge a foster family too. Foster kids have found the weak spot in a universal law about parents and children; they'll keep pushing for that weak spot again and again until someone stands up and says, "I will love you anyway. Stay."

The problem with child welfare, Mary says, is this: "It's a tradition in foster care — that whenever you're bad, you have to go." Even when you land with parents like Bruce and Allyson Green who want to keep you.

One afternoon, when I was sitting in the car with Bruce and his son Jaleel, I witnessed a particularly heartbreaking scene. We were parked in the shade of a leafy tree, waiting for Dominique to come out of some appointment or another, when a chubby, shy-looking kid ambled up to the front passenger window. Bruce rolled it down.

"Hi, Dad," the boy said. He looked about fifteen, though Bruce said he was younger, and he had swirls shaved into his closely shorn hair.

"Hey, Clarence," Bruce chirped, a huge smile on his face. "How are you?"

Clarence muttered one-word answers to all of Bruce's questions: school was "bad"; the new foster home was "fine"; but when Bruce asked if he missed the family, Clarence's eyes filled. He looked down at the van's open window and picked at the glass in the frame.

"Clarence was with us for three and a half months," Bruce said to me. "But he was a runner. He took his bike on the subway and ran away. Right, Clarence?"

"No. Four," Clarence answered.

"What?" Bruce asked. Jaleel watched intently from the back seat.

"I was with you for four months. From November seventeenth to March sixteenth."

"Well. And you'll always be my son," Bruce said, shaking his head. "And I love you."

Clarence, openly crying and half punching at his eyes, walked around to the driver's side to hug Bruce. "We'll see you Sunday?" Bruce asked. Clarence still showed up at the Greens' for the free bi-weekly haircuts, donated by a barber friend of theirs.

"Yeah, Dad, I love you," Clarence mumbled, into Bruce's shoulder. And he opened up the back door to sock Jaleel in the stomach. Jaleel laughed as Clarence loped away.

Clarence was more than a runner. He had been in five foster homes before the Greens', as well as a psychiatric hospital. He used to tear up classrooms in his junior high school, arriving early to rip bulletin boards off the walls and destroy furniture. When he ran away, he left a note threatening to kill the family, so by law Bruce had to act. Because Clarence threatened violence, he had to be placed with a different agency, in a "therapeutic home" — with parents who had had more hours of psychiatric training. Still, Bruce said, "You don't stop being a dad just because the kid's not in your house," and he welcomed Clarence back for visits anytime.

The law requires foster children to be housed in the least restrictive home possible, which means ideally, kids begin their tenure in a foster family like the Greens'. When they act out, and test, the parents can send them back to the agency and the case manager will decide: Does the child need more supervision in a therapeutic home? Sometimes, if a child has already filtered through a lot of homes (therapeutic or otherwise) or if he has exhibited aggression or psychiatric problems, families won't take him, and then it's time for an institution. Sometimes, a case manager will just decide it's time for an institution right away.

And sometimes, when a caseworker doesn't know where to send a child, she'll put him in one of the city's "diagnostic centers," which kids unequivocally hate. Mandated to sequester kids for a maximum of ninety days (usually after some sort of upset at another placement), diagnostic centers are generally serious, lockdown places designed for both restraint and observation. They're also designed to be temporary, but they're not always; even nonaggressive kids have been known to stay in punitive diagnostic centers for months and months.

The first institutional rung after a foster family is the group home. A group home is basically a modern term for an orphanage. Clusters of ten or twenty or sometimes more kids live together in group homes, with adults paid in eight-hour shifts to watch them. There are low-restriction group homes, and high-restriction group homes, group homes for gay kids, young kids, teenagers, kids who have been accused of sexual assault and so on.

But kids push and test their way out of the group homes too, and from there they go in one of two directions. If their behavior seems psychologically rooted (and sometimes if they've just broken curfew or run away), they may land in a hospital. If the kids are rule breakers, or aggressive, or if they've timed out their stay in the psych ward, they'll be sent to a residential treatment center. This is the last stop on the foster care train. RTCs are locked, highly regimented facilities, often with their own schools. In New York they're outside the city, on large plots of land upstate, and they're the places where foster kids learn criminal behavior, because juvenile delinquents live there too.

Nationally, the RTCs themselves lack a set definition, but generally, they're places for kids who have behavior, psychiatric, or substance problems but don't merit psychiatric hospitals or correctional facilities. This is a pretty broad description, but it's all we've got: the General Accounting Office has claimed it's difficult to get an "overall picture" of the facilities because there's no standardized definition to differentiate them. Somewhere around 15 percent of kids in out-of-home care live in RTCs.

You've got kids who need families, kids who need criminal rehabilitation, and kids who need psychological treatment, all living together in upstate farmland, rubbing off on one another. One study that looked at 221 kids in New York RTCs in 2001 found that 41 percent came from a criminal conviction, 31 percent came from child welfare, and 28 percent had a history of psychiatric hospitalization.

A major problem is trying to meet such divergent needs all under one roof. Services can range widely: some RTCs may have group therapy; others may simply chart rules for behavior on the wall. Despite one study that showed 83 percent of the kids in RTCs having serious emotional disturbances, psychological treatment isn't regulated or necessarily overseen. In fact, there are currently no performance measures that the state of New York uses to ensure that the RTCs are providing a certain, regulated standard of care or supervision — in *any* category, psychological or otherwise.

Jonathan Cruz was raised by the city and state of New York. Remanded into care when he was five years old, separated from three of his siblings when he was nine and from his only remaining brother shortly after that, Jonathan was sent to a residential treatment facility at twelve. He skipped the group home phase completely; he never committed a crime but was placed in one of the toughest facilities for young delinquents — in an institution so violent and poorly managed it was later closed by the state. When this happened, Jonathan was sent to another RTC, where he was kept for five years until he became an adult.

I met Jonathan when he was twenty-two; he was slim and mild-mannered, if a little shy. He didn't know his heritage because he never saw his parents again after ACS removed him; he remembered his father being "short and bald-headed — yellow, really light," and his mother was dead. Jonathan had golden skin and even more golden eyes; they glinted with flecks of rich brown and amber. His black hair was shorn close to the scalp and across his forehead in a sharp, even line.

Although he doesn't remember much about what his parents looked like, he remembers the fighting, and his first memories are of being "kept captive" in the two-bedroom apartment he shared with his parents and two younger siblings. (Two more babies were yet to come.)

"The first people I really remember coming into the house are the police," he said of his early childhood — mostly, he figures now, to break up domestic violence disputes, though he also witnessed his parents using various drugs. He remembers that once, his mother threw him a birthday party, and his father burst through the door, furious for a reason he never understood. "He started getting violent, and throwing things, and people were running to get out of there. My moms and pops were going at each other with scissors."

The police visits yielded calls to child welfare, and Jonathan and his siblings were removed. Jonathan was the oldest; the youngest three were adopted, and Jonathan and his brother went into foster care. By nine years old, Jonathan had earned a reputation as a troublemaker, mostly for sneaking outside to play with other kids. By twelve, he said, "all I wanted to do was play baseball, stay out late. Families didn't want me no more, and they ran out of options for me." So Jonathan was ordered into a residential facility for juvenile delinquents. Except he didn't know it.

"They lied to me. I was with two social workers, who told me I was going into another home," Jonathan said, anger edging into his normally neutral tone of voice. "We drove for like three hours and the next thing you know I'm in the woods, on this weird-looking campus, like an army training base. I see these big dudes, but also these teenagers running around like crazy."

The "weird-looking campus" was the Holy Cross Campus of Pius XII, a 120-acre facility for boys ages thirteen to eighteen, in Rhinecliff, New York, named after the controversial pope who reigned during the Holocaust. "I remember crying for a couple of nights because it was so scary. These kids weren't my size. I was twelve and still growing — and in my eyes, the other guys were like grown men," he said. "Here I was, going from thinking about cartoons, to suddenly being in prison."

His description wasn't far off. In Jonathan's first two years at Holy Cross, state police responded to three hundred calls and formally investigated ninety-seven criminal incidents, some of which led to arrests. There were cases of staff-to-resident violence, cases of assault, escape, and robbery, drug cases, and four sexual assaults by staff members.

"There was a lot of gang retaliation, stuff like that," Jonathan explained. For him, the other residents were far more dangerous than the staff. Still, he knew he couldn't complain, "or I'd have a drill sergeant up my ass. I felt like I was sent to Iraq. Or hell."

An official audit from the state comptroller's office reveals that staff members at Holy Cross didn't necessarily have the training to be sergeants — or group home employees. The nineteen-page document, detailing "unsanitary physical plant conditions, insufficient staffing levels, un-implemented recreation programs ... and high levels of vandalism," also described a sampling of twenty personnel files. Fifteen failed to include a high school diploma — required for employment at Pius — and none indicated that references had been checked.

In 1996, Pius XII had contracted with the state agency, the Office of Children and Family Services (OCFS), as opposed to ACS in New York City, to operate two campuses for delinquent boys: Holy Cross and another called Chester, in nearby Orange County. When the state caught wind of the allegations against Holy Cross in June of 1999, it conducted site visits at both facilities. By August, the state required Holy Cross to come up with a "corrective action plan" to improve safety.

Despite all this, resident allegations of abuse and neglect surged during Holy Cross's corrective period — perhaps because residents sensed that finally they'd get some response. Also, while under official scrutiny, Holy Cross fired a staff member for bringing a gun to work, and authorities arrested another for marijuana possession. And one more counselor was convicted of sexual abuse. In March of 2000, the Office of Children and Family Services gave Holy Cross sixty days to improve conditions. They didn't make it. Holy Cross closed its doors in May of 2000. By June, Pius XII shuttered the Chester facility of its own accord.

Jonathan was delivered from his "hell" when Holy Cross closed — and was sent to another residential treatment center. "I did five years there," he said of his transfer to Graham Windham at Hastings-on-Hudson, as though it were a prison. A lot of foster kids talk about their placements as "doing time." But Graham Windham was, for Jonathan, comparatively tranquil. "I saw pools, I saw trees, I saw girls, and there were these college-looking houses. And the staff people said, 'Welcome.'"

Because I could no longer visit Holy Cross, I took a trip to Graham Windham. I tried to imagine being a thirteen-year-old kid like Jonathan, arriving for the first time — with no family or adult allies on the outside (his social worker, after all, had been the one who drove him to Holy Cross). About an hour outside of New York, Graham Windham sits on a forty-acre bluff, overlooking the Hudson River. Two schools, high school and elementary, are nestled at the bottom of a large hill, along with a gym. Little brick cottages with columns and names like Percy, Rogers, and Morris face a paved path that dips and circles around a grassy knoll, some boulders, and a scrappy basketball court. The numerous garbage cans scattered about are painted with the slogan "Show Your Tiger Pride!" for the school team. Jonathan was right; the place was pretty, and it did feel a bit collegiate.

But it was also an RTC — this one, an uneasy alliance of roughly 150 kids with very mixed backgrounds. About 35 percent were regular foster kids, 60 percent were kids who had committed crimes but were sent to Graham Windham as an alternative to juvenile hall, and the remaining 5 percent were a mix of special-ed kids and kids whose parents just sent them there for the restrictive environment. All of the residents attended the schools at the bottom of the hill, joined by another 135 day students who were bused in — all for special ed.

This educational model isn't unique to Graham Windham. Many RTCs have to tailor their schools to the lowest common denominator, or special education. And because kids generally can't leave the campus, special ed is all they get. If they stay for years, the way Jonathan did, they're in no way prepared for college.

Jonathan arrived at Graham Windham not knowing a soul, and I imagined him trying to make friends. As I sat on a boulder in the center of campus, four girls with West Indian accents walked by carrying volleyball netting and shouting, inexplicably, "Lisa, Lisa, Lisa!" Five minutes later, they were back, still carrying the net, still calling for Lisa. They were circling the cottages. Some boys appeared and played a halfhearted game of basketball. One of the girls paused to single one out.

"What's your name, boy?"

The boy, tall and gangly, jogged up to her. "RudeBoy."

The girl turned up her nose and went back to her friends. The boys, around sixteen or so, chatted as they took turns shooting the ball.

"I saw your girl; she went down on my nut."

Shoot, dribble, shoot.

"Like some bitch-ass nigger!"

Shoot, basket. Shoot again.

I went up to talk to RudeBoy; he seemed approachable. Turned out, he'd been at Graham Windham only five days, which was why the Lisa girl asked for his name. When I asked him how he liked it, he shrugged.

"It's a facility, you know," he said, his expression purposefully weary, as though he'd been asked the question a thousand times before, and he was tired of the paparazzi. "It's better than LaSalle School, because it's less restrictive, but you still gotta get a pass if you want to leave your house."

The two other boys, who had wandered up to join our conversation, had also bounced around between facilities and agreed that Graham Windham wasn't as bad as some of the places they'd stayed. That didn't mean it was *good*, they stressed; it just wasn't as violent as other RTCs they'd known.

I spoke with one of the directors at Graham Windham, who said the campus didn't have any riots (unlike, say, the Randolph Children's Home, about fifty miles from Buffalo, where a dozen kids staged a riot in 2009). The director also said that if a staff member was even accused of hitting a child at Graham Windham, he'd be removed right away.

The biggest complaint RudeBoy's companions had about Graham Windham was that it was isolating. "It's kind of lonely," one of the kids, a light-skinned boy with pimples, admitted. "Especially because sometimes you get your own room. I guess the worst thing is, you've gotta stay here."

"I've been here six months, and there's nothing really bad about it," said his friend, a short Latino kid with disturbingly yellow teeth. "Except if you get modified [for bad behavior]. This means you get sent back before another judge and sent to another facility."

Jonathan was never modified, and he grew to adulthood in the little brick cottages at Graham Windham. He told me he experienced the full range of emotions on the campus — "happy, sad, mad" — but at the end of five years, he didn't feel as if he had any truly close bonds with any of the counselors or staff — and he certainly didn't consider them family. His final assessment of Graham Windham was that it was "just a place to rest your head."

What Jonathan didn't know was the cost of his headrest: in 2009, each child in an institutionalized placement facility cost taxpayers an estimated $210,000 per year. This was about $156,000 more than a year of room, board, and tuition at Columbia University — the place where I teach, and one of the most expensive schools in the country. And after his five-year tenure at Graham Windham, Jonathan hadn't even graduated from high school. If Jonathan had been placed with a therapeutic foster parent, one who had been trained to work with psychiatrically troubled children, the cost to the state would have been half of what was paid out to Graham Windham.

Ten years after a surgeon general's report that showed kids in therapeutic foster care are less likely to run away or become incarcerated than those in residential treatment centers, the state of New York began to scrutinize its residential treatment facilities for both their effectiveness and their safety. The first decade of the new millennium had been a troubled one for OCFS, which contracts with both residential treatment facilities like Graham Windham and juvenile detention facilities, which are exclusively for young criminal offenders. A teenager died at the hands of two adult aides at the Tryon School for Boys, leading to a Department of Justice investigation of Tryon and three other facilities. The investigators discovered extensive abuse; for instance, the forty residents at an all-girls facility were restrained an average of fifty-eight times per month, resulting in 123 injuries like concussions, knocked-out teeth, fractures, and shoulder separations and displacements.

The governor convened a Task Force on Transforming Juvenile

Justice to probe more deeply, and to propose improvements. Composed of local and national nonprofit directors, commissioners, judges, and professors, the task force made a clear recommendation: Stop sending so many kids to institutions. They called institutionalization a "choice of absolute last resort."

But the group homes, which are the next rung down in terms of restriction and are run by the city, have come under fire too. In 2003, investigators from three major advocacy and legal organizations launched a study of New York City's group homes and found that kids needed, but were not receiving, "family-like settings." Instead they were living with poorly trained staff, in subpar facilities. Mental health services were lacking, as were the systems to help kids stay connected with their biological families. The report's authors were blunt. They recommended that ACS stop sending so many children into group homes and instead find them families. If group homes were to remain open, they said, they would have to turn them on their heads, demanding that "the current group residence model with its focus on behavior control must be replaced with a service-based, family-like model."

By 2005, ACS had closed more than fifty group homes with close to six hundred beds. And in 2010, ACS announced a further reduction in group home beds — by about 25 percent — by April of 2011.

I thought that both of these trends — closing the RTCs and the group homes — were undoubtedly good signs. But it would have to mean more than shuttering buildings. ACS would also have to find enough new good foster parents. And they'd have to train the parents to weather the children's inevitable storms. It would mean viewing the kids as traumatized, rather than oppositionally defiant; seeing coping strategies rather than delinquency. And it would mean changing the entire culture of child welfare, so kids no longer tumbled down the ladder of more and more punitive placements. As Jonathan said, and all system kids know: "When you're a foster kid, an RTC or a group home is the last stop for you before jail."

I had hoped, when the first group homes began to close, that the link between child welfare and criminality, both perceived and actual, would begin to fade. But then the mayor made a big announcement in 2010, which collapsed this hope. In New York City, juvenile justice would be merged with foster care, under ACS.

City officials said the reason behind the move was to provide better services: so many of the kids were dual-involved. They were juvenile offenders who were also foster children, and if their needs were met by one big umbrella agency, they could have one case manager, one lawyer, one judge, and one goal: to clear up the troublemaking and get integrated back into a family and community. The big idea was to reduce recidivism and close more juvenile jails, reserving the locked facilities for only the most serious or violent offenders.

At the state level, a merger like this had already happened twelve years prior, with the creation of New York State's Office of Children and Family Services. Progressives generally applauded the move because it meant the judges who sentenced adolescents had more options. Rather than facing a short list of locked facilities or detention centers, these judges could now rely on the services of foster care too; they could send a kid back home with extra monitoring or counseling; they could send him to a foster or boarding home; they could bring in social workers and shift the general approach from one of punishment to one of support. And fiscal conservatives liked the fusion as well, since one agency was cheaper to run than two.

When the mayor made his announcement, there was almost no negative response from the press. The numbers were clear: abused or neglected children were more likely to be arrested, so providing them one large pool of services made some kind of intuitive sense. But I felt the low hum of dread beneath all the logic and evidence-based practice; there was nothing visionary in this move. It was entirely reactive, predicated on the belief that many foster kids would, by necessity or design, become criminals.

I met with the new ACS commissioner a few years after the merger had been announced, and he had inherited this combined agency — as well as a radical, and exciting, new plan. All of the juvenile delinquents from the city who had been housed in RTCs upstate (save for the more serious criminal offenders) would be handed back to ACS. Whether or not they were foster kids when they committed their crimes, they would become foster kids now. When we spoke, Commissioner Richter was just about to move the first wave of 250 kids into brand-new urban facilities.

"They'll be residences with six to twelve kids each. The largest will be twenty-four," Commissioner Richter said. "All of the residences are required to have a strong program model, like the Missouri Model." The Missouri Model is an approach to juvenile justice that favors a high staff-to-child ratio, therapeutic group treatment, individualized attention, and supportive peer relationships rather than harsh and punitive coercive techniques. The main thing, the commissioner said, was that the kids would be closer to their families, who could be newly involved in their lives. And they could take regular classes in accredited schools, earning crucial credits toward a high school diploma.

But the foster kids at places like Graham Windham wouldn't be coming home, wouldn't be getting new programming or higher-level education. The "last stop" foster kids would still be going into the RTCs that contracted with the state and housed their own mix of kids with records and substance problems and mental health needs.

So in these early stages, it looked as if the delinquent kids would get more perks from the agency merger than the foster kids. I know it's not a competition between the groups, but I worry about the philosophical implications of foster care sharing its administrative home with juvenile justice. Without the managerial and cultural divisions between the two, will a new foster kid envision jail, even more, as the next logical link in the chain? So many feel already imprisoned by their status as wards of the state and shackled by the stigma of being wild, unlovable foster kids; an expanded ACS mission expressly contrived for delinquents may only deepen this notion — for the kids, the workers, and the foster parents too.

8

Arrested in Development

WHEN I MET KECIA PITTMAN, she was serving a twelve-year prison sentence for burglary. She had a BA in sociology, which she earned while she was locked up, and her thesis was on the connection between child welfare and criminal justice. Her teachers brought her books about discrimination in foster care, books like *The Lost Children of Wilder*, and *Shattered Bonds*, and *Nobody's Children* — the same ones I'd read over the years — but the links Kecia made to the justice system were her own.

When we talked at Bayview, the medium-security prison where I teach writing, Kecia had just turned forty. She was long and lean, with clearly defined muscles roping around her arms and shoulders, evidence of her daily workouts in the prison gym. She kept her dreadlocks tied in a loose knot behind her head. Kecia explained that the first of her theories was the most basic and obvious: group homes led to jail because of the connections that you made in care. The kids you met could lure you into trouble, and the adults were strangers you couldn't trust. One thing led to another.

"It's much easier to deviate in a group home," Kecia said, blandly. "You're not held to anybody's standard. I mean, there's not enough

love in a group home to keep a kid loyal to any particular person."
Even with adolescent rebellion, depression, experimentation, and all
the rest, a teenager in a family can be bound enough to another's af-
firmative view of herself to pull through the tough years. Sometimes
friends provide the positive mirror. But in a group home, that all goes
awry. A teenager makes herself anew, in anyone's image.

"There's a lot of movement, they pull you out of school all the time,
and you never feel stable. It's easy to jump into anything because
group homes promote that kind of lifestyle," Kecia said. "You're always free to do mischief. You don't owe anyone anything anymore —
that's really the connection to the criminal justice system."

Kecia and I were alone in Bayview's conference room, though the
door was open and a guard was stationed right outside, listening to
gospel music on a hand-held radio. Like most of Bayview, the room
was depressing: scuffed beige walls and floors tiled in a sickly green
linoleum, sealed and barred windows, an old wooden table, and then,
randomly, some stuffed floral chairs in the corners. We sat as far from
the guard as we could as Kecia described the way her mother dropped
her off at the child welfare offices when Kecia had just turned fourteen. By Kecia's telling, she was going through ordinary teenage rebellion, but her mom couldn't handle the challenge and filed a petition in
family court to have Kecia declared a Person in Need of Supervision,
or a PINS kid. Her mother was free of all responsibility; the city would
take over from there.

Kecia sat back and started counting off the group homes she'd lived
in: Edwin Gould, Hegeman Diagnostic Center, Graham Windham,
"a house on Park Avenue and 21st," Saint Barnabas, Ashford, Mount
Hope, Euphrasian, and then, for a stint, Bellevue's psychiatric unit.
She said there were others, but she couldn't remember all the names.
At first, Kecia said, she cried and cried for her mother. Then she got
angry at what she felt was abandonment; she refused to even look
at her mom when she came for visits. "I felt like she didn't love me
enough to hold on to me, and then I felt like nobody could love me
enough. Now I got twelve to life, and it all started from the group
homes."

• • •

There's one commonly cited statistic — that 80 percent of all inmates have spent time in foster care — but when you look more closely at the data, you see that it's limited, and that little analysis has been conducted on the causal relationship between the two institutions. The 80 percent figure actually comes from a study on a single state (Illinois), though reputable sources have extrapolated the figure to represent the entire country. A California State Assemblymember, pushing through new legislation, claimed that 70 percent of the state's adult inmates came from child welfare, and Connecticut officials determined that 75 percent of the youth in the state's criminal justice system were former foster kids. Nobody has really conducted a full national count, so some people guess more conservatively; ABC News, for instance, ran a series on foster care and put the number at a careful 25 percent.

Even more significantly, nobody is looking at what *type* of foster care these inmates are coming from. Kecia pegs the blame squarely on the group homes and the RTCs, but what about the kids who have more stable placements, or live with families, or keep connections with their parents? Does the trouble lie with foster care as an institution, or with certain things that happen in foster care and not others — or is foster care just the fall guy for a child's earlier traumas?

Doreen Soto's daughter, Shameka — the little girl who was removed when Doreen left her alone in the apartment to buy drugs — did not live in a group home. Shameka was immediately placed with a loving family in Brooklyn who eventually adopted her. She lived with them until she was nineteen. And then she went to jail.

I met with Doreen many times, both when she was an inmate at Bayview and after she was released. At first she lived in a halfway house in Harlem, and then another one in Queens; eventually she got her own single room with a shared kitchen in Brooklyn, which meant she could qualify for the apartment in the Bronx. Each time I saw her, Doreen looked happier and healthier. She had always marshaled a hearty laugh, but she emanated a deeper kind of contentment and equilibrium once she was free, had found a job and a church, and could attend twelve-step meetings every day on her own. She was losing weight to take pressure off her knee, and she was growing out her hair and getting manicures. She wore big pink polo shirts and khakis for her full-time job at a telephone answering service, and her ever-present pinkie ring was soon accompanied by a gold chain at her neck and sparkly studs in her ears, all bought on sale at Macy's. Still, Doreen saved most of her extra spending money for presents for Shameka's daughter, whom she was hoping to rescue from foster care someday.

Talking about Shameka was a visible struggle for Doreen, but she did it a lot. She volleyed between worry and resentment; whenever Shameka called her mother now, it was to demand money. Still, Doreen didn't blame foster care for Shameka's sour attitude or her run-ins with the law — she blamed herself, and the early separation.

"When she got taken, that was the best family she could have went to, but she was still placed in a home she didn't know," Doreen said one day when we met up in a diner for matzoh ball soup. Shameka's family, the Taylors, lived in the projects in Williamsburg, Brooklyn, near the Navy Yard. They were religious and community-minded: Mr. Taylor served as the sergeant-at-arms for the building's tenants' association, and Mrs. Taylor turned on lights and appliances for her Orthodox neighbors every Sabbath. They easily folded Shameka into their large family, composed of eight biological and four adoptive children.

Mrs. Taylor encouraged contact between Shameka and her mother, but for more than a year after the removal, Doreen was preoccupied with drugs and never made a visit. She rallied for Shameka's third birthday, though, when she met Shameka and Mrs. Taylor at the agency. Shameka didn't recognize her.

"She walked all around that room, looking at me, for about an hour," Doreen told me, tearing up at the memory. At the agency, Doreen placed a picture of herself on a low kids' table, and Shameka picked it up. Carefully, Doreen called out the name she used for Shameka as a baby: Muu-muu. "Her reaction! She snapped her head right up. She remembered that."

After hearing her name, three-year-old Shameka walked up to Doreen and stood between her legs, staring at the picture. "You?" she asked. She let Doreen hold her and call her Muu-muu for the rest of the afternoon. "She still has that picture today," Doreen said.

Mrs. Taylor told Doreen that as long as she wasn't high, she was welcome at the apartment anytime. But the birthday visit was all Doreen could muster; at first, she was "smoking dope, smoking crack, running like a madwoman," and then she was arrested for possession and sentenced with three to five years. Doreen was sent to Bedford Hills — about fifty miles away by car, and a long trip for the Taylors to make with twelve kids at home. Doreen sighed heavily over her soup. "So from age three to six, Shameka had no contact with me. She was probably always thinking, 'Where's my mother?'"

Parents in prison traditionally don't have many rights. When a mom like Doreen is incarcerated, she has to abide by both the rules of her sentencing, determined by a criminal court judge, and the tenets of the foster care agreement, determined by a family court judge. The family court judge usually requires visitations, which are almost always up to the mother to initiate; she must navigate prison bureaucracy to place phone calls to her caseworker to both coordinate and pay for a visit. Most inmates are jailed more than fifty miles away from their children, and gas money and travel time can be too burdensome for a foster parent to shoulder. Then there can be cumbersome clearance problems, or prison personnel who view child visitation as a privilege for good behavior.

That said, in 1983, prisoners in New York State won the right to monthly visits with their children, as well as to attend their family's hearings in family court. This law, however, often butts up against reality; again, caseworkers may be required to facilitate visits between parents and children but don't have the resources to travel long distances or accept exorbitant collect calls. To appear in court, an incarcerated parent must be ordered there by the family court, and then transferred to and temporarily housed in a local jail like Rikers Island. The Department of Corrections may not process the order in time; they may fail to notify the inmate of the transfer; the court date can get changed; the potential breakdowns between an order and an appearance are endless. The end result, for a judge, is the specter of an absent parent. And then there's ASFA — the federal law that mandates that children who have been in foster care for fifteen out of twenty-two months either return home or become available for adoption. Even if a parent has managed to demand, coordinate, and pay for the visits with her kids, she can't demand to shorten her sentence. In the five years after ASFA's passage, the parental termination proceedings for incarcerated parents more than doubled.

In a way, for a parent who gets arrested, it comes down to the luck of placement, both for herself and for her child. If she lands in a "good" jail — like Bedford Hills or Taconic in New York — she may get to live with a newborn in the nursery programs and learn critical mothering skills. Prisons like these partner with programs such as the Children of Incarcerated Parents, which provide transportation for older kids to and from the facilities. But if the parent lands in a worse jail, or gets assigned a caseworker who won't return calls, she's stuck watching the clock tick by on ASFA's deadline.

Doreen was a lucky one. She was sent to Bedford Hills, and Shameka was placed with the Taylors, who kept up a connection by taking calls on holidays and making Shameka draw cards and pictures for her mother. This was a few years before ASFA, but still, Shameka's caseworkers looked at Doreen's trajectory and didn't see much hope. Shameka was still a young kid, and they needed to place her somewhere permanent.

About halfway through Doreen's sentence, Mrs. Taylor showed up at Bedford Hills. She was worried, she said; the agency wanted to move Shameka out of foster care. If Shameka, who was six then, was moved into an adoptive home, the agency could lose tabs on her. Doreen might not ever see her daughter again. Better, Mrs. Taylor thought, that Doreen voluntarily give up her parenthood and sign Shameka over to her. That way, she said, they could always stay connected.

"Ms. Taylor always made me feel safe and secure about seeing my kid," Doreen told me in the diner. "I didn't know what she was talking about, with this open adoption thing; it was like she was speaking a foreign language. I felt like I didn't have any choice, though, because I was only a year and a half into my sentence. I didn't want them to put

Shameka back into foster care—where, who knows where she'd go. So I gave her up."

Like many inmates, Doreen didn't know she had any rights and didn't know she could ask for them. She didn't know she could have fought for custody again, when she was slated to be released on good behavior within eighteen months or so. She felt the despondency, the drag and shame of prison, and the sense of profound failure as a mother. She took Mrs. Taylor's advice and gave over her daughter.

Looking back now, from a position of sobriety and stability, Doreen thinks she made the right choice. When she was released from Bedford Hills, she went back to using heroin and was in no condition to take care of her daughter. What she doesn't know is how much her three state bids in prison—and subsequent absence from Shameka's life—affected Shameka.

There are studies that link parental incarceration with increases in a child's inclination toward aggression, isolation, and depression, but research doesn't often show the nature or degree of these effects —especially because the circumstances kids find themselves in after a parent has been locked up can vary so widely. Despite being raised by sober and devout parents from the age of eighteen months, Shameka ended up mirroring Doreen almost exactly.

As a small example, Doreen told me the story of the day Shameka delivered her first child at sixteen—a bright, healthy baby she named Sharisha. It was Mrs. Taylor who called Doreen to the hospital; Doreen was out of jail at the time but still, as she said, "high as a kite." Doreen showed up at the hospital loaded down with gifts. She had a bassinet, bottles, a bottle warmer, baby clothes, diapers—all for baby Sharisha. And she brought one new outfit for Shameka. Doreen realized, when Shameka complained that her mother hadn't arrived with more presents for her, that Doreen had said the same thing to her own mother sixteen years before.

"My mother brought me one new outfit, and everything else was for the baby. I was like, 'Hello? I didn't die!' My mother said, 'All right, but you got the baby now,'" Doreen said. "And I realized I just did the same thing to my kid." She shook her head. "Damn. History keeps playing itself."

When Doreen was released from jail for the final time in April 2008, she didn't know where Shameka was living. She knew Sharisha, her granddaughter, was staying with one of the Taylor daughters, who had been named Sharisha's official foster parent. And just as Doreen had done when she was her daughter's age, Shameka was running the streets, using drugs, and a warrant was out for her arrest.

There were things, outside of the Taylors' or Doreen's control, that had happened in Shameka's life that made it harder. She suffered from epilepsy, which was controlled by medication, and from learning disorders, Doreen told me, which she thinks might have been brought on by the crack she smoked during pregnancy. (This latter suspicion is likely unfounded; in a major *Journal of the American Medical Association* review of dozens of articles, doctors found no evidence that children's language and motor skills, as well as attention and behavior, are connected with cocaine exposure, though they didn't look at learning disorders per se.) These conditions may have made Shameka more isolated or withdrawn, or less confident.

Whatever her circumstances, at sixteen, Shameka ran away — though sometimes she said she was abducted. She also said she was forced into prostitution, though when she found out she was pregnant with Sharisha, she made her way back to Brooklyn. Doreen said Shameka was traumatized but didn't want to press charges or go through an investigation. And, Doreen said, after the runaway/abduction, her daughter was never the same again.

In this respect as well, Doreen sees a reflection of herself. "She's definitely a photocopy of my behaviors. Definitely. Used to be, you gave me a little bit of attention and I ran with that. Shameka's the same way — so easy to be lured."

Doreen thinks her own need for physical attention came from the lack of it in her own household when she was growing up. Her parents loved her, she's sure of it, but they rarely touched or hugged her. It was the same in the Taylor household; there was guidance and moral teaching, Doreen remembered from her visits — but not a lot of affection.

Maybe, I countered — but plenty of people grow up without hugs and they don't get "lured" into drugs and prostitution. So call it a perfect storm: some emotional neglect mixed with neighborhood access, mixed with genetic disposition, and *blam:* you've got Doreen's life trajectory. Compound it all with an early traumatic separation and a mom in jail, and you've got Shameka's.

But then, Shameka endured a second major loss in her life — underscoring the notion that, although there may be a pipeline from foster care to jail, individual lives are so potholed with particulars they're impossible to typecast.

Doreen told me about the fire almost as an afterthought. "And then, of course, when the Taylors died in that fire . . ." she said to me one day when we were talking about something else.

"What?!" I sputtered.

"Yeah, from two years old to nineteen, that was the only family she ever knew," Doreen said. "That fire took a big toll on her, and she probably never grieved that."

The newspaper report claimed there were seven people at home in Shameka's childhood apartment when a kid, possibly a grandchild, started playing with matches. He dropped a lit match between two couch cushions, and the fire caught. The family hid in a bedroom to escape the smoke, but Mr. and Mrs. Taylor, as well as two of the youngest grandchildren, were already dead by the time firefighters arrived.

Doreen was between prison bids at the time of the fire and went to the funeral. She said Shameka was furious. "Shameka said, 'I don't know what the fuck you doin' here,'" Doreen remembered. "And I ate that. I know I kept coming in and out of her life, promising to do the right thing, only to end up back in jail."

But that evening after the funeral, Doreen said, Shameka softened. She and her three-year-old daughter, Sharisha, stayed with Doreen for two nights, all curled up in the bed together. Despite the circumstances, Doreen remembers those nights as the happiest she'd ever known; she hadn't slept in a bed with her daughter for seventeen years.

"Shameka is still a baby, 'cause after she's been with me after five minutes, that kid comes out of her," Doreen said. "It's like, 'Mommy, I want to play this; Mommy, let me hold you; Mommy, pick me up.' You want me to pick you up?! You fuckin' two hundred pounds!"

If she could, Doreen told me, she would take Shameka back, let her live with her again, let her be a baby, and try to repair what was broken so long ago. "I'd keep her under my supervision at all times, put her in the bed with me at night. All that. Because Shameka never slept in a crib, she only slept with me."

Doreen let herself fantasize but quickly cut it short: she knew her daughter was using drugs; letting her too close could mean a relapse of her own. Shameka may have been vulnerable at the funeral and on prison visits when she read to her mom or babbled about boys, but she could also be vicious and demanding. At the time we talked, Doreen was living in a subsidized halfway house for the formerly incarcerated; she couldn't have visitors, let alone overnight guests. And there was a warrant for Shameka — even talking with her on the street would be a violation of Doreen's parole.

"She could be with me and a cop comes by and they'd call my parole officer to let her know I'm with a fugitive; I can't have that. I'd kill myself before going back into the penitentiary," Doreen said, her eyes hard and fierce. She sat for a minute, and the anger on her face twisted into pain. "She's my kid, and she's fucked up. I don't know how to help her."

Kecia and Doreen were not friends when they were incarcerated together. They both took my writing class, though Doreen needed it and Kecia attended to stave off boredom. Doreen was jovial with everyone; if she were a tree, she'd be an oak — strong, solid, and welcoming. Kecia was more wary; her taut musculature and stony expressions said "Don't touch," and she was wound up tight inside, her fierce intellect doing battle with her grief. I don't know if their differences developed from their backgrounds: Kecia came from foster care and Doreen did not. But Kecia said all the previous foster kids she knew who were now serving time projected a similar kind of remove.

"There's an attachment disorder that happens in foster care, that creates a sense of instability, even if everything is sitting still around you," Kecia said to me that night we were talking in Bayview's conference room. "Even if everything is secure in your life, you'll always have that insecurity."

But how does that lead to crime? For Kecia, it's a process, a long chain of damage (self-inflicted and otherwise) stemming from an original violation of trust. She's read a lot of Erik Erikson, a social psychologist who wrote about a person's developmental stages. She said people don't go from foster care to jail because they don't have resources and need to steal (though that is sometimes true), or because an institutional life is the only life they know (though that may be true too). They move between the systems because a life stage has been irreparably damaged. They can't trust enough to care, and they can't care enough to hold on to a better life.

The attachment begins in infancy, goes the theory, and with it something called "basic trust." "Babies cry, and they learn that somebody comes, and they calm down," Kecia explained slowly, as though she were teaching a class. "In that, babies learn that they have some type of power. This is the basis for some very important psychological things later on: you need faith, you need hope, and you need confidence that you can manipulate things to get what you need." When parents are negligent or, as Kecia suggested, so poor that long work hours or suboptimal child care keeps adults from tending to a baby's cries, this "basic trust" is broken.

This is what happened with Kecia — and a lot of the women she interviewed in prison for her thesis. Kecia's mom was a single mother forced to work long hours, and Kecia was the only child. "I remember going to babysitters, always being in a room alone. I was always crying. I remember that; it never leaves you."

Despite the fact that Kecia had already graduated from college and her writing skills were excellent, she wanted to take my precollege writing class anyway. I let her be my teaching assistant, which mostly worked out well: she was quietly constructive with her feedback on student papers, but she occasionally butted heads with the stronger personalities in the room — like Doreen. When Doreen had a point to make, which was often, Kecia would lean back in her seat and purse her lips, staring hard at a distant corner of the chalkboard.

"I'm like a broken thing; I'm always watching — looking for the hurt, looking for the pain. People want to get close to me, but I can't. I look for pain, because that's my escape into isolation. I'm better off alone," Kecia explained. I saw this in classroom dynamics a lot; when Kecia could ensure that she was the smartest pupil, she was fine. But when somebody like Doreen met Kecia at her level, and challenged her on a point, or simply wanted to connect with her, Kecia was insulted, and retreated.

"Whatever stages you haven't resolved, they will keep popping up again, and every stage is contingent upon the last one having been resolved," Kecia said, explaining that this can mean big trouble during adolescence. Adolescents are famous for testing limits, and those with attachment disorders may push even harder. This is why, she theorized, so many kids — including her — enter foster care as teenagers. "If you don't have the basic trust, the basic confidence that you can make things happen in the world, then when you come into adolescence, you experience identity diffusion."

Erikson coined the term *identity crisis* — a natural process wherein teenagers "try on" different identities (hairstyles, musical or religious affiliations, and so on) and use their friends to reflect these characteristics back to them. If they've had healthy attachments early on, the theory goes, the crisis resolves into a stable identity. If they haven't had these attachments, they can develop identity diffusion — or an unstable, threatened sense of self. They don't have the inner security to hold on to a single identity, or perhaps the faith that loved ones will see them through this second infancy, of sorts.

This may be what Doreen was describing when she said that Shameka was "so easy to be lured" during her teens. Kecia, who hit her own identity crisis at fourteen, was abandoned by her mother and deposited in a group home. Group homes are hard for anyone, but for someone like Kecia, they are a disaster. Said Kecia, who had once planned to be a scientist, "Have you ever heard of failure to thrive? It happens later on, in its own way, with adolescents. They're not going to die, literally, but they might, psychically."

Kecia's mischief was fighting, and isolating herself. Once Kecia had stopped crying for her mother, she said, she "became very well defended." She didn't trust anyone around her and she argued with staff, once even landing in a fistfight with a counselor. These fights would yield new group homes, new schools, more strangers, and bigger defenses. Once, Kecia climbed into the back of a truck, riding it all the way into a garage where it parked for the night. It was full of dolls for sale. She tried to steal the dolls and sell them but was caught. Kecia was a minor and slapped with a reprimand, but it marked the beginning of her criminal record.

By seventeen, Kecia had been pulled in and out of schools so much, she no longer had a workable transcript, but she heard of a place in Brooklyn that administered the GED. She hadn't attended a single school for more than a few consecutive months, but Kecia took the test and passed. Without telling any group home staff, she registered for New York Technical College. Her dream of being a scientist had dissipated, but she figured she could become an electromechanical technician; Kecia was good with numbers. She got a job at McDonald's but knew it wouldn't cover tuition; a counselor at the college helped Kecia apply for financial aid, and Kecia faced down her mother to sign the forms.

All of this, Kecia said, was below the radar of the group home. But when they caught wind of the student loan, she said, they told her she had to go. No children at their address could be receiving large sums of money; it was liable to cause problems.

"They called my mother and asked her if she wanted me, and all of a sudden she said yes," Kecia said. But Kecia was still burning from her mother's betrayal; she wouldn't stay there. "The group home put me out, and I've been on the streets ever since."

At first, Kecia said, she tried to make it work by finding a boyfriend and moving in with him. She went to school and to her job, but things quickly deteriorated. "I didn't know how to live in a house, after moving from place to place to place. It was beautiful, this house with the boyfriend, but I just didn't feel comfortable in it. I was so detached from everything," Kecia said, adding, "You have to practice being stable."

Kecia didn't have the practice, and she fell into a depression. She stopped going to school, which made her more depressed, and pretty soon she had to find a way to dull the pain. The answer, for a while, was cocaine. She lost the job and the home and the boyfriend, but she was still a quick study; she had lived in enough places to know how to pick locks and dismantle alarms, and she turned to burglary to support her habit. She never robbed people when they were home, and she always worked alone. Only once, she said, a woman came to the door in the middle of a burglary. "I pretended to be a cop," Kecia said, though the ruse didn't work. "I didn't want to scare her."

Kecia was caught when she was twenty and did a year at Rikers Island. She got out, got sober, fell in love, which lasted for a while, but the breakup sent her back to drugs and crime. The next sentence was two years, followed by more sobriety, then more depression, more drugs, more burglary, and another arrest. Because of her two prior convictions, Kecia was ultimately sentenced to twelve years to life, culminating at Bayview, where we met.

Kecia said this last sentence was different and if she got out, she wouldn't be going back to jail. "Because I finally got my degree. And I got psychological help," she said, referring both to all the books she read and the intensive therapy she asked for and received — therapy that often enraged her, but pushed her to the point of accepting her many losses. "I've addressed my depression," she said. But then she paused. We could hear the thrum of the cars racing on the West Side Highway, just beyond the windows of the prison. "The residual effect of it is not gone. I'll never be able to love in a normal way."

Even Kecia admits that her theories provide only a scaffolding for the complexity of a single human life; thin lines that suggest, rather than contain, the forms they demarcate. And anyway, the theory and the therapy are what have helped her now; what would have helped her back then, when she was a kid, was more direct.

"You've got all these scholars making these big, big proposals about whether to close the group homes; you're putting a proposal together and you've got all these legal teams," Kecia said. We had been talking about recent studies of New York City group homes and their innumerable failings. "And you've got all these professional psychologists.

The question to be asking is 'What do you do in your house? How come your kid finished college?'"

The answer, Kecia said, is you stick by him. "If you have a family, and you have five kids, are you going to throw one out because he fights more than the others? No, you're going to keep him in the house, and eventually it's going to get worked out." For Kecia, it would have been best if her mother kept her at home, but a close second would have been a group home with staff who could have seen through Kecia's defenses and loved her anyway. Or the next group home, or the next. By Kecia's fourth, fifth, sixth, and seventh group homes, she was already too shut down to find.

Tolightha Smalls was a caseworker at Edwin Gould, where all the Green foster children get their services. (I met with Tolightha in 2007, and sadly, she passed away in 2012.) She fit her name: she was short and small, with tiny hands and a nearly unlined face, although she claimed to be "somewhere close to sixty." When we met, her current caseload was fifteen kids — all teenagers — and every single one of them had both her office and her cell phone numbers so they could reach her anytime, day or night. She used to work in adoptions, and these kids had her number too, and they still called her, even though they've found permanent homes. "They still send me pictures of themselves, now with their parents," she said proudly. "I worked with thirty-five homes and did thirty-three adoptions."

Like Kecia, Tolightha believed that foster kids need one solid adult in their lives to stick by them, and as a case manager, she stepped out of her job description to play that role. But she also believed kids should receive the kind of consistent, personalized therapy Kecia had in jail — without having to commit a crime to get it.

Tolightha and I met in the same Brooklyn conference room where, once before, Bruce and Allyson attended their "emergency preparedness" meeting with the firefighter who never showed up. On a bulletin board outside the room, a sign claimed the city was in "urgent need of foster parents who would take in teenagers"; next to it was a poster advertising the minimum wage in 1997.

Edwin Gould was ranked the top foster care agency in New York in 2004 by ACS's review process, then called EQUIP, which stood for "Evaluation and Quality Improvement Protocol." (The review process has since been renamed Scorecard and uses letter grades to evaluate child safety, permanency, well-being, and foster parent recruitment and support. In 2009, Edwin Gould earned three Bs and a C and was still among the higher performers. No agency received straight As.)

At the time Tolightha and I talked, Edwin Gould served two hundred kids — about half of them out of the Brooklyn office. Like Francine Cournos, the Columbia psychiatry professor who spoke with me during the blizzard, Tolightha felt that many of the kids would be better served in therapeutic homes with better-trained foster parents. But despite being a top agency, Edwin Gould didn't offer such homes. If a child needed a therapeutic placement, he'd have to leave the agency and his caseworker. This was tough on Tolightha.

"A kid'll say to me, 'I don't have parents, I don't have foster parents; the only person I have and trust is my social worker,'" Tolightha said, pursing her lips for emphasis. The fluorescent lights buzzed audibly. "These kids have been in so many placements that if they have someone they can attach to, like a social worker, you can't turn your back on them."

Officially, Tolightha was supposed to make home visits to each of her fifteen teenagers twice a month. Every six months, she had to hold a formal "consent meeting" with each family to reaffirm the living arrangements, as well as go to court with them for their twice-annual permanency hearings. This meant she was in court or an official meeting more than once a week, visiting two homes at least every other day of the week, and filling out extensive paperwork for every encounter she had. Much of her time, though, was spent providing de facto therapy for the kids she'd bonded with.

"You have to start where the client is. I mean just sit back and be a good listener — give them an opportunity to express themselves," she said, sitting back in her metal folding chair. In her brown turtleneck and creased brown slacks, Tolightha looked like a young grandmother — not the kind who would bake you cookies, but the kind who would take an interest in your appearance, ask you about your school-work, remember whom you asked out on a date. "I've been told so many times not to get too attached to the kids, because you have to be able to separate yourself, but I get attached to every last one of my clients, and that's why it works."

At first, Tolightha said, this devotion took its toll on her marriage — as she started coming home at six, then seven, then eight and nine o'clock at night. But she and her husband had been married for over thirty-five years, and she said he realized that this job was a kind of calling for her. It takes that much time, she said, to really understand what a foster kid needs — and then try to build the services up around him.

"We all know that the kids come into care with different issues — physical or sexual, neglect or abandonment. The mom might or might not have been involved in drugs; the mom might have a mental illness," Tolightha explained. The mental illness component is a big one: one study of nearly five thousand kids showed that those with moms who had a mental illness were more than twice as likely to be placed in care. And even though it's not directly within her job outline, "I'm the one that has to make sure that mom gets the services that are needed." Otherwise, she said, it just might not get done.

Tolightha had a BA in urban studies, which, she explained, helped her to look at child welfare from an economic perspective — but it didn't provide much assistance with the deep psychological trauma that her clients presented daily. She'd been thinking of going back to school to get a master's in social work, so she could offer them real therapy. Right now, there simply wasn't enough to meet the need.

"We have so many kids who come into care who have been physically or sexually abused — but you can't just make a referral to a psychologist or a psychiatrist that doesn't work in that area," she said. "We have a good gynecologist if the child is pregnant, and a good substance abuse therapist — but you can't send every child to the same person."

In fact, she said, the entire agency retained only three psychiatrists for all of its children — and most of their work was in medical prescriptions. There were no therapists practicing in the neighborhood of Bed-Stuy for outpatient referral, where about 45 percent of the population lived on some form of public assistance in 2008, so when Tolightha wanted to send a child to a specialist, she had to send him to Schneider Children's Hospital in Long Island. Since many foster parents in New York don't drive, that's just too far away.

Still, she said, most of her clients didn't want clinical help. "They always say, 'I don't need therapy; I'm not crazy,'" she said, smiling at first, then tightening up when she mentioned how many times her kids' privacy had been violated. They worried that their files were always available for any new stranger to see. "They say, 'I don't want my business all over the agency. I'd rather talk to you.'"

A group of therapists in New York City, called the Fostering Connection, offer their time and services to foster kids, and their families, pro bono. Francine Cournos is on their board. The night after Barack Obama won the presidency in 2008, I went to one of their meetings, where a few psychologists were presenting case studies of their work in a plain gray conference room on West 57th Street, above a Gap.

It was a room full of mostly women, with kinky hair, funky earrings, and canvas bags. It was already stuffy and overheated when I settled in and listened to the opening remarks.

"Much the way lawyers have a mandate to give a portion of their time to pro bono work, we dreamed up the Fostering Connection ten years ago," one of the cofounders said into a microphone. She claimed the idea was to provide long-term, consistent relationships from the "soothing" comforts of the therapist's private office — mostly located in Manhattan. I prickled at the presumption: one person's comfort may be another's inconvenience. And with foster kids, I knew, you had to go to them — very few, I imagined, would travel to unfamiliar neighborhoods to spill their sadness to yet another stranger.

The codirector confirmed my suspicions. "What we've found is that foster kids don't always want, or can't even imagine, a long-term, open-ended relationship," she said, adding that the nonprofit often had more therapists on call than it had clients. I thought of Tolightha Smalls lamenting the dearth of qualified therapists in her neighborhood. "I now joke, 'Build it and they *might* come.' There are many mismatches in terms of time, and respecting one's time."

What this meant, according to the next speaker, was that patients just didn't show up. Their parents, or caseworkers, didn't bring them. She'd make calls to ACS, and nobody would return them; she'd set an appointment, and then sit in her empty office, frustrated. Why didn't people value what she was offering?

The mismatch, I thought, wasn't about time. It wasn't the gift they had that was wrong, nor, as one speaker insinuated, was it the recipients or their "cultural understanding of time." It was the way that gift was packaged and presented. The final speaker, thankfully, reflected on some of these themes.

"We need to think about our assumptions," she said, leveling her gaze across the room, "that when they don't show up they don't value it. We need to think about what people have internalized and what we represent."

For kids, a therapist could represent a lot of things. A good percentage of foster children are on psychiatric medications to control their mood swings or hyperactivity and could view a therapist, with a raised eyebrow and a cocked hip, as yet another doctor in the lineup. Others, like the kids Tolightha encountered, were afraid of therapists spreading their private business around; respecting confidentiality hadn't been in their realm of experience. And others, like Fatimah at the Greens', wanted therapy, but wanted it to be convenient and familiar. Fatimah had been searching for a therapist, she said, to help her sort through the abuse and the jangle of memories so she could write her book, but she said, "I don't want to go somewhere far where a lot of white people will be looking at me like I'm crazy."

A few years after this meeting, I spoke with a therapist who had been volunteering with the Fostering Connection for three and a half years; she had been seeing the same teenager the entire time, and he'd shown tremendous progress. TFC's model worked, this therapist told me, though she had learned to be flexible: she found her client was more comfortable meeting her in a diner than at her office, so they talked, every week, over turkey burgers and omelets. This long-term, individualized therapy also worked, she said, because her client really wanted to be there. With the luxury of free weekly appointments over several years, they had time to build trust; at the beginning, they played cards and talked about snacks.

This kind of gentle start makes sense, as Francine Cournos says therapy might not always be the best idea for foster kids anyway — at least not while they're in the tumult of transitions. "When you're feeling unsafe, it's not a good time to explore your emotions; you're too enraged and disorganized to fall apart a little bit," she said in her talk on foster care at the School of Social Work at Columbia. "These kids don't need uncovering therapy; they need adults who understand the natural processes of bereavement and trauma."

It's the parents who are the real "healing agents," as Francine called them; they're the soil into which the kids can root. But really, she said, anyone a child attaches to can do the trick; it's a matter of them "seeing in you the capacity to become something good." It could be a teacher, a mentor, a therapist, a nun. It could even be an employee at a group home.

When I talked with Tolightha Smalls, she lamented the change in tide and the city's decision to close more of its group homes. Tolightha watched kids who lived with individual foster families struggle with all manner of psychological troubles, and she thought about service implementation. If the kids lived together in more cohesive groups, she thought, it might be easier to provide them with more consistent psychiatric care. And keep them under closer supervision.

"If we had better service delivery in the group homes, we wouldn't have all these kids running away, running out to prostitute, because they'd be in these therapeutic settings," Tolightha said. Her concern about prostitution was especially serious. Domestic trafficking of minors for sex work is on the rise, and pimps — in New York they're often gang leaders — target girls in homeless shelters or group homes where the adults in charge often have no training about these types of predators who run brothels out of apartments. The number of teenage prostitutes in New York is hard to gauge (a recent estimate gathered by various state agencies was three thousand, but many experts claim that's too low), but the district attorney's office in Brooklyn recently created a Sex Trafficking Unit to target people who sexually exploit women and girls. I knew one foster girl in Brooklyn whose story was fairly typical. She wanted to keep her identity a secret, but she told me that she was approached one day by another girl about her age who promised to take her somewhere for a job interview. The girl I know was locked in an apartment with several other kids and forced, via beatings and rape, to take Ecstasy and sleeping pills and have sex several times a day for no pay. She escaped six months later and ran from the foster care system entirely.

Tolightha believed that well-staffed group homes could counter all this. Behind her head a brightly colored poster advertised the "Five top reasons to foster parent a teen." It promised a teen could teach you the latest trends and help you program your cell phone. "But we can't make the group homes look like storage. We have to implement services where kids can see they're being assisted — give them group therapy, family therapy, tutoring. A kid could go back to his family from one of these places."

Unlike Francine and her sister, Francine's brother was placed in a group home, and he did fairly well there, Francine said to me during our talk. He found an employee with whom he could connect but wasn't expected to love on command, the way she was expected to love her new mother. But while services can be better consolidated and coordinated from a central location, Francine cautioned that the central service for a traumatized child will always be a primary, human attachment. In group homes, workers would have to be trained to offer this — and step up as family figures, with all the loyalty and consistency that implies.

From her experience, Kecia was skeptical that group homes could provide such a thing. "There are just too many kids in there, and group home staff changes every eight hours," she said simply. OK, I pressed, but if they *were* to work, what would have to change?

Like Francine and Tolightha, and like the recommendations in the report on ACS, Kecia thought the solution depended on people more than place. "Why do we get away from the humanness of things? How do we get away from it and then expect it to work?" Kecia said, playing with a crease in her state-issued jeans. The trouble with group homes, or with any institutionalized care, she said, is that kids feel they're being thrown away. But a person, she believed, inside that institution could change that perception. "I do believe love conquers all. But that means you've gotta rock with the kid — whether it's a little baby or an older child — rock with whatever they get into, no matter how bad they get."

It was dark outside the room where Kecia and I sat talking; we could hear the evening guard ordering takeout chicken just outside our door. Kecia said that if she passed the parole board in the coming spring, she would go back to live with her mom, who was failing in health. Probably sign up for some computer classes, try to get a job in tech support. She looked forward to the little things — like her skin clearing up, and her hair softening again; the dry air and state-issued soaps in prison were driving her crazy. She looked at the bare walls, the barred windows, at me. Healing could happen anyplace, she said: a group home, a foster home, a bio home. "It's very simple — it's just the way life is. You don't leave people," she said. "You stay."

9

Taking Agency

BRUCE AND ALLYSON GREEN don't use Kecia's terminology, but they basically embody the mission of "rocking with kids, all the way." Dominique, the curfew-skipping, trash-talking, angry teenager straight from a psychiatric hospital, was by far the toughest to rock with, but they were managing. Allyson had agreed to let Dominique enroll in some fashion design classes after school, and once, when I stopped by, Dominique confessed to regularly hanging out with Fatimah, who loved SpongeBob and sports and was undoubtedly a good influence. Things seemed to be settling.

But then, just after Dominique hit her seven-month mark at the Greens', the agency called. There had been a mistake. The Greens were supposed to be a temporary placement, since Bruce and Allyson weren't authorized to care for a child with documented therapeutic needs like Dominique. She would have to move.

Apparently it wasn't the first time Edwin Gould had tried to take Dominique away. "The first time we spoke up for Dominique, it was because we were out of compliance," Bruce said. He was with Allyson and Dominique in the kitchen on a Saturday morning, wearing his customary baggy jeans and T-shirt. He pulled some orange juice from the refrigerator and poured himself a tall glass; Dominique watched him closely. "State rules say we can only have six [foster] children but we had seven, so they had to move her. This went on for weeks."

"Dad, can I please have some juice?" Dominique asked from the kitchen barstool, tipping up her face. She was still in her pajamas. She looked pretty and soft, her almond-shaped eyes fluttering in a sleepy way.

"No," Bruce answered. "You're watching your weight." He turned back to me and explained that Tonya's sister had been living with them for a bit, but once her biological dad regained custody, he thought they were in the clear with Dominique.

"Can I please have some in a cup?" Dominique whined.

"No," Bruce said. "At this point, Dominique was arguing with everybody in the house. I mean everybody. Even Russell. Even Allen. She'd argue with that spider crawling on the ceiling."

Dominique was pouting. "I'm just thirsty."

"She found a reason to dislike something about everybody. Turn up the TV, turn down the TV, turn the channel." Bruce paused. "Drink some water if you're thirsty."

Dominique slumped on the stool, but she stayed quiet. Bruce said a few more months passed, and slowly, quietly, a transformation began. Dominique's storms softened; she stopped reacting quite so bitterly; everybody went to bed a little earlier, slept a little better. And that's when the agency called: Dominique had to move not only to a different family, but to a different agency — one that had licensed therapeutic homes on its roster. It should have happened long ago, they said, but like all things in child welfare, the clocks are set in months, not minutes.

Bruce was angry. "Bad as Dominique may be — hardheaded, stubborn — she's gone through all her trials and tribulations here and become acclimated to this household and all its rules and regulations," he said, setting his empty juice glass on the counter with a soft thud. "How can they just play with the emotions of a child?"

Allyson thought this hurdle would be a good time for Dominique to learn to advocate for herself. The agency was recommending her removal, but a judge would decide Dominique's fate. Allyson believed if

Dominique spoke to the judge herself, she would have a good shot at staying.

"I told her, 'Your lawyer is getting paid to represent you. The court is getting paid to sit on that bench. But you have your life in your hands. These people won't know what's going on if you don't tell them,'" Allyson said. Even this early in the morning, Allyson was dressed up in a silky blouse and boots. "I would have been right there with you and together we could have let them know. But I can't do it on my own because it's not my life at hand, it's hers."

I watched Dominique track Allyson's brisk moves around the kitchen, warming a bottle for the baby, stirring some fruit and cereal for herself, and wondered: Can a child whose whole life has been commandeered by a string of faceless lawyers and judges and social workers, a child who has been driven to strangers' homes in strangers' vans for unseen motives, have any faith in self-advocacy? At seventeen years old?

Dominique didn't show up at her court date, and the judge ordered her out of her agency and into the therapeutic home. Allyson drove her to the woman's house, in what was supposed to be a series of longer and longer visits, until Dominique felt acclimated enough to pack her Hefty bags and move in. But Dominique shut down. Normally alert and ready to fight with anyone, Dominique simply visited her new foster mom and refused to say a word.

Dominique did, however, talk to Allyson. She told her if she had to relocate, she would run away. This is the kind of self-advocacy she knew: like many foster kids who have little experience getting, or even imagining, what they really want, their only power lies in saying no.

"To hear her speak like that, I was like, wait a minute. I have a conscience. This is my daughter, and this is going to rest on me," Allyson said, her rising voice echoing around the kitchen. "When I got into this, I got into this fully. I came in here fully committed. I thought, 'Something has to happen.' And I told Dominique not to worry, something is going to work out."

Allyson called ACS and asked if there was any way they could get the training to be a therapeutic home. They told her no. Their agency didn't offer the training, and they couldn't just switch agencies because all their other children were with Edwin Gould. Allyson said they would adopt Dominique.

"The woman on the phone said, 'Are you sure?'" In the retelling, Allyson's eyes blazed. "I said, 'Lemme tell you something. When I say something out of my mouth, I am sure. Because regardless of how this turns out, it ain't gonna be nobody's problem but mine.'"

On the eighteenth of that month, Allyson said, she, Bruce, and Dominique were scheduled to go to the agency and sign paperwork. "And that's it. They can't move her from here. This is Dominique's home."

I asked Dominique, who hadn't stopped staring at Allyson throughout her entire speech, how she felt. She looked shyly down at the countertop. "I can't stop smiling because I feel loved. And it never happened before. They're so passionate about keeping me here and welcoming me. It's kinda weird. It's scary. I don't know." Dominique trailed off, but then picked up again, louder than before. "Honestly, when I first came here, I was like, what kinda Cosby thing is this? I'd never been in a house with two parents before. I didn't ask them to adopt me — I had always asked for people to adopt me, but I never had no one volunteer. I'm about to be signed out of foster care, and someone's going to adopt me? It's really strange."

To hear Dominique tell it, her path to assimilation at the Greens' was smoother, and speedier, than Bruce or Allyson claimed. Dominique had been with the Greens for only two days, in fact, when she did something that would cut her off from her past life and would, if only in her own mind, lock her securely into the house on DeKalb. She called her biological father.

"I was kind of getting comfortable here, so I called him," Dominique said. At this point, she and I were the only ones in the kitchen, unusual for a late Saturday morning. "I said, 'Why you put me in foster care? I know you! Most kids don't know their fathers. Most kids don't have the chance to go back. Why can't you get me out of this situation?'"

She was trying to see if she had options. If she didn't, she wanted to commit to where she was. In her entire life, Dominique had lived with her father for only one month; he had eleven other kids, with various women, and two other kids with her mom. Dominique ran away from her dad's place because she couldn't abide some of his behavior. She didn't want to discuss it.

"I asked him if he loved me and he said no," Dominique said, describing the phone call, her eyes boring into the countertop. "He said he can't love me because I remind him of my mom too much. And he loves his stepkids more. So I cursed him out and told him I hope he goes to hell. And that I hope someone murders him. Then I hung up the phone, and I haven't called him since."

After a moment, Dominique gave away her last little lie. "A week later, his phone got turned off."

The notion that foster parents would pull through for Dominique in a way her own father hadn't was vital for Dominique's fragile and burgeoning trust. That they had stood up to the agency was even more radical; every important connection Dominique had ever made, she felt, had been destroyed by ACS.

First, ACS took her from her mother when she was five years old. This may have been reasonable; her mother was using cocaine, her older brother was violent with her, and Dominique was too young to remember much else. Dominique moved in with a woman who, Dominique said, would have adopted her if she could. She was loving and kind, and Dominique called her Grandmother. But Dominique's mom got better, and after living with Grandmother for five years, Dominique went back home. It lasted only three months. ACS decided the kids weren't safe and rolled them into a different agency — likely whichever one had space on its roster. Grandmother didn't know Dominique was back in care, and Dominique didn't know how to find her. Dominique's next placement wasn't as good; she missed Grandmother, she missed her mom, and, as adolescence hit, her bitterness became quick bursts of rebellion — the "devil's advocate" as Bruce would say later — against anyone who got too close. When she was told her mother died, Dominique felt entirely alone; she rarely talked to her brother, who was living in another borough, and ACS and its agencies had betrayed her. When she was fifteen, she looked up Grandmother on her own.

But it was too late. In Dominique's absence, Grandmother had fostered another little girl and adopted her. Still, she let Dominique move in. Dominique switched agencies yet again to do it, but once she got there, Dominique felt displaced. Dominique picked fights with the girl, who was about her age, and then in a particularly jealous fit, she threatened to kill her. Dominique was sent to a psychiatric hospital, and then later to the Greens.

Dr. Francine Cournos has written and spoken extensively about child welfare since she was a foster child herself in the late fifties, and she says that still, workers focus too much on rules and protocol rather than on kids' emotional attachments. I told her about Dominique, and she sighed; she'd heard it all before. Foster parents, like Dominique's "Grandmother" or even Bruce and Allyson Green, are often viewed as "interchangeable parts," she said. She volleyed with a story of her own, about a foster mom whose child was sent back to his biological parents. When the parents were deemed unfit a number of months later, the foster mom wanted him back. Unfortunately, the agency said no: she had since fostered another child, and there wasn't enough bed space. "It's such a remarkable thing that people think about furniture and square feet instead of attachment — when there are children all over New York City who live in crowded places," Francine said. "If the system was following the child's attachments, the child's continuity . . ." She trailed off. "The day somebody asks a foster child, 'Where were you living before your biological mother's? How long were you there? How did that work out?' — that will be a very good day."

It's partly because the system treats foster parents as "interchangeable parts" that they don't do the critical work of attaching to their children. Or they do it and then they stop. They're just like the foster kids: they get burned out on the system's entrenched disregard for their love.

This disregard, while deeply felt, isn't intentional. It's just that agency workers have so many rules to follow. To get their money from the state and the federal government, they have to make sure the kids are in secure placements with the proper square footage and so on — not that they're with someone who loves them. And this money, skeptics say, is the real reason agencies don't follow ASFA guidelines or work harder to reunite kids like Dominique with their biological families or with foster parents who might eventually adopt them. Money is the elephant in the room; money keeps the kids in limbo year after year after year, with family after family. And here's why: every day that a child is in care, the agency makes an income. When the child goes home, the cash flow goes with him. Foster care agencies — the private and independent businesses that contract with the state — need the foster kids to stay foster kids so they can stay in business.

All across the country, foster care payments are issued on a per diem basis: the federal government provides money to cover each day a child lives away from his parents. Take New York as an example, where there are more than thirty agencies contracting with ACS. To get their funding, each agency has to track each child, garnering a different type of payment depending on his age, disability, special needs, and so on. The agency then tracks which type of "bed" he's in: a foster home yields one payment, a psychiatric foster home yields another, a group home gets another, and so on. And they have to do this every day, for every kid, if they want their money from ACS. And ACS has to check all this accounting and reenact a similar process themselves if they want their money from the government.

In one way, cumbersome as it is, this makes sense. This is public money, and there has to be accountability for the way it's spent. And matching each child with each dollar ensures, in theory, that there will always be enough. If more kids come into care, because of a drug epidemic or a media blitz, the laws are designed to flow more money in from the government to cover them. But it also means a lot of paperwork, and audits, and child welfare personnel pulling at their hair because they're spending more time on forms than on people.

Rudy Estrada, the lawyer who now works for Legal Aid but had been hired by ACS in 2007 as the first LGBTQ coordinator, likened the fee structure in child welfare to that in health care. "It's like an HMO, fee for service; everything is being contracted out. There are these elaborate formulas that are used to figure out how much each agency will get from the city each month based on how many kids and which kind of beds, so they're running all these numbers constantly," Estrada said. "Half of what ACS is doing is counting those beans."

Forty-nine states and the cities within them are counting those same beans, zapping away critical hours and manpower while kids languish in care. But one state recently challenged the model, with results that suggest it might show the way for a better system.

In 2006, the state of Florida struck a bargain: it would become the first state in the nation to drop the per diem pay structure in exchange for a flat sum from the feds of around $140 million a year for five years. The risk they were taking was this: if there were to be a sudden surge in the foster care rolls, they wouldn't have the per diem/per child pay structure to weather it; they'd have to make do with their capped income. But the benefit would be all the extra time and energy their workers would have — freed from the burden of filing what were, essentially, overly complicated payment requests. They'd have the time to ask questions of a kid like Dominique and track down her past connections, rather than racing to assign her the next open bed. And more than that, the plan was to focus this energy on neighborhood-based preventive programs, so fewer kids would need foster care at all.

Alan Abramowitz was the state director for family safety for Florida's Department of Children and Families (he's now the executive director of Guardian Ad Litem). He's a big man, bald and plainspoken, with a hearty laugh. He's known in house as "the firefighter." I met him at a conference in New York in early 2009 and spoke to him on the phone some months later; he said the wild risk they took was paying off.

"We're still removing the extreme cases," Abramowitz said, claiming that they'd reduced removals by 29 percent in the last two years. Many people, including Abramowitz and other officials in Florida, did see the per diem pay structure as a perverse incentive to bring kids into care, and to keep them there as a way to meet their budgets. Without that incentive, Abramowitz said, "we're able to put millions of dollars into the front end, into home services, which is far less expensive so you end up serving far more children."

While the idea of a flat sum, called a "waiver," has been kicked around by child advocates for years, Abramowitz says the idea was especially embraced by the then head of the state's child welfare department, Bob Butterworth. The first thing Butterworth did when he took office, Abramowitz said, was interview kids who had aged out of foster care at eighteen. "These kids said they would have rather been abused at home with their parents than abused by the state. We realize now that the outcomes for children in foster care are going to be worse than if they had stayed in the home," Abramowitz said. "*Even* if there was some neglect."

And decisions about which kids get to stay home are far too subjective and random for Abramowitz's taste. While Abramowitz was working in Palm Beach County, he compared removal rates between his sets of investigation teams. He found that the most experienced investigators removed 4 percent of their kids, and the least experienced removed 18 percent. "The biggest decision in a child's life wasn't based on the kind of abuse they were exposed to, but whichever investigator they were assigned to," Abramowitz said. "And we assign our caseworkers randomly."

So now, he says, with Florida's increased spending flexibility, investigators can allot more time to the nuances of each individual family. "If it's a substance abuse case, talk to a substance abuse expert; if it's a poverty case, there are a lot of poverty people you can bring to the table," Abramowitz said. "Before you make the decision to remove, there are a lot of experts you can involve, a lot of services you can look at."

In Florida, county employees still handle the initial investigation, but everything else has essentially been privatized. Abramowitz said his agency has reached out to community-based organizations that were already in place — drug rehab centers, domestic violence agencies, child care centers, prenatal care organizations, and so on — and let them contract with the state. They also let private "lead agencies" take over all the kids in foster care, handling all the case management — from initial placement to adoption — everything, in fact, except for the initial abuse investigation. The overall philosophy, he said, is this: "We believe the state can't raise a child very well, but the community can."

The trouble with buzzwords like *community*, and the privatization it connotes, is that every community is different. The state may be a bureaucracy, but it's big and public and, in theory, it treats everyone the same. Private agencies (even if they're nonprofits, governed by outside boards as they are in Florida) can raise their own money and thereby range widely in terms of quality or breadth. And dropping the fee-for-service model can also mean dropping accountability or tracking measures for each individual child. Critics of privatization in child welfare — and there are many — argue that although there may be a kind of perverse incentive to retain kids in foster care to retain the day rates they incur, when you change to a flat rate there is the *dis*incentive to provide higher-quality, expensive services. In other words, when you're handed a flat sum (rather than a budget that changes every month based on changing client numbers), you'll tend to run the least expensive programs. You'll also target the broadest common denominator, and kids with specialized needs will fall off the map.

Privatization is a strange word, lacking clear definition in child welfare. Sometimes it's used to signify Florida's choice: swapping out the fee-for-service model for a flat, nonnegotiable sum. But this isn't really the privatization part of Florida's radical overhaul. The funding shift is called a waiver, and five other states — California, Indiana, Illinois, Ohio, and Oregon — have accepted waivers too, though on a smaller scale, in select counties. Privatization, in its strictest definition, is when the government seeks competition from private bidders to perform government activities. And this has been happening in foster care since its inception.

In New York City, for instance. Foster care in New York was founded on the private religious institutions and charities that took in foundlings and orphans and destitute kids, and although ACS still oversees all the kids who come into care, it contracts out all of the actual housing provisions, foster parent recruitment, and so on, to private nonprofits. Eighty percent of all states do this — it's nothing new. What is new, perhaps, is the growing trend toward outsourcing more of the big-picture thinking and action in child welfare. The state of Kansas, for example, now uses private agencies for all aspects of its child welfare, including investigations and child removals — trumping even Florida in terms of government involvement. And, as more states and counties experiment with the waiver system, and thus have flexible funds at their disposal, they may look even more to the private agencies for broader, or more creative, or more business-oriented services.

It's hard to tell, exactly, how the dual and sometimes intersecting trends toward privatization and waivers will pan out, but they seem to signify the beginnings of systemic change. Casey Family Programs, a national organization that provides child welfare services in five states and conducts major nonpartisan research on foster care as a whole, advocates the waiver system. Casey's goal is to reduce foster care by half by 2020, so to them, tying funding to children who have been removed is entirely counterintuitive. Waivers allow states and agencies to spend their money as they choose — on more front-end support, say. Florida, on the whole, seems to be doing well with its choices. The secretary of Florida's Department of Children and Families, and one of the key waiver advocates, was appointed head of child welfare at the national level. And shortly thereafter, President Obama signed an act allowing more states to apply for waivers, lasting through 2016. Florida applied for another five-year waiver.

Even still, one county that adopted the waiver option has garnered deep reproach. Los Angeles County, which shifted to the waiver payment in July 2007 and cut the number of kids in foster care by 23 percent in nearly three years, was criticized in a scathing series of articles in the *Los Angeles Times*. The reporters claimed Child Services didn't share vital information across agencies or follow policy and noted that deaths from abuse or neglect went from eighteen in 2008 to twenty-six in 2009, and they questioned whether the waiver system, and a renewed focus on family reunification, contributed to the increase.

But there were critics of the critics, who claimed the data wasn't contextualized, that publishing wrenching tales of child fatalities instigates agency panic and unnecessary removals from other, safer homes. Amid the furor, the county transferred the director to another job.

I lived in Los Angeles in 1998. That was when I took in Christina, and the system made me send her to a group home for sex offenders because they had nowhere else to put her. I met caseworkers and foster parents and kids in that city who had the same demoralizing experience of their system as people do anywhere else. I'm hopeful about waivers, because a change in money can mean a change in philosophy, it can mean some freedom of movement, it can open the windows for new ideas to circulate in. But I know the windows are still housed in an old, tired building, so change will take time. The federal administration for children's services basically said the same thing in a 2011 report — claiming that the first round of waiver states and counties looked hopeful — but the experiment needed to go on longer to really tell. A main problem, so far, in using the waivers to try new approaches is recruiting and training qualified staff.

In the first year of the waiver, LA's child services spent $5.9 million on 2,400 new tablet computers for its social workers, so they could carry case files with them and access information about a family remotely when they did investigations. Armed with more knowledge, investigators could make more nuanced decisions or find resources for families on-site. But the department purchased only four hundred wireless cards, so mostly the social workers left their computers sitting on their desks.

10

Homespun

FOSTER KIDS WHO LIVE in places without waivers, which is to say most of the country, know about the day rates they incur. Fatimah, the sixteen-year-old track star with the SpongeBob necklace, calculated her value that way.

By the time she arrived at the Greens', just a month after Chanel and Tonya, Fatimah knew she had one thing going for her: she came with a good price. She knew she would qualify for the high monthly payments from the government, post-adoption, because she was "special needs." In the state of New York, a "special needs" child is one who hasn't been adopted within six months of becoming available, is part of a sibling group, is over eight and part of an overrepresented minority group, or is of any race and over the age of ten. Fatimah hit three out of four. In addition to the $6,000 one-time adoption incentive her new parents would receive, they would garner $678 a month to take care of her, plus a $62 monthly clothing allowance. Fatimah thought, after she met and eventually grew to love the Greens, that this cash would be the carrot to get her wish.

Although many foster kids say that even adoptive parents are in it for the money, in reality, outside of the one-time adoption incentive payment (which was initiated under ASFA in 1997), the government's monthly payments for an adopted child are roughly the same as for a foster child. Each state has its own complex rate system, depending on where you live and what physical, developmental, or psychological problems your child might suffer, and each prospective parent can petition for extra stipends before an adoption is finalized. In the Greens' case, the kids aren't wanting for much; it's clear by the abundance of new sneakers and iPods and video games, as well as Bruce's forty-hour work week, that Bruce and Allyson aren't hoarding government money for themselves.

Maybe Fatimah leaned on the financial aspect of the arrangement with the Greens as a defense: if they didn't end up wanting her, even after the adoption they'd promised, at least they'd get her money. Or maybe she had to construct them as paid caretakers because Fatimah believed, unconsciously, that one day she might return to her "real" mother. That business wasn't over; that wound hadn't healed.

Rudy Estrada, the lawyer at ACS and Legal Aid, told me once, "They always come back." Foster children are sometimes called "orphans of the living," and it's a particularly apt designation: they've been abandoned in some fundamental way, and yet the biological bond is very much alive. Even if their parents' rights were terminated long ago. Even if they want, desperately, to be adopted by somebody else.

On June 17, 2008, two months shy of her seventeenth birthday, Fatimah and Bruce and Allyson stood before a Queens family court judge. In the car ride over, Fatimah listened to the song called "Officially Missing You," by Tamia. She was a little nervous: the night before, she and Bruce had had an argument over nothing, probably because of the tension. Fatimah was the first foster child (aside from Charles, who was already a biological nephew) to get adopted. The fight from the night before was quickly swept aside; Allyson woke her up that morning with tears in her eyes.

"I cried," Allyson said, making breakfast for Allen and Anthony about a month after the adoption was finalized. "The job of being a mom is never-ending. You understand? I could be a mother to every child but when the moment came, it felt like 'Wow. This really happened. Now I am really a mom and she belongs to me.' It's a beautiful thing."

Fatimah sat on one of the kitchen stools, toying with the Sponge-Bob charm on her necklace and describing the judge. "He was like sixty-five. And he said to me everybody was five before. Everybody was ten before. Everybody was fifteen. And he said we all have our own experiences. And we all have that childhood but we have to learn how to be a child and also, you know, be mature. Right, Ma?"

Allyson nodded her assent. Baby Anthony had just spit up on the floor and she was busy rinsing out a rag. Fatimah continued. "I guess to me it meant I got to learn how to not take everything serious and like just relax and just let things flow easy inside. I'm a child but I can't relive my childhood obviously. I need to grow up."

After the judge's speech, Fatimah said, everybody signed some papers and the judge officially presented her with her new last name. She also added a name of her own, the middle name Imani, because she liked the sound of it, and because she wanted to do something strictly for herself and outside the bonds of family on that day.

Fatimah couldn't feel much, she said, at least not right away. "I was just looking around like *wow*. I don't know, I can't explain it," Fatimah said, shaking her head as though trying to jiggle the words out. "I don't know — it just felt — it felt regular. It didn't feel like permanency."

"But then the next day you couldn't sleep the night," Allyson reminded her.

Fatimah nodded. "Yeah, I was like walking around all night. Because I was so shocked," she said. "I remember one day, I was about to leave one of my homes. I was staring out the window with my 3D glasses, and I was like, I wonder if I'm ever going to be adopted? I thought that I was never going to get adopted because I always heard stories about kids that go astray. I just can't believe it; I really can't believe it."

Fatimah knew she'd have to come up with a new title for her memoir, *Until November,* about her twenty-one foster homes. The original adoption date had been November 2007, but like so many things in family court, the date got pushed back. So far, she'd settled on *To the*

End of June. She planned to open the book with the scene of the adoption and then go back to her first memory, of hitting a piñata, and wanting candy but getting a whistle. Then she'd move chronologically through all her foster homes until she ended up where she started the book, in the courtroom with the Greens.

Fatimah said a central theme to her book, and her life, was going back to all of her foster parents and asking them that ever-present "why" question. She'd already done it with a handful of them. "I want to ask them why they kicked me out. And I want them to feel bad," Fatimah explained. "I'll just be like, 'Remember the time you sent me here, or remember this, remember that?' Because they should be ashamed. How you put a child in care but then you're the abuser?"

So far, Fatimah said of her former foster parents, "they always deny it." A foster mom who called Fatimah greedy screamed with joy when she saw her, and then wanted to hug her and catch up on the last ten years. A lady with an all-yellow house didn't remember punishing her foster kids by stepping on their hands, but, Fatimah said, the sheer act of facing these women down was enough. "It made me stop hating them," she said. "I'm not even mad at them anymore."

Fatimah hadn't asked her biological mother any fundamental "whys" and didn't feel the need; her mom, she said, was just "whack." Fatimah told me she didn't care what her mother felt or thought, but in the next breath she said she wished her mom could have mustered a reaction to the adoption. When Fatimah called to tell her about it, she said her mom sounded blasé. "She just said, 'Oh, congratulations. How are you?' She acted all fake," Fatimah said. "I wanted her to be jealous, because she should have been doing her job."

And then, as soon as Fatimah went back to school after getting adopted, she promptly lost the first twenty-five pages of her book: everything she'd written so far. That day in the kitchen, she told me she planned on rewriting it all, but not right away. The loss of all she'd created had been a hard, and disorienting, blow.

And there had been other losses too. For example, her friendship with Chanel had taken a sour turn. When Fatimah got home from court, she tried to show Chanel her name change documents. "She was just like 'Oh, OK,'" Fatimah said, shrugging her shoulders and imitating Chanel's indifference. "I was like *wow*. You see people's true sides when something good happens to you, basically. It's like when a person becomes rich after they was poor. After they was in a struggle. And then they want to shun on you."

Tonya, too, seemed to have reacted to Fatimah's adoption. Shortly after the papers were signed, Tonya ran away, though neither Fatimah nor Allyson saw the link. They both thought she was merely sowing the seeds of her recent adulthood; Tonya took off just before her eighteenth birthday, and she hadn't yet returned. And although Allyson dutifully phoned the police and the agency, she wasn't about to chase her. Increasingly, it seemed to me, Allyson's strategy was to surrender to her faith. "I pray for every last one of my children and I pray for the world's children. I pray for everybody. But that's all I can do," Allyson said.

The one person in the family Fatimah didn't talk about that day was Dominique. Maybe she was mad at her; I would later learn that Dominique had betrayed Fatimah's confidence. Or maybe she was ashamed. At the last minute, Dominique's own adoption — the adoption that she had so happily plotted from that very same kitchen just a few months before — fell apart. Dominique was gone.

At the end of that summer of 2008, I met Dominique on the boardwalk at Coney Island. I had heard from the other kids that she'd carved "I hate the Greens" into one of their wooden bureaus, and then her social worker showed up to drive her away for good.

"What happened?" I asked her, offering her lemonade from Nathan's, the famous hot dog stand at the boardwalk's entrance. She wouldn't take it. Dominique drinks only from cans, because she worries about the germs that can fester in soda fountains, and whenever she takes a sip, she has to drink the whole thing straight without letting it touch the table — part of a long list of obsessive-compulsive rituals that began long ago. We sat on a bench and watched the water.

"They wanted me to change," Dominique said, her voice steely and her gaze focused on the horizon. She was more dressed up than I had ever seen her at the Greens' — possibly because we were out in public, and she had tentative plans to meet a boy later that afternoon.

She was wearing bright pink jean shorts and a white T-shirt covered by a black lace vest, which protected her large breasts from too much scrutiny. Dominique hated being so curvy. A baseball cap shielded her eyes, and she sealed her lips tight over her protruding top teeth before she spoke. "Bruce told me if I didn't change in two weeks he would just call the adoption off."

Apparently, that slipped out in one of their arguments; despite Dominique having stabilized and adjusted to the Greens' rules over the seven months she lived with them, she still regularly fought with Bruce. And as soon as they planned to adopt her, the tension escalated.

Allyson sensed a kind of ambivalence about the adoption, Dominique said, and tried to talk to her about it. "She said, 'I just want you to be sure this is right for you,' and I felt rejected." They had been driving in the car, and Dominique had broached the topic by informing Allyson that it was *Fatimah* who didn't want to be adopted — she was just going through with it because she didn't have any better options. Fatimah was later furious about this admission, but Dominique needed any ally she could find. "I was doing so much questioning in my mind — like I didn't want to rush into adoption, because once you're adopted you can't turn back."

She had wanted Allyson to rally for her, to meet her ambivalence, and her attitude, with unconditional love. She wanted, perhaps, for the Greens to chase her just a little. The day after Allyson signed her adoption papers (but before they went into court to make it official) Dominique got some things off her chest. She told Allyson how unfair it was that she aired everybody's business during the church lessons on Sunday afternoons. Except for Sekina. When Sekina had a problem, Dominique argued, she was whisked into private talks with Bruce and Allyson. Nobody else in the house received such preferential treatment. "I told her, because of Sunday church, Sekina still feels like the real daughter and we're the foster kids. And without her even trying to see the positive in me telling her that, she saw it as a negative!" Dominique shook her head. "She said, 'Since you feel this way, you have to question whether or not this is the best place for you.' From then on, I was like, I don't care no more."

After that, she said, the whole mood of the house changed. Fatimah was mad at her, Bruce was arguing with her, and she herself stopped answering to anyone. "I felt abandoned, and I was so angry, but I became like a robot — blunt and everything," she said. Soon, Allyson called a meeting. "We all three agreed that it was the best choice for me to leave. I didn't say, 'Yes, I want to leave,' I just said I didn't care anymore. But I cared, you know?"

Allyson tells the story differently. She and Bruce and Dominique did have the final meeting about adoption, but it was at the agency. And Dominique was professing she didn't want it. "Right there at the meeting, she was saying, 'I was just testing them — to see if they really want me.' She was being defiant," Allyson said to me in a phone call shortly after the adoption disintegrated. "And then no sooner did we walk out of there, she became disrespectful, disobedient, loudmouthing. I said it was time for us to go home. She said she wanted to stay at the agency; she starts showing off. They said: 'That's it for you' — they turn around and say she needs a therapeutic home."

Despite the different accounts, Allyson and Dominique agree that she tested the family on their love. "Once Allyson came to therapy with me, and I told my therapist how I test people in order to trust. And Bruce failed that test so many times," Dominique said, tipping back her baseball cap and taking in the sun.

But it wasn't Bruce's fault that Dominique was the way she was, I countered; he didn't inflict any of the original damage. True, she said, but he was like everybody at the agency — who didn't want to let her feel her rage. "I don't have an anger problem," she said, turning to me, her face getting red. "I'm supposed to be angry. I'm supposed to be mad at this situation, because it was not supposed to happen this way."

Dominique stared back out at the sea. "Every day of my life I wish I could die because of how angry I am," she said. "And with foster parents, we're not asking them to buy us anything, or do anything, just understand."

Allyson understands the anger, she says, but her loyalties are spread thin; she doesn't have time to give someone like Dominique the innumerable nuanced responses she needs. "I told Dominique, 'You've got to see what people are doing for you — you've got to change yourself.' She's not a baby," Allyson explained to me on the phone. "I can't stay focused on one person — I have so many other children in the house. And when you're so stressed out over one person, you can't focus on everybody else."

When I met with Dominique, she had been living with her new foster mom for a few months, and things weren't looking so bright. Despite its being a therapeutic home, she said, the mom rarely talked to her. Unlike the house on DeKalb, this new place didn't have many restrictions and Dominique could come and go as she pleased, but she was bored. School was out, and when we met on a Monday, she thought it was a Saturday. She said she fought with the one other foster child, a girl around her age, every morning — just because it made her feel better. Allyson told me the foster mom had already called her to say Dominique was defiant and was stealing the other girl's clothes. "I was passionate about finding that family," Dominique said glumly, meaning the family that would keep her, and love her, no matter what. She said she didn't think she would last long at her new home. "Now, looking back, I would have changed it all. But I just wasn't ready."

That year, Bruce and Allyson were the only foster family honored at their agency's annual fundraiser — a black-tie affair where the other Green kids took the stage and praised their parents. Bruce told me about it afterward. "We were called Foster Family of the Year, and a very generous family out in California donated $10,000," Bruce said, lamenting the fact that despite their best efforts, they were struggling with the older teenagers. Dominique's placement had failed, Tonya had run away, and even Fatimah was acting more sullen since her adoption. Chanel was planning to move out early, into an apartment of her own. He was feeling sort of bitter and briefly considered keeping the award money for himself. "I could have spent that money any way I wanted — they didn't specify. I could have bought things for me, for Allyson. But we decided to buy an entertainment center for the family, and then computers for all the teenagers, for them to do their homework."

So it turned out that Tonya did get a laptop for her eighteenth birthday, though it wasn't from the agency and it wasn't because she was a foster kid. Tonya just happened to land at the Greens', and she happened to stay there, so she happened upon her laptop after all. She also happened to run away for thirty-three days during the time that Fatimah was adopted, though she hadn't planned it and hadn't considered the repercussions.

"I went to the Bronx and I was having fun for two days, and those two days turned into two more days, and it was like, I don't wanna be in trouble. I just didn't want to go through that," Tonya said to me after she returned. We were sitting in the bedroom she had once shared with Dominique, where one whole wall was neatly stacked with shoeboxes; she could wear a different pair every day of the month and then some. Like Fatimah with her SpongeBob toys, Tonya also favored a cartoon icon; hers was Dora the Explorer. There was a Dora pillow on the bed and Dora folders for her papers. "I thought, 'I might as well have all my fun now.'"

I suspected there was more to it. Adoption may be the explicit goal for foster kids with parents who have lost their rights, but it can also be a trigger. *This is it,* adoption says. *You can never go home again.* A pending adoption pushed Dominique right to the edge and out of the house. And Fatimah's adoption may have made Chanel jealous and sent Tonya scurrying back to her mom and childhood neighborhood, just to make sure she still mattered somewhere else.

In any case, Tonya went to visit her mother, who was drinking again, in the Bronx. She was about to check herself into a six-month rehab, and Tonya could have the apartment to herself. There, Tonya said, she had other people to look after her. "I didn't have no clothes. Thank God I had the friends I had because you know they was lending me outfits and stuff like it's nothing," Tonya said, explaining that she hadn't packed a bag because she hadn't planned to stay. "We grew up together so it's just like I'm a family member. And their moms is all looking out for me all the time, saying, 'You can have money. Did you eat today?'"

Tonya said that summer in the Bronx looked like this: "Get up at three in the afternoon, eat, take a shower, do my hair, get dressed, and leave. Then I wouldn't come back 'til the next morning." Her best friend bought her new clothes for her birthday party, which Tonya didn't particularly remember. "It seems like when my mom relapses, I relapse too. Every single time she goes back into alcohol, I go back into drugs. And it's not good, 'cause I feel like I'm dealing with her problems, and mine too."

Tonya's drug of choice was marijuana; she said she used it to calm down, though she also got into four fights in her thirty-three days away. One time, she said, she almost got shot. Mostly, though, she just partied, and she was sleeping off a particularly late night when the cops finally banged on the door. "There was a guy with the police, a representative from the agency. He said, 'Do you know how many times I've been here in this building, in this neighborhood, doing surveillance on this block?' He started hugging me and stuff," Tonya said. She told the cops that she was a legal adult; she didn't have to go anywhere. "But the agency guy said, 'Look, if you don't want to be in foster care, there are ways of going about it. We can take you down to the agency and you can sign yourself out.'"

At first, this is what Tonya planned to do. But then, at the agency, they showed her a photograph the Greens had provided them. "It was a picture of all three of us together: me, Chanel, and Fatimah. And I started crying, crying, crying, 'cause I hadn't seen them in so long," Tonya said. "And I realized it would have been stupid to sign myself out because I didn't have nowhere to go, didn't have no money, you know what I'm saying? I couldn't live my life like I was living in the summertime."

To hear Tonya tell it, Allyson was all love and "How are you, baby?" when she called her from the agency. And Bruce yelled, "Don't move!" into the phone and rushed to the Bronx in the family van.

Allyson had a sterner version of things. "I told her that what she did was unacceptable," Allyson told me on the phone, two days after Tonya returned, "and that our curfew was reinstated. She can't have any more weekend visits with her mom, and if she breaks the rules, she can go back to the agency and find somewhere else to live."

If that happened, I thought, Tonya would probably return to her mom's place, despite the way she believed her mom's substance use affected her own. She had lived there, after all, for about half of her eighteen years.

Mike Arsham, the executive director of the Child Welfare Organizing Project in New York, told me that as foster kids gain their independence and thus run out of options, they often return to their birth parents. "ACS and the court seem oblivious to these persistent relationships because the case record says something different. Yet it is not uncommon at CWOP to see women raising the children of children to whom they lost their rights years prior," Arsham said. "The system lives in denial of this reality."

I've certainly seen kids reconnect with their biological parents beneath the agency's radar. For example, my foster daughter, Christina, to my ongoing dismay, would repeatedly visit her mother and return shipwrecked and furious, nicking her arms with a razor in self-contempt and confusion. And even though Dominique believed her mother had long since passed away, she'd still wander past her mom's old apartment in Coney Island, "just to look." I know another Domineque, in California, who's serving twenty-four years in a maximum-security prison for armed robbery. It wasn't the foster care that screwed her up, she thought, though that had delivered its share of traumas. It was the desire to understand her own mother, to really *find* her, on some primal level — and to do that, Domineque had to do the things her mother had done. She had to commit the same crimes, ingest the same drugs, feel the same terrible way about herself, to locate her mom inside. Just like Tonya, she had to go back to her mom.

The agencies and the foster parents (myself included) don't know how to manage what every single foster child seems to need — that need to go back. Because, whether physically or psychologically, they will go back to their parents and what hurt them, if only "just to look," as Dominique says. We need to get better at this part of the foster care trajectory because that journey back is land-mined for self-destruction.

The next time I really got to sit down and talk with Fatimah Green, a full year and a half had passed since her adoption. She wanted to meet me at the far corner of DeKalb, opposite the house, because she wasn't living there anymore. She had moved in with her "whack" mom. The adoption — while technically finalized — had fallen apart. But she needed to go back to the Greens' and pick up one last thing — her mom's drawings, which still hung on the walls. She wanted me to go with her.

I was happy enough to act as a buffer for Fatimah's art heist. I didn't understand what had happened in the adoption breakdown; I only knew she'd been missing for the past six months and then turned up at her mom's. In the year before she ran away, we had barely spoken; mostly, she just wasn't around when I came by the house, and she never returned my calls. In that time, Allyson told me, her grades were slipping; Bruce told me she had become "more materialistic" and was picking fights with him. Once I spotted her on the way to the Laundromat wheeling a cart stuffed with clothes, her hair tied back with a bandanna. She gave a tired wave and pushed on but didn't want to talk. Another time I caught a few minutes with her at the Baptist church that the family had recently joined, one Sunday that Allyson invited me along. Fatimah whispered that things had been "pretty bad." In the past week, she said, she slept at three different friends' houses for three different nights "as an experiment" to see how other people lived.

Fatimah knew how other people lived. She was a foster kid, with twenty-one placements in her past. But I couldn't remind her of this because we were in church and were supposed to be quiet. And we couldn't talk about it later, because then Fatimah ran away for good.

We met on the corner one morning in January. Fatimah had lost weight since the last time I'd seen her, and she was wearing a pink T-shirt and jeans, with a thin black trench coat, cinched at the waist. The SpongeBob necklace was gone. Her teeth chattered as she clacked up to the door in her low-heeled boots; it was freezing outside.

Allyson was expecting us, and she barely glanced up from her place on the couch where she was busy stuffing Anthony into his baby snow parka. "We're about to go out," she said, leaning her face up for my greeting kiss on the cheek. "Happy New Year." Fatimah disappeared, hunting for a bag in which to carry out her mother's artwork.

Anthony, looking like a puffy marshmallow doll, reached for Fatimah as she whizzed by. "Feemah!" he said.

Fatimah paused. "How's he know my name?" she asked, angling toward Allyson. "You been showing him my picture or something and saying that's your sister?"

Allyson ignored her. Anthony's and Allen's adoptions still hadn't been formalized, despite the latest promise of the prior November. Allyson told me the boys' maternal aunt had suddenly turned up, wanting to take the kids, "but the courts said no way. They're staying here."

The surprise appearance of a biological family member had stalled things and inspired the judge to ask that one last newspaper ad be placed for the biological mom since her rights, at least for Anthony, had not been terminated. The mom hadn't responded to the ad, Allyson said, and the termination would happen in three days. And then, finally, the adoption proceedings could really begin. Allyson sighed. "I've had to become more faithful since the kids came to me."

I know, I told her; I'd seen it.

Even Allyson's grandmother, who always featured strongly in her dreams, was now delivering more direct religious communication. "The other night, I had a dream where my grandmother brought me a black box and on it was written 'Romans 4:6–16.' I didn't know this verse," she said, settling back into the couch. Fatimah had come back into the living room with her mother's artwork wrapped and bagged, and she perched on the edge of the loveseat. Allyson stared hard at Fatimah. "At the time of the dream, I was very worried about this or that child running away."

Fatimah didn't flinch. The verse was about Abraham, Allyson explained. "The verse said that righteousness doesn't come to you by what you do; it comes to you by faith. Against all hope, Abraham became the father of many nations," she said. Anthony squirmed, overheating in his coat. "That freed me up to know that I can continue in my faith, and God will handle the work. My calling is to have faith and to take care of the children in that way."

Allyson noticed Anthony and scooped him up. "Come on," she said. "Let's go pick Sekina and Charles and Bruce and Jaleel up from school."

She waited at the front door for Fatimah and me to go out before her; it was clear we wouldn't be staying in the house alone. As we bent to gather our things, Fatimah whispered, "How's she gonna pick Sekina up when she's on her way here? How come she doesn't see *that* in her dreams?"

It was true; as soon as we hit the stoop, we saw Sekina on the corner, her hair newly bleached white and pink and shaved up the back of her head. Fatimah ran up to her, happily shrieking her name.

"Her hair looks *horrible,*" Fatimah said, once Allyson had pulled away and Sekina had disappeared again around the corner. She pulled out her cell phone to show me the dozens of Twitter messages the two had been exchanging all day, as well as the night before. A few were from two in the morning. "Sekina didn't come home last night, and she wasn't in school. How's she in school if she's on Twitter with me all the time?" Fatimah was thirsty and she paused to take a sip from a grapefruit juice I had in my bag. She'd never tasted grapefruit juice before. "Ugghh! That's disgusting! Anyway, how are Miss Green's dreams real if she doesn't know about her own daughter?"

It was a complaint I'd heard often, from Fatimah, Dominique, and Tonya: they said Sekina also snuck out and broke house rules, but because she was a biological daughter, her parents looked the other way. I never knew how much jealousy was tingeing these grievances, but I had certainly seen Sekina flaunting her status. In any case, Fatimah believed all of Allyson's dreams were lies, manufactured to elevate anxiety in her children and keep them in line.

Fatimah's loss of faith in Allyson's integrity was only part of the reason she ran away. The final straw came when both Bruce and Allyson forgot the anniversary of her adoption.

"On June seventeenth, the day I had been adopted in the previous year, they didn't even remember it. They didn't say anything about me, about it, or anything. That's the anniversary and you don't remember that? So that's the day I ran away," Fatimah said. "My friend, she told me about a quick way to get money. It was during Regents week, and I would have done so good if I had gone, but I didn't."

The Regents are the state examinations that every New York high schooler must pass to be granted a diploma and considered for college. They're administered in June, August, and January, and by the time Fatimah and I met, she had missed every one.

By this point we'd hailed a cab and were heading toward the ritzier part of DeKalb, in Fort Greene, to a South African restaurant Fatimah had been to once. Fatimah lowered her voice, so the driver couldn't hear. For those missing six months, Fatimah had gotten herself into heartbreaking trouble, which she now doesn't want to talk about anymore. When she did talk about it that day, her voice was monotone, her former lisp almost entirely gone.

I must have looked sad as Fatimah spoke, because she told me not to make her cry. "You're supposed to pretend that it's OK," she said. "What I do is: everything that robs me I smile about it. That's what I've been doing all my life. It stops me from crying. It stops me from getting mad or angry. I always smile and laugh and try to make people happy."

When Fatimah got sick of the trouble she'd found, she called her mother.

"I guess I missed her," she said. Or she missed the idea of her. When Fatimah's mom said, "I know you been going through something; why don't you come and stay with me?" she took it as a sign. Maybe her mom had changed; she'd been sober for eight years, though Fatimah conceded she'd relapsed the year before. And maybe this was the chance to save her little sister, Kimberly, who was eight years old and lived at home. At least, with Kimberly, she'd have something to live for.

Fatimah pulled out her phone to show me a picture of Kimberly. She said their mother was either depressed or barking orders, and both were ineffective at getting Kimberly to bed on time or to do her homework. Fatimah felt it was up to her to get food in the cupboards and to walk Kimberly to and from her elementary school; she'd recently applied for food stamps because her mother had been too depressed to bother. She also had to prod her mother to attend her AA and NA meetings because, after the relapse, ACS was closely monitoring the family.

"You know, I had plans but it's hard for me to — I'm struggling with money," Fatimah said. She hadn't been back to high school in months but planned to re-enroll in February. She didn't want to write her book anymore, now that it didn't have such a happy ending, but she was still interested in becoming a writer; her newest idea was to create her own magazine about international families. "My intention is to travel across the world to report on how families live in Afghanistan, how families live in Uruguay. It'll be a magazine about the different kinds of chances people take."

But for now, Fatimah had to focus on more immediate crises. "I have to feed Kimberly. I have to feed myself and, like, make sure that everybody's happy. That's why I go crazy," Fatimah said, playing with her new hair weave that cascaded to her shoulders. "Sometimes I just want to go in the bathroom and cry, but it's like I told my little sister: don't ever cry."

Fatimah felt bad about dispensing this last bit of sisterly advice. "Now, when she gets hit, she laughs about it. In class, the teacher says, 'Stop talking,' and she laughs. When she's yelled at, she thinks it's funny. And now they really want her to go into a facility for it because she's acting so crazy."

Fatimah had been worried about other things too. The other day, she said, she caught Kimberly torturing the dog. She had dragged him into the bathtub and was burning him with the tap water. She also found Kimberly sifting through porn on the Internet, which Fatimah thought was a little intense for eight years old.

But Fatimah didn't have many places to turn for help. ACS was the only agency she knew of with resources for kids, and she viewed them as a terrorizing force, one that had pushed her through twenty-one bad homes and was casing the apartment as we spoke. If Fatimah talked to anybody official, they'd likely tip off ACS. Fatimah's biological mother was no help; she was teetering on her own kind of edge. And her adoptive mother, Fatimah felt, didn't have any answers either. Since Fatimah had left DeKalb, Fatimah said, Allyson never called her, even though she had left her new phone number several times.

"She's just focused on the babies. And scripture. Even if you ask a question about something, she'll answer, 'What does the Bible say?' No matter what it is. I have a headache. She'll say the reason's in the Bible." Fatimah rushed her words. "The only thing she does is send me fucking Gospel texts."

Fatimah pulled out her phone to show me the latest. "'Be healthy in the Lord and serve him in all your faithfulness. Throw away the gods your forefathers worshipped beyond the river in Egypt,'" she read. "Come on. Like that has nothing to do with what I'm going through. It's just copy, paste, send it to everyone, you know? Resend, forward."

The next time I saw Dominique, she too was thinking a lot more about her biological mom. As she had predicted, her placement in the therapeutic home in Coney Island bombed. But while she lived there, she could walk by her mom's old apartment every day, and Dominique had decided *that* mom should have been her answer. When she was placed with a new family in Queens, Dominique crossed adoption off her list of goals for the first time in her life. Even though her mother was long gone, Dominique wanted to hold out for the real thing, if only in her mind.

"I've been in five pre-adoptive homes, and I've never been adopted, so I decided to take adoption off my plan," Dominique said, as we wandered around a makeup store near her new home, picking up fake eyelashes and bottles of glitter nail polish. This meant she had decided, like the other 80 percent of kids her age in ACS, that she would just age out on her own. "I still want a mom, but I realized God is not going to bless me because I ruined that relationship with my real mom. And honestly, since I took adoption off my list, I feel like I've been blessed with more. There isn't the pressure to find adoption, and I've learned family is about blending in with people who love me."

Dominique wasn't sure if her new foster mom would love her, but without the stress to live with her forever, she had more hope. The first thing Dominique showed me was her new tattoo on her left hand, of a small butterfly taking flight. She'd had it done down the street.

"I didn't think I liked butterflies, but subconsciously, I liked them, because I have them all over my room," Dominique said. I noticed that her stutter, normally so prominent, seemed subdued. "I think they symbolize freedom, because I've never seen them standing still; they're always flying. And I've always wanted that freedom — not as far as having space but as far as feeling like, 'Dang, I'm loved.' So I don't have to think about anything. That's freedom."

Dominique admitted that the first butterfly she ever saw was actually "standing still." It was in a box, when she was in second grade, and her teacher had brought it in as part of a lesson about the butterfly's progress from caterpillar to chrysalis on up. But what impressed Dominique was the box.

"I felt like that," she said. "Like I always had an obstacle surrounding me, keeping me from moving. I got this tattoo because I wanted to set down the box. Set down all of this pain, all of this hurt. Just let it go, so I could move on with my life."

Dominique was hungry, so we left the makeup shop and the fast-food chains of Sutphin Boulevard to find something quieter and homier. Despite the winter weather, Dominique was wearing only moccasins on her feet, and her head, newly adorned with raspberry-colored hairpieces, was hatless. I thought she might be cold, but Dominique brushed me off. She liked to walk; she liked exploring new neighborhoods, and she was warm enough when she was moving.

"My mom was not perfect, but she did try," Dominique said softly, once we had found a small Spanish diner and ordered rice and beans. A telenovela was blaring in the background, so it was difficult to hear her. "I've been in the system a long time, always looking for someone who could replace my m-m-mom, and no one has yet to. So now I'm like, maybe she was what I needed in the first place."

Dominique's stutter returned; it cropped up when she was angry, or remorseful. She said she wished she could turn back time. She was the one who made the call to ACS and turned her mother in. If she hadn't done that, she said, maybe her mom could have continued to improve.

"It was me," Dominique said earnestly into her rice. "It was me in my anger and me in my hatred of the situation of how she allowed my brother to get abused — it made me resent her and not really allow her to try to get back to where she could have been in our lives."

So now, Dominique said as the waitress cleared our plates, she was trying not to speak up quite so much. Her quick mouth had ruined her chances with her own mother, and it had ruined her chances with the Greens. She was now consciously trying to stuff her feelings or, at least, not voice her fury at all the injustice she saw. But it was hard. She was feeling "phony," and often "frozen." To her friends, she said, "Don't tell me what you do, because I don't want to tell you something you don't want to hear," which was making her feel, for the first time in her life, like a false friend. And with her new foster mom, who called to check up on her "like twenty times a day," Dominique also bit her tongue. The strategy led to a more peaceful existence, at least superficially, but Dominique admitted the loss. "I'm holing things up inside," she said. "This mom doesn't really understand me."

Lei, the former foster kid who graduated from an Ivy League university, didn't have to chase her mother down. Unlike Tonya, Fatimah, and Dominique, Lei had a perfectly competent mom; she just lived in China. And when Lei turned eighteen, her mother came to her.

By then, though, it was too late. Lei had already survived foster care for five years, and the mom she missed was the mom she knew in childhood. Her father had already died, and when her mother immigrated alone, Lei said she could hardly relate to her at all. "I feel like, to this day, my family still doesn't understand what foster care really is. I feel like they think I just went to some hangout place," she said. "As soon as I went into college, they were like, 'You're fine.' But I was not fine. I felt like dropping out, withdrawing."

Despite all of Lei's accomplishments, there were just too many disconnects, too many parts of her life that didn't fit together. She was at an Ivy League school, but there were no other kids like her there, nobody from foster care, nobody to understand what she'd endured. And then there was her mother, who took going to a good school as a given and expected her daughter to major in economics or business. "I come from an immigration family, so they wanted me to graduate with something where I could make money. They were not happy when I told them I wanted to be a youth worker. They were like, 'Nonprofit, what's that?'"

When we met at the Starbucks, Lei had accomplished her vision.

She had been out of school for a year and was working at an agency in Brooklyn helping low-income teenagers make plans for their futures. But despite her e-mail quote about knowledge and humanity, Lei's experiences had destroyed her faith in people. "I don't trust anyone. Even my family, mmm-hmmm," Lei said. "I felt so betrayed. They weren't there for me when I needed them, and they pulled me down."

So even Lei had to go back, to find the mom of her memory — the one who had been there for her way back when. About a year after I met Lei, she sent me an e-mail, to say hello. She still had the same quote on her signature line, but she had moved to Taiwan and was teaching English to school kids. She was doing fine, she said, adjusting to the heat and humidity, and to her new hectic schedule. She had moved back to the region of her childhood, where love had been constant and abundant. But she'd moved to a city she'd never seen, where she knew nobody, and nobody knew her, and nobody could break the reverie of what might have been.

Three

RELEASE

We may either smother the divine fire of youth or we may feed it.

— Jane Addams, *The Spirit of Youth and the City Streets*

11

Fantasy Islands

EVENTUALLY ALL FOSTER CHILDREN, if they don't go home or get adopted, will be declared legal adults and released from the system. This is called "aging out."

In New York, there are over six thousand adolescents under ACS supervision. At fourteen, these kids get to set their own "permanency planning goal"—meaning they, rather than their caseworkers or guardians, get to map their futures. If their biological families aren't an option, they have two choices: they can continue trying for adoption, or they can give up on the whole family idea and opt for "independent living" as soon as they reach legal age. In 2009, ACS reported that 7 percent of the fourteen- and fifteen-year-olds wanted to try for independent living; the rest were still vying for adoption or to return home. By the time they turned seventeen, though, they'd given up hope: only 6 percent were still asking for adoption; most of the rest had shifted their goal to independent living.

Most foster kids I know do not use the term *independent living*. They call it getting "discharged"—as though foster care were military service. And every year, the thousand or so youths "discharged" to the streets of New York City, even according to ACS, "must rely primarily on themselves." They have nobody else to turn to.

ACS doesn't track the whereabouts of its kids past their discharge date, but many don't have the skills, or the money, or the education, or the support network to live on their own; it's why so many end up homeless. And they don't have the experience: 70 percent of these young people are discharged directly from group homes or institutions — places with strict rules that hardly mirror all the options and temptations of real life in New York City.

To bridge the gap between the authoritarian world of the institution and real life, where a foster kid has to suddenly be self-motivated, independent, and responsible, most states have created a supervised living arrangement for kids in their late teens. They're often apartments or dorms, where kids live in clusters of twos or threes and learn to cook and clean and budget for themselves, with social workers checking up on them a few times a week.

In New York, this is called the Supervised Independent Living Program, or SILP, and there are programs like it all around the country. They can vary slightly in approach and amenities, but generally kids in SILPs get money for food and household expenses, they get television and a telephone and their own bedroom and usually only one or a few other housemates, and as long as they hold down a job (any job; it doesn't matter the hours or the pay), they get to stay. Until they turn twenty-one. Critics of SILP programs say they're all carrot and no stick; kids don't learn to save money because they don't have to work for their rent, and when they're released, they only know how to order takeout and hide a party from the landlord. It's a kind of faux adulthood that's administered too young: when kids taste early freedom, they can't muster discipline later on. Proponents of SILPs say kids learn how to budget with their stipends and how to shop and cook and clean for themselves while they still have a social worker to rely on, before the stakes are raised and they're all alone.

Over at the Greens', Chanel had already gone this route; it seemed, at least to me, that she was no longer considering adoption. And after Tonya came back from her month-long runaway in the Bronx, she wanted a SILP apartment too.

"I'll probably go this week or next week," Tonya told me confidently, her small white teeth flashing a Cheshire grin. "They already have the apartment ready for me. I just need to get a job."

Tonya and I were talking in her bedroom with the Dora pillows, which she would probably take with her when she left. She said she met two out of the three requirements for the placement: she had a bank account, and she was in school. Although she was failing three of her senior-year classes, Tonya thought an independent apartment would actually improve her chances for higher education. "It's gonna prepare me, being on my own. I'm going to college. There's no ifs, ands, or buts about it. Mr. and Mrs. Green have been preparing us to be independent — as in washing our own clothes and all of that. But I want the whole thing. Like what I eat is determined by how I budget my money, how I cook, you know what I'm saying? I don't know how to cook and I'm eighteen years old. I want to crash test before I go and everything falls apart in college."

To budget herself, Tonya's only plan was to direct-deposit the money from the job she didn't yet have; that way she wouldn't spend everything in one shot. "Because I don't have to pay rent, my paychecks are just gonna stack up and stack up, and then I can just get whatever I want from an ATM," she explained, adding that the first thing she intended to do was decorate. "My bathroom, it's gonna be brown, 'cause I want it to be warm and inviting. And I want scented candles, and not like the little ninety-nine-cent ones that you buy on the road. And in my kitchen, I want all the little magnets on the refrigerator, but not a whole bunch. And towels and curtains that match everything. For my room, I want a big flat-screen TV, with surround sound."

I interrupted her reverie: what if the lack of structure in a parent-free apartment proved too tempting for Tonya's wilder side? I had heard stories of parties, drugs, fights, and pregnancies all occurring under SILP roofs. Tonya wasn't concerned. "It's called the Supervised Independent Living Program because basically they supervise. They come out twice a week to make sure that you don't move nobody else in with you," she assured me. As for a roommate swaying her intentions, Tonya said the agency made its matches carefully. "They put you with someone who's your polar opposite, basically. Like they'll put me with someone who's thinking about not going to school, so I can influence them and encourage them. I'm always a good influence. And they put you with someone where your schedules are opposite to each other. Like if that person has to be at school at ten and I have to be to school at eight, I just probably won't see them. And it'll be less chaos because I can be in the bathroom alone, curling my hair, and not have to worry about someone."

Tonya said she often worried about people in the Green household, and she felt burdened by them coming to her with their problems. "Everyone comes to me because I'm the most able to be talked to without giving out information. And I give good advice, which is one of the reasons I want to be a psychiatrist," she said. "But I need to learn how to say no sometimes. In my own apartment, I won't have to say no, and I won't hurt anyone's feelings."

Mainly, Tonya wanted to say no to her mother, who, she said, was constantly calling the Green land line, as well as everyone's cell phone, to track Tonya down. That was the reason she never got a cell phone herself. "If I'm on my own, then she won't be able to reach me at all. Like, I don't want to hear any negative things while I'm trying to get myself together," Tonya said. Her mother's drinking was the subtext, though she didn't mention it outright. "It's a way to get away from everybody. I won't have to worry about anyone until I'm mentally stable. It's so I can grow. You know how you get one of them trees that's laming and you build a net so they won't fall? That's how I am. I'm really fragile, even though sometimes I don't show it. On the inside, I'm kind of crumbling."

Allyson thought that giving Tonya her own apartment was a terrible idea. But Tonya's social worker didn't work for Allyson or coordinate goals with her. She just worked for Tonya.

"They're telling her she's going to live in her own apartment, but she can't even handle school?" Allyson fumed, when we were alone in the kitchen. Tonya had blown a scholarship to Virginia State, contingent upon her completing high school with top grades. Allyson had been the person to place Tonya in the charter school, encourage her on her homework, tell her she was smart. "The children don't listen to me, but I have to understand that what they're doing is not against me," Allyson said. "If they don't pass their classes, it's affecting who? Not me. So I teach them — I pick out pieces of information from the Bible and show them what will happen to them if they go down that road."

Still, that the agency could promote a road that was so counter to the one she and Bruce had been paving for years enraged her. "They tell her to get a job at Victoria's Secret on 59th Street — but she's supposed to be in school from eight to four. She wants to party, to be with boys, and they're allowed to go out as late as they want in these apartments." Allyson sighed, deep and long. "Now, you tell me the system is not designed to fail."

Another person in the Green family who seemed destined to failure at that particular moment was a teenage foster boy named Russell. Among all the screech and squeal of the girls in the house, it was easy to overlook Russell; he was a quiet but lurking presence, and he had perhaps the broadest set of needs of all.

Russell moved into DeKalb around the same time as Tonya, Fatimah, and Chanel, diagnosed with autism, Asperger's, and something called a "developmental disability not otherwise specified," which Russell carefully wrote out for me on the back of an envelope. He also, in my (unclinical) opinion, suffered from some type of delusions. And yet, like Tonya and Chanel, Russell was being encouraged to go the SILP track.

The first time I met Russell, he had just gotten caught stealing books from a Barnes and Noble. He was eighteen at the time, and handsome, with long straight hair that he pulls back into a ponytail. Russell talks a little like a nursery school teacher, in a high-pitched monotone; he sounds patient and gentle, though he can slam into rages when he doesn't get what he wants — a hallmark of both the autism and Asperger's. He stole the books largely because he didn't understand why he shouldn't; he didn't have the money to buy them and he had fines on his library card so he couldn't check out books there. Morals and consequences were a tough sell for Russell's psyche; mostly he just knew he had to avoid the security guard. When the Greens checked Russell's bedroom that night, they found fifty-nine more stolen books. They were all history and religious texts; he said he wanted to get smarter.

"Russell wants to get his own apartment, but he can't because he's autistic," Allyson said when I talked to her about it. I remembered the way Russell had panicked when Fatimah once showed him a new route to school; like a lot of people with autism, he needed a strict ritual order in his life. Surely, I said, he'd find the demands of an apartment, a job, *a real adult life*, overwhelming to the point of breakdown?

"Of course," Allyson answered. But Russell was nineteen already, and his agency was pressuring him to move into the next phase for foster kids who come of age without getting adopted. The problem is, the kids usually don't have enough money saved to sustain the apartments once the gig is over; many haven't graduated from high school, their job prospects are grim, and they have no families to fall back upon. For a kid like Russell, the problem is even more layered; although he was going to college, his disabilities prevented his grasping a sense of consequence, or even cause and effect. (I want the books, I take the books, his logic goes.) So, while he could perhaps hold a menial job with few stressors and no daily alterations, he couldn't handle things like budgets, bills, and a refrigerator without premade sandwiches tucked inside. Foster care does poorly by kids who reach adulthood with all their survival skills intact; those with disabilities can face even steeper challenges.

But that didn't stop Russell from wanting to live on his own. Unlike the other Green children, who have had to temper their demands for the latest sneakers or video games, Russell often gets his wishes granted, Allyson said, because it's easier than managing his outbursts.

"Everything Russell wants, Russell gets, but he's still not satisfied," she said. "He's happy for the moment, but the minute you turn around, he starts flipping again."

She knows this is part of his disability, or his spectrum of disabilities; after all, Russell was placed in foster care after he physically assaulted his biological mother and had to spend time in the psych ward. And Allyson was taking baby steps with Russell, preparing him for the life he said he wanted. She was trying to teach him some basic budgeting — by giving him $10 a day and talking to him about saving it. So far, though, it hadn't worked.

"My girls, I teach them how to shop, how to buy good-quality clothes and make their money work. They've begun to embrace this. But Russell — he'll take his money to Taco Bell and eat so many burritos. He doesn't know how to do anything constructive with what he has."

Several times, I had patiently indulged Russell's monologues about moving out on his own, complaining that he was an adult and was tired of being babied. He was going to college, after all, and the other students in his classes had their own places, or lived with roommates. He also told me it was probably time for him to start having sex; he had urges, it was natural, but he thought maybe God and Mrs. Green wouldn't like it. (Russell didn't recognize the standard filters in social conversation — another hallmark of autism or Asperger's.) He did know, however, to whisper when he told me that the chairs around the dining room talked to him and told him what to do; many inanimate objects spoke to Russell — he heard voices all the time. He named the voices after cars; one was Dodge Caravan, one was Ford Crown Victoria, another was Ford Van, and so on. He said everything talked to him, "cars, faucets, soaps, chairs, doors, the trucks," and these voices would "be talking on the phones to their own imaginary friends." Although it got pretty noisy, Russell said the voices kept him "preoccupied and happy," and he claimed to have heard them every day of his life since he was two. I wondered about a secondary diagnosis of psychosis or some sort of schizoaffective disorder (Russell said his doctor gave him "psychotropic medication" that controlled his mood swings but didn't take away the voices), and I just nodded mutely along with Russell's dreams of independence.

Inside, though, I was worried. Bruce and Allyson knew Russell far better than I did, and they didn't even let him go to church with them because he might act out.

"Mr. and Mrs. Green say I have to wait for church until the time is right," Russell told me one afternoon. He was wearing a white T-shirt onto which he'd scrawled the letters *ECW*, which stood for Extreme Championship Wrestling. Russell was obsessed with wrestling. "I always used to get angry at church, and also I get bored sometimes and I hate when that happens."

Russell talked about God with whoever would listen. "Mr. George, he's this guy who used to give me the 411 on religion, and he said religion has no validity to it. Is that true?" Russell asked, with his characteristically quick but monotone speech. I deferred with something cheap and hobbled — I was no expert, everyone has his own experience, blah blah — but Russell pressed on. "This guy I'm interested in says religion is a form and a fashion. What does that mean?"

I paused. I had misunderstood him. I thought he said, "a form of defense." It would have made sense; Russell told me Allyson had been getting more religious lately, confirming my periodic observations with his more continual ones. I wondered if he made the connection: Allyson was defending against the increasing difficulties at home with a fortress of scripture. Then I realized Russell's complaint was more concrete: she now had the television tuned to the Word Network all the time, and it interfered with his wrestling.

"I just can't get enough of it," Russell said, though he conceded that wrestling was better when he was younger and the sport was more extreme. "Now there are about twenty-nine good wrestlers left, including on TNA. TNA is a little bit more violent. I like them in tights — that's what makes me feel good."

Russell never stayed on one topic very long; he talked a lot about living independently but would easily switch over to wrestling or celebrity gossip, and in this way, too, I was concerned that Russell couldn't sustain focus without the Greens watching over him. "I've been praying to be able to have sex soon. I've been praying and praying and it still hasn't happened yet," Russell said to me the day we talked about church. Then he quickly changed the subject. "The Undertaker is still in the WWE. He's been wrestling for almost nineteen years — that's a long time."

Russell thought he would go to hell for being gay; throughout our conversation he kept bringing up the ideas of hell he'd gleaned from books or from Allyson or from an aunt of his who was very religious. Then he told me his plan to get to heaven: it came from what his voices, the cars, told him.

"You know Ralph Fiennes? He killed almost sixteen million people," Russell said, as though he were discussing tomorrow's weather forecast. The comment came after a perfectly lucid discussion of Russell's desire to join a gym. "He keeps killing all these people because I didn't get what I wanted soon enough. That's what my imaginary friends tell me."

What Russell wanted was to have sex, as well as to find a white boyfriend, for whom he'd been waiting for "more than sixteen years." He also wanted unlimited access to free books; Russell still didn't understand why he couldn't simply take them from bookstores when he didn't have the money, and he confessed that he'd stolen even more from a Barnes and Noble. But Fiennes's murderous rampage would stop, he said, as soon as these injustices were reversed.

"When I get what I want the most, he'll die, and I'll go automatically to heaven," Russell explained. "What could happen is I could change my ways, I could be the richest person, and get a girlfriend. Instead of liking boys, I could start liking girls again."

Thankfully, right around the time Fatimah ran away, something shifted. Maybe Allyson's talks sank in. Maybe his social worker caught on to the depths of Russell's struggles. But Russell stopped talking about independent living and switched to something more reasonable.

"They're going to put me into assisted living, which means they'll help me with certain things and give me SSI [Supplemental Security Income]," Russell said. He was a little fuzzy on the details as to how and when this might happen, but he had relinquished the dream of following Chanel and Tonya to SILP apartments. And then, shortly thereafter, ACS announced it would stop funding the SILP program entirely by the end of 2010; the agency believed kids were better off with families as they aged out of the system. Elsewhere in the country, however, Independent Living Program apartments are very much alive, and someone like Russell, with his disabilities, can go right from them into a free fall of independence, or else be institutionalized well into adulthood. "I'm scared because they say I'm in for a rude awakening. They'll have me doing a lot of things — cleaning, cooking, washing, working, traveling back and forth to the places I need to go. Here, I clean up my room. I take a shower every day, brush my teeth, I do my laundry, and that's it."

Russell wasn't so keen on leaving anymore for any kind of new housing, because a new foster kid named David had moved in; room had opened up for another foster kid with Dominique gone. "Guess what?" Russell gushed, eager to change the subject from assisted living. "I find David handsome!"

David had responded to Russell's admission with an "Awww." (Russell did an imitation of David's reaction — he looked as if he were wincing at a kitten or a baby.) But Russell wasn't discouraged; he had a host of new prospects since Allyson and Bruce had started allowing him to visit the gay and lesbian center in Manhattan, on the advice of his caseworker. "I go to a young men's group; we play some games there, have community discussion, and everybody goes into a circle and you take turns to answer questions," Russell explained. He was allowed to go as often as he wanted, and although it was fun, it was also sometimes uncomfortable. "This past Friday, they had an open mike and there was a guy who had a blond wig on and a short dress and he was dancing in front of everybody! I was so embarrassed. You may see that in the Village but not in this neighborhood."

At the center, Russell told me, he learned the term *entrepreneur*, and he thought he might like to be one. He'd somehow managed to pay off his library fines and could now check out "twenty-nine books" at multiple branches, so he was planning to read up on famous entrepreneurs. He also was thinking about joining the YMCA around the corner from the center, so he could lift weights and play basketball. Russell had been losing some of his paunch by cutting down on the Taco Bell, and he wanted to continue the positive trajectory. Also, he said with a grin, "at the YMCA they have a locker room where I can watch the guys get naked and change. And when that happens I get so nervous and crazy."

• • •

Sometimes even when kids aren't delusional or saddled with disabilities, fantasies can help them face an encroaching discharge date. I saw this a lot with Dominique, who had been transferred to yet another foster home. (The foster mom who "called twenty times a day" took in a second girl, with whom Dominique battled, and Dominique had to leave.) Dominique's plan for aging out was to move to New Haven, Connecticut. "Oh, my God, it's so quiet, so beautiful there," she said. "I can just see myself living there — the beaches are wonderful, and the sand is so golden."

She imagined living with a cat and a fish, and having a wedding on the beach, but after that, the fantasy faltered. "I mean, I want someone I would be with for the rest of my life, but I don't think I want to be married," she said. I must have looked confused because she continued: "I would love a wedding, but I don't think I would want a husband. There's a difference. I could see myself on the beach with that white little nice dress just flowing and my hair so beautiful."

In the meantime, Dominique had been placed with a single parent; I talked with Dominique's caseworker, who thought placing her with a grandmotherly type, who could fuss over Dominique alone, might be a good solution. But while the kids over at the Greens' were still running away and rebelling against parental control, Dominique found herself in an odd role reversal, and she wasn't too happy about it.

"I feel like I've been hired to be a home health care aide," Dominique complained to me about her new placement. "She's eighty-three and I'm always taking care of her because she has a lot of health problems. Honestly, she can't do too much for me."

Without anyone pushing her to go to college, Dominique had decided to take a break from school. She picked up a full-time job at a Walk Shop, which was "fine," she said, and she was interested in learning about the bones of the feet and good posture. She took off a shoe to show me her latest purchase. "See?" she said. "I have orthotics in my moccasins."

Beyond the Walk Shop and her loose ideas about Connecticut, Dominique was considering becoming a flight attendant. There was only one hitch: she was scared of flying. She had been polling Facebook to see if her 1,298 friends thought she could overcome this fear.

Dominique's plans may have sprung primarily from her own imagination, but as foster kids get closer to aging out, they're often promised things they couldn't possibly attain on their own. Like Russell's independent apartment. Agency workers may overpromise out of guilt or a desire to overcompensate; they know what these kids have been through. Rudy Estrada has seen this a lot. One teenager he used to mentor just knew he was going to be on *America's Next Top Model*, and his case manager told him he had a good shot. But the kid was overweight and unattractive; Rudy was encouraging him to fill out a job application at Starbucks. Rudy's mentee was offended; selling coffee was beneath his supermodel status, and he wouldn't consider any job offer unless it came from a big-name producer. I had a similar experience with Christina. She got her first job when she came to live with me, at seventeen, at a tourist shop in Hollywood. She was scandalized when the manager upbraided her for taking extra-long breaks and ogling boys on the street. She quit a few days later. At her next job, stocking shelves in a vitamin store, she argued with her boss in the first hour and was let go within the week. In foster care, Christina had been told she was responsible only for *getting* a job; she had neither the training, nor the emotional resilience, to actually keep one.

Part of the problem is that so many foster kids grow up in a kind of alternative reality, especially in the group homes — with too much structure, and too little love. When they're discharged, they're shocked to discover that the world of employers and landlords doesn't operate with the same uniform predictability that their group homes once had. Christina was appalled, despite the extreme injustice of her early life, that the people at her jobs "just weren't being fair." And she didn't have the softness inside her, the plasticity and adaptability that come from being cherished, to bear it.

The reason these kids are pushed so hard into independent living comes from a national effort to help them. In 1999, a Republican senator named Chafee noticed that it was the aging-out teenagers who were getting short shrift, and he put through a bill to allocate more funding for them. Probably the biggest change to federal foster care since ASFA, the John H. Chafee Foster Care Independence Program, or "Chafee laws," essentially doubled the federal funding allocated to kids who are likely to age out of foster care without families, providing them with housing, training, and health care.

But the legislation — or its implementation — is flawed. Despite a mandate to collect data on Chafee spending and programs, states didn't report much so nobody knew how well, or even if, the programs were working. Nine years after Chafee was signed, the federal government published a "Final Rule," requiring states to present their programs' outcomes by 2011 (or else face a financial penalty), which would result in a national report later that year. As of mid-2012, that report still hadn't materialized.

Still, there have been a few independent studies, and the results don't look good. One organization did a Web-based survey in 2008 to see how states were using their Chafee funding, and nearly a third of the respondents *didn't know* how many of their kids had aged out in the past year. The largest longitudinal study is called the Midwest Study, and it has followed a sample of 673 former foster kids who received Chafee-funded independent living services from Illinois, Iowa, and Wisconsin, comparing them to nonfostered adults. At last count, these kids were twenty-four, and more than half weren't employed — and half of those who did work had earned less than $8,000 in the past year; nearly 40 percent had been homeless. Five percent of the men and 7 percent of the women had earned an associate's degree — a tiny fraction of the general population their age who had graduated from college.

Looking at these numbers, it's easy to say that independent living training and services don't work, that we're giving these kids too little, too late. Or it may be that the agencies just aren't good at it yet. One researcher conducted interviews with child services experts in Massachusetts and found that they commonly described not being able to serve transition-age youth because that wasn't the mission of their agency. Foster care was designed to serve children, they said, and its purpose was to protect them — not prepare them for adulthood.

But just as ASFA forced child welfare workers deeper into the adoption business, Chafee pushed them into the world of young adults. Rudy Estrada has worked in adolescent foster care for more than fifteen years and has a bird's-eye view of the change.

"Several years after ASFA, there was such a reduction in case-loads — like in New York we went from thirty-five thousand kids to seventeen thousand, and what happened was it skewed the demographics. We moved the little kids out," he said, explaining that, as always, the youngest children were the easiest to connect with adoptive parents. This left the teenagers filling out the caseloads, and administrators wondering what to do with them. "Chafee's had a dramatic effect — where it's pitted independent living against permanency," he said. "Suddenly, caseworkers had a beautiful carrot to offer their kids: like, 'You can have an apartment! And college! Or, would you rather get adopted?'"

For many caseworkers, who have to monitor their kids only until their final exit meeting, the new Chafee subsidies must have felt like a welcome relief, as suddenly they had real benefits to offer their kids all the way up to their twenty-first birthday. (In 2008, more legislation was passed that allowed kids to stay in care, at states' discretion, until they turned twenty-one.) If the kids in their caseloads chose to sign themselves out, the laborious hunt for adoptive families could end. And after these kids turned twenty-one, they wouldn't be their problem anymore.

"As a lawyer for these kids, you want to say, 'Give a family a chance.' You want to say, 'It might sound nice to get your own apartment now, but this family represents a lifetime of connection, a place to live, a place to go home to. This apartment's only for three years,'" Rudy explained. "But to a kid who's eighteen, three years sounds like a long time. They think, 'I get an apartment for three years? By then I'll be a recording star.'"

12

There's Something
About Mary

MARY KEANE, THE WOMAN WHO adopted the Rosario clan and ran the parenting classes, didn't know about the Chafee laws when she set about adopting teenagers. When we first talked about the trend toward giving teenagers apartments, she only rolled her eyes. "They say they've eliminated the homeless problem — because they can say we've placed a thousand kids in apartments," she said. This is, some claim, the grand delusion of the Chafee funding; it provides some help up front, but former foster kids don't have the skills, or the safety nets, to weather young adulthood. "They're not following the kids nine months later to see if they can keep it up."

Mary provided what the city would later say the kids had needed all along: a stable family to stick around long past the discharge date. When I talked to the new commissioner of ACS, the agency had shuttered all its contracts with SILPs: foster kids would no longer live in supervised apartments. The commissioner said ACS would still be providing independent living services, meaning the classes and the training that would help kids get jobs and housing on their own. After all, some of them would still be aging out of group homes. And parents like Mary were hard to find.

Mary is an understated person with a wry laugh and sparkling blue eyes; she wears a sweatshirt that reads "Nouveau Poor," and despite housing eleven kids who always need rides someplace, she drives an old Miata two-seater. Irony is one element that sustains Mary; the other is imagination. Politics aren't a big part of her impressive fortitude.

Mary's imagination was first sparked more than ten years ago, when she saw the twelve-bedroom Victorian house in Yonkers and decided to pour her life savings into what everybody now calls "the mansion." Mary was fifty-two at the time. She had just broken up with a longtime partner and retired early from her job as a health care consultant. Call it a midlife crisis or an inspired vision; it was the start of a new millennium, and Mary wanted a family.

To get there, Mary planned to open a group home, of sorts, for lesbians in foster care. She had heard that these girls had it worst, that foster parents didn't want them, that they were especially singled out for harassment in institutionalized care. Mary was a lesbian; she figured she could provide a haven.

When I first visited Mary in her cream-colored mansion across the street from a park, I felt a pleasant shiver of recognition: there was the rainbow flag in the dining room (which Mary uses as an office), loads of tea and mismatched mugs in the kitchen, a chore wheel taped to the refrigerator door, and a cat mewing underfoot. A pot of rice boiled on the stove. I went to college in Santa Cruz and have lived in several lesbian households; this could have been a transplant from any lesbian collective I've seen. But in this house, big men in baseball caps lumbered about, and in a collective of thirteen members, only three — including Mary — were gay.

In this house, Mary parented eleven kids from the system, all over the age of eighteen, save for one who was just under. Many were from the Rosario family, the kids whose mom had called them names like "Daughter of Satan" and "Fucking Idiot" and left them in an abandoned apartment for months. Mary had adopted several of the Rosarios, along with other kids who still lived in the house and even more who had moved on. Sometimes she practiced what's known as "moral adoption," meaning she committed to a child for life, without the formal documentation. She did all of this because she had the house and the means (Mary worked for an agency that trained foster parents, and she got a little money from the state for the kids who were still under twenty-one). Mostly she did it because she saw the privation: early adulthood is when system kids most need, but so rarely receive, a family. But she never got the houseful of lesbians.

"I first went to Westchester County and said I wanted lesbian teens. They said, 'We don't have any. But we've got pregnant teens!'" Mary said. She had completed her ten-week class to become a foster parent and filled the rooms with beds and linens, ready for her girls. We sat at the big wooden kitchen table, bathed in white winter light from the window, drinking tea. Mary was sixty then, though she looked ten years younger with short gray hair and only light smile wrinkles. "So I went to an agency in the city. They loved the idea of me taking lesbians. But they didn't have any either."

Just as the Greens wanted a baby and got a teenager, Mary wanted a lesbian and got a "little fourteen-year-old straight out of Children's Village crisis unit." Still, Mary didn't want to sit and wait in an empty house for lesbians to materialize when there were other kids in need, so she changed her criterion to girls only. Soon, she said, "they were sending the most challenging, the most runaways."

To Mary's dismay, the girls would run away from her house too, and a handful never came back. "And the agency was basically no support. When I would call to say so-and-so ran away, what do I do, they'd just say we'll send you another kid."

It was Mary's first child, Jennifer, who helped her understand why all the kids ran. "They didn't think it was going to last anyway," Mary said that Jennifer explained. "They thought this was too good to be true, and they wanted to be the ones to leave before they were thrown out."

While the mansion didn't look like a group home — there was art on the walls, and a bird in the master bedroom, and Mary lived there all the time — it was still a big house, with a lot of kids. It would take a while for everyone to adjust to the idea that Mary was offering something radically different. When the first big fight broke out, between two girls, in the front yard and in full view of the neighbors, those two girls both responded the way they had in homes past.

Mary can't remember who started the argument, or what it was even about, but two of her earliest foster kids, Amy and Anni, politely went outdoors when they came to blows.

"A crowd gathered and was shouting, 'Kill her! Kill her!'" Mary remembered. "I called the police to break it up because I didn't know if they were really going to hurt each other."

Both girls went to their rooms, and Mary called their agency, as parents are required to report any serious trouble. "The agency just said, 'Who should we pick up?' Amy and Anni thought the same thing. They were upstairs, packing up their things, ready to go."

But Mary wasn't running a standard group home; she was creating a family. Both girls were shocked when she told them to unpack their bags and stay. And then she signed up everyone, herself included, for weekly family therapy. A fight that big never broke out again.

Looking around Mary's home, I could see why a kid accustomed to harsh conditions would panic — for the same reasons Tonya and her brother tore up the first nice place they landed in Mount Vernon. Mary's house feels like a song on an old acoustic guitar — comfy, settled, and soothing — but entirely too peaceful if you're used to the noise and chaos of thrash metal. Even the kids who have lived with Mary for years still call the house "the mansion." Although the original tin tiles on the ceiling are falling in places and all the walls need a coat of paint, there's a big bowl of fruit on the kitchen table and pictures and notes from the kids scattered around. Once I visited near Christmas, and Mary had hauled up a big box from the basement filled with glass ornaments that the kids had decorated in years past, and she'd brought out permanent paint markers for them to do it again. Everything in Mary's house seemed to say, "You belong here."

Through the Chafee funding, some ACS agencies provide classes in independent living, often held in downtown offices, once a month. Kids over sixteen get a small stipend if they attend, and in these classrooms they learn how to write checks, pay the rent, and balance budgets. For kids accustomed to institutions, this information can seem pretty obscure (or too hard to get to; subway travel to and from the classes can take several hours), and many choose not to go. If they do attend, however, they learn that they're entitled to a few things: they can get a $300 monthly rent subsidy for up to three years, and they can receive priority status on the waiting list for public housing.

This can be helpful, but it's not enough. The assistance checks are notoriously months late and far too low for New York rents; the figure was set in the eighties and never increased. And, while there aren't sufficient public housing units to go around, there also isn't proper coordination between ACS and the New York City Housing Authority. Applications are frequently lost or misprocessed. Still, if kids don't go to their independent living classes, they might not know what's out there upon discharge. They might, like Tonya at the Greens', think they're getting a laptop.

One of Mary's kids, a girl named Fannie (she's one of the lesbians; Mary calls her the "chosen one"), decided not to go for formal adoption because she too had heard about all the bounty she'd inherit if she aged out of foster care independently. She had lived with Mary since 2004 and had been "morally adopted," but she didn't tell the agency; she was nineteen and was waiting out the last two years. Why, she reasoned, had she endured the nightmare of foster care if there wasn't going to be some reward at the finish line? Fannie expected her reward to be college tuition.

Arelis Rosario-Keane was in college, and she told Fannie not to bet on it. Arelis was home on spring break; she'd just trekked in the night before on the Chinatown bus from Boston to New York, and her fleshy face was rumpled with sleep. The girls were sitting at the kitchen table; the snow outside was piled in heaps.

Fannie had heard about the $5,000 voucher program that foster kids can access for college or vocational school expenses, as long as they're in care after their sixteenth birthday. But like so many foster kids who have heard rumors of their aging-out entitlements but never had them fully explained, Fannie was misinformed. And like the rent stipend and other entitlements, the voucher program is inadequate.

In truth, Fannie could access the $5,000 whether she got adopted or not, since she passed her sixteenth birthday in care. But she'd have to choose a school with expenses that topped out at $5,000, since that's the maximum grant — and a school that could wait until November for payment since, as of 2011, that's when the checks were cut. And she'd have to enroll before her twenty-first birthday and finish before her twenty-third — a time frame that renders most foster kids, who age out without high school diplomas, ineligible.

Arelis scoffed, "Wait 'til you have your exit meeting. Then you'll see. There's no security for you."

The exit meeting is the last formal step for a child in foster care, and it signifies her legal discharge from care. In the meeting, the kid, the case manager from her agency, and someone at ACS discuss the child's future. The child is supposed to have somewhere to live, a safe adult she can call upon, and a written plan for income and stability. She then signs papers, and her file is officially closed.

Arelis remembered signing herself out of care at her exit meeting; she was twenty-one and hadn't yet been officially adopted by Mary. "They make you sign this yellow paper that basically says Forget This Address. Once you sign it, it says you can't ask them for nothing," she explained. "But the thing is, I like to read what I sign. And on this paper, they check off everything they *say* they've given you. I'm like, 'This is a lie!' Like they say they gave me money for vocational training. When did that happen?"

The ACS pamphlet *Preparing Youth for Adulthood* claims that, prior to discharge, youth should have the opportunity to participate in internships, career fairs, and vocational training. Their agencies should train them in money management and in strategies for obtaining documents — like birth certificates and immunization records. Youth ideally should know about the educational resources available to them — where they can go on to get a GED, say, or a mentor referral.

"I kept reading and I was like, 'I didn't get this, and I didn't get that' — and they were all sitting there, claiming I had gotten these things and I hadn't," Arelis said, the memory making her voice rise again. "And, of course, those are all the things that are supposed to make you successfully age out of foster care and know that there are other resources out there. I never heard any of that stuff before."

Fannie was outgoing, with close-cropped hair and defined muscles, with a kind of happy, coiled energy that seemed ready to spring. She was wearing a baseball cap and a tank top, like the boys in the house. As she stared at Arelis, her strong will started to wither. Maybe college tuition was out but, she said meekly, "I heard they give you Medicaid?"

"They lied!" Arelis shouted. "They lied!"

Arelis softened her tone. "They say they give you Medicaid, but it doesn't work," she said, shaking her head at Fannie. Before the New York State Assembly in late 2007, Legal Aid lawyers testified that far too often, foster kids' Medicaid coverage is simply dropped as soon as they leave care — even if they are still poor enough to qualify. ACS is supposed to help kids transition from foster-based Medicaid to community-based Medicaid, but as Legal Aid testified, "ACS and foster agency staff are woefully untrained on this vital issue." Kids don't realize their coverage has been terminated until they receive bills in the mail. Arelis didn't know about any of this, but she told Fannie, "I have bills from going to get my eye checked out, and I have to pay them."

The only preparation for adulthood and independence that Arelis received was her independent living classes, which, Arelis said, were a joke. "I had to go all the way from Yonkers to lower Manhattan to find out they just really waste your time," Arelis said. "They just put all these kids in a room, and what do we talk about? About how long it took us to get there, and why isn't the pizza there yet."

Arelis made the trek primarily for the $35 stipend, but that too wasn't worth it, because it was distributed in installments: $10 here, $17 there, along with a Metro card for her ride home. In class, the kids watched movies that felt irrelevant and obscure. "They showed us videos about how to buy an apartment — like how to knock on the walls to make sure you couldn't hear through the other side. It was like, 'How am I going to buy an apartment? I don't have any money,'" Arelis said. "They set you up for failure. They really do."

Mary's house, and Mary herself, are antidotes to that setup. Mary doesn't push her kids into adulthood with prescribed sets of expectations; she lets them live with her as long as it takes to grow into a kind of faith in themselves and family again. There are a few rules: no overnight guests; everybody has to go to school and do their chores. If the kids want jobs on top of that, they can save the money for themselves. When there are arguments, people talk it out. Nobody ever, under any circumstances, gets kicked out.

Jonathan, the young man with the golden eyes who lived for five years in the Graham Windham RTC, never imagined he'd wind up with someone like Mary. He didn't think he'd want to.

"I already had my run with families, and I was like, 'Nah, I ain't doing that no more.' I just wanted to get out on my own and be free," Jonathan said to me. Like most other foster kids nearing their discharge dates, Jonathan had chosen independent living as his permanency goal.

Jonathan was placed in a SILP apartment, after five years at Graham Windham. And even though he didn't have to pay his own rent or buy his own food, he couldn't take it. "I thought I had already tried it with families and it didn't work. But it wasn't until I resided in a SILP that I realized I didn't want to do that. I was already twenty," Jonathan said. He knew that by his twenty-first birthday he'd be put out, and he started to panic. "I didn't graduate from high school and I didn't have enough money to be stable. My agency was pushing me to save money, but I was being rushed. I really felt like I wasn't going to do well when I got discharged — like I was going to keep falling behind and struggling and struggling. I got so frustrated, I called Mary."

Mary had talked with Jonathan several times, when he had lived at Graham Windham. "She wanted to recruit kids who were free for adoption and connect them with adults who were interested. She was always trying to introduce me to that concept," Jonathan said. Back then, he always said no; he was rooting for the free apartment. But once he had it, he wished he'd planned differently. "I asked Mary if she could set me up with a family, just until I could get myself together. Two weeks later, she came to the apartment and said, 'Would you like to come and live with me?'"

Four years after this talk, Jonathan was still living with Mary. He didn't know, when he was younger, to fight for a family, he said, because he had never been in a good one. "I live in a different world now, that I didn't expect. I didn't expect to be at peace," he said. The straight line of his haircut looked like a lid on the top of his head. "It's no longer a matter of run to this place, run to that place, so I can get my mind together. There's no more discharge states for me, no more computer life — where I'm just a name and a number with an expiration date."

And Jonathan was making up for lost time. He was twenty-four years old, taking high school classes and working nights at a Dunkin' Donuts. "Before, mostly, I didn't go nowhere for Christmas, didn't go nowhere for my birthday. Actually, everything I didn't have before — it's the opposite. The house, my mother, my family — now I have it," Jonathan said. "Eventually, I'll get my own place, but now I like this."

When kids are sixteen or eighteen, they don't know they have other needs than the practical. And foster care has always favored safe housing over psychological stability, so kids follow this model into adulthood too. But what Mary has found, and what the kids discover once they've been out of the system for a while, is that they all need to regress.

"When they get here may be the first time they're able to go back and relive some of what they've lost," Mary said. "These kids will sit on your lap, have to sleep in your bed; one of my kids had to have a baby bottle for a while. She was fourteen."

Mary thinks the group home orthodoxy of rules and consequences doesn't work for foster kids; it's too standardized, and as Kecia intimated, kids are often emotionally stranded in a life stage when they were first traumatized. Said Mary, "We say an eighteen-year-old should be doing such-and-such, but you can't have milestone expectations like that. They can't all go at the same pace, and they're stuck in different places. They might be twenty, but emotionally fourteen."

This was a different day and, as usual, Mary and I were sitting in the kitchen, drinking tea. One of the non-Rosarios, a skinny girl named Tamara, stumbled in, rubbing the sleep from her eyes. Tamara was twenty and had lived with Mary for four years. When I was around,

Tamara barely talked — she sat in the corner of the kitchen on a stool, glancing up from her hand-held video game whenever anybody said something funny or loud, but she rarely cracked a smile.

"Did I do a good job?" Tamara asked quietly.

"A wonderful job, wonderful!" Mary said, beaming at her. Tamara didn't take her eyes from the phone she held in her hand. "I'd like to come down and see the kitchen looking like this every day."

I caught a tiny upturn at Tamara's lips, but she kept her gaze on the phone and shuffled away. *That* was what the literature didn't promote, Mary said, once Tamara was out of earshot: intense, direct praise for even the smallest accomplishment, like a chore well done. "They have to know first and foremost that they're loved and have value — so you have to think of one thing every day that they did well, something they can feel good about. They're so desperate for positive feedback," she said. In the early years, when her kids' trauma was more raw and recent and they were regressing to baby bottles and front-yard brawls, she had to dig. "I would say things like 'I'm so proud you went to school today.'"

But most group homes focus on responsibilities and consequences, not safety and praise. Kids start at zero and run in a deficit. Mary said all of her kids came to her "in absolute panic and fear that they were being judged." Even if they wanted to please Mary or follow her rules, they couldn't always prioritize the things she asked them to. "Their head was going through absolute trauma, and chores were the last thing they're thinking about."

So Mary grew patient and imagined where her kids were coming from. "If I knew their heads were spinning, and they were freaking out," she said, "I could just be there for them and relax."

And then she had to train them — something else a lot of group homes don't consider. "If they didn't come from a clean house, they never saw clean, so clean for them might mean push everything to one side," she said. "You have to go in and show them, 'This is what I had in mind.'"

I looked around at Tamara's swept kitchen and thought — no way. Kids are crafty and self-involved; give an inch, and all that. They'll play sick, play dumb, play any card that'll yield them some favor. My daughter, Christina, for instance, would leave takeout containers scattered all over the kitchen and under her bed, but her own backpack was as tidy as a military locker. She had selective vision, trained on her own needs. Mary's kids may have loved her, I thought, but they could also prey on her kindness.

Later that afternoon, though, Mary's unofficial foster son Anthony shifted my perspective. Unlike everybody else in the house, Anthony had never been in foster care. His mother died when he was three months old, his father when he was six, and he lived with his grandmother and many cousins and other foster kids for some years after that. When this grandmother passed, some aunts and uncles scooped up the cousins, and the grandfather drove the foster children to South Carolina, but he didn't take Anthony. He remembers waking up to an empty house one morning in 1996, after everybody else drove away. He was eleven years old.

I could almost see traces of the little boy in the face of the twenty-three-year-old man who sat at the kitchen table with me, quietly laying out his story. A dimple in one cheek and crooked teeth belied the kind of quick charm he must have had as a leggy adolescent, though his eyes were sad and serious. He wore sweatpants and a crisp white T-shirt, covered by a plaid flannel shirt buttoned once at the neck. Perched high on his head was a baseball cap, its brim carefully cocked to one side.

The cap, too, was a tease at the kid he'd been; before his family abandoned him, Anthony had played baseball. There had been money for uniforms and team dues, and dreams of the major leagues. But after the death, Anthony said, "happiness ended right there. After my grandmother, that was it."

"It" was the streets. No school official, social worker, or government agency caught up with Anthony from that day forward; he simply fell off the grid and no one ever caught him.

"I stole drugs, hurt people, robbed people," Anthony said, explaining how he survived. He joined the Crips for a while, lived for some time with an older teenager who'd inherited an apartment from his father who had died. "I didn't get a job until I was nineteen, at Circuit City, because before that, I was just too young."

Anthony didn't like to talk about the ten years he lived on the streets; in the one year he'd been with Mary, he said, he'd changed too much, and it hurt him to look back. "Some of the things I did, I can't forgive myself for, 'cause I can't see myself doing it now. Every day I wake up and ask myself, 'Why did I do that?'" Anthony said, his words determined and flat. "Now, if I see someone getting robbed, I'm going to run and help him, but I still can't make up for what I did before."

What he can make up for, at least a little bit, is playing the child's role. He revels in Mary telling him what to do and at first, he affirmed, he did in fact need help learning how to clean. "Once I got here, I could only stay a night or two, and then leave, because I wasn't good with authority or having rules," he said. He arrived at Mary's house directly after years of squatting in abandoned places or on the couches or floors of older friends. His brother, who had been in jail for most of Anthony's childhood, was living with Arelis Rosario-Keane's sister down the street, and he introduced Anthony to Mary. By then, Anthony was twenty-one. He had nowhere else to go and figured he'd give stability a try. "After a while, I started getting comfortable here because I realized this was how it was supposed to have been as a kid. I was supposed to have rules — to clean my room, have chores. I started relearning what I was supposed to get, what I missed out on. And it feels good."

During another visit with Anthony, he told me that if we had more Marys around, the world would be entirely different. Mary's model is unique, and if others had her patience and dedication, it could be replicated. Because even when kids age out and do well, even when they can conjure the American dream of college, they still regress. They still have to contend with lost parts of their childhoods. Arelis Rosario-Keane feels that her mom stole something crucial from her.

"I can never live up to myself because I don't know who that is. I feel like I will always be missing a piece, no matter where I am in life," Arelis said to me one day, her eyes briefly filling. "I think she has that piece."

I pointed out the ways Arelis was doing so well; here she was, in college, living in Boston, living out what I imagined she always dreamed for herself. She told me she never had those dreams. "I never thought I'd live to be this old. I never thought I'd live to graduate high school. And because I never dreamed of things like college, they still seem unreachable," she said.

The things that do seem reachable, Arelis said, are more familiar. Before college, Arelis spent some time doing drugs, going to rehab, experimenting with the substances her mother used — things she promised herself she'd never try. "You can say, 'I don't want to be like my father because he was drug-addicted,' or 'I don't want to be like my mother because she was drug-addicted and she did alcohol and she was just a bad person,' but still I walked down that road anyway. I did those things anyway because I was around them my whole life, and if they were going to take away the pain, I was going to do them."

Arelis isn't using drugs anymore, and she's doing well in school, but she still feels as if her life is in a fragile balance. "My brain is messed up," she said. "You know how puzzle pieces can fit together, but they don't belong? That's how I feel. The pieces are shoved together. The thing functions but there are cracks — and all it takes is one bad experience and everything falls apart."

I asked her what the bad experience might be. After all, Arelis had already been through hell and survived. She'd survived an abusive home and then foster care, and then was awarded with foster care's one shining promise: a stable, adoptive mother who loved her. With her siblings. By foster care standards, she'd lucked out.

But it was the instability of foster care, Arelis reminded me, which couldn't find a "Mary" soon enough and kept sending her back to her mom, that did the damage in the first place. Now the danger came from inside her. "Foster care makes you feel like you don't deserve anything," she said. "And now I'm the self-destruct button of myself."

The work at Mary's was slow, ineffable, improbable. Mostly, it took place in the kitchen, with kids long past the age when the system had let them go. And even when they insisted, as Arelis did, that they were past saving, I watched the steady hand of unconditional love work its power on them. I saw the healing inherent in what Mary provided, and in what they gave to each other. This was beyond any system or program or mandate; it was, as Kecia said to me in the prison, just the humanness of things.

One day I was talking with the three men of the house: Anthony, who'd grown up alone on the streets; Jonathan, who'd grown up in group homes and RTCs; and Arelis's brother Jay Jay, who'd used his sisters as mother figures for most of his life. They'd lived together for a year and, so far, Jay Jay and Jonathan considered Anthony family, but Anthony couldn't go there.

"Me and Jay Jay are really cool, but I can't trust yet," Anthony said, nodding in Jay Jay's direction. Anthony's hands lay open in his lap, and his eye twitched with grief as he described his yearning to return to childhood, so he could fix what had hardened him against these men who clearly loved him. Jay Jay, leaning forward, nodded back. "I mean, my own family did this to me, so imagine what a stranger could do." Anthony looked at Jay Jay straight on. "I would love to trust you one day but . . ."

Jay Jay, despite his round belly and soft face, did look as if he could be Anthony's less muscular brother. They shared the same skin tone and similar deep brown eyes. Jay Jay tried to rescue him. "I have a hard time trusting too," Jay Jay said, "because people have stabbed me in the back so much."

But Jay Jay had a girlfriend, Anthony countered. There's no way he could risk that. "I mean, it's kinda bad for me — I'm twenty-three years old and I don't have a girlfriend, not that I don't want one," he said. "I don't know if I'm going to be faithful, I don't know if I'm going to hurt her; I don't know how I'm going to react in any situation, so I distance myself."

Jonathan, strikingly handsome with his honey skin and gold-flecked eyes, didn't have a girlfriend either. But he thought trust was something different. He looked at Anthony with a kind of tenderness that bordered on maternal. Outside of a church or a funeral, I had never seen American men this soft, this gentle, with one another. "At a certain point in your life, I think it's worth it to trust," he said slowly, measuring his words for their effect on Anthony's face. "Because you can be more at peace with yourself and with others. You gotta trust yourself first. I think I can trust myself first. I can live with my own skin."

Anthony considered this. "That's what I want, I'm hoping," he said; his faith had been buoyed by the growth he'd experienced already in the year and change he'd been at Mary's. "You can now give me $100 and tell me to put it in your drawer. I can do that."

It was his own gut-level, instinctive reactions, he said, that he couldn't predict. He'd been in survival mode too long; it was hard to slow down and imagine his impact on others. Or imagine that they'd care. "I don't mean to say anything about you guys, but I like to keep to myself. I don't want to hurt nobody." He looked at his hands. "If I had trust, I could have a lot of things. Like I would love to have an enemy. Because you have to trust to have even that."

Despite Anthony's assertions that he couldn't connect deeply to anyone, at least not yet, he listened carefully to both Jonathan and Jay Jay, as we sat talking for more than two hours. When Fannie came through to get something from the cellar and Jay Jay locked her down there, giggling all the while, Anthony calmly crossed the floor and un-hitched the latch to set her free.

And when Anthony talked about his mother, and divulged his long-nursed suspicion that he was responsible for her death, I thought he should reconsider his narrow parameters for trust; what was trust, after all, if not sharing one's earliest, most fragile secrets over a kitchen table?

I kept these musings private; I know the almost mythic power of believing oneself impervious to loving. On the day we talked I may have been especially vulnerable to intuiting connections between non-blood family members; I needed them myself. Five days before I made the trip to Yonkers, I received a call from a lawyer telling me that my mother had died; he was looking for next of kin. She'd already been dead fifty-six days; I had missed the funeral. Though I hadn't seen my mother in twenty-five years, I felt lost and strange, and infinitely to blame — my child self returning to me in waves.

But when Anthony said that his birth probably killed his mother, I spoke up. "You might have always felt that way, even if you weren't a baby when she died," I said. "I just found out my mom died on Tuesday, and I feel guilty too."

Jonathan chimed in. "It's so weird, right? Getting a call from a stranger saying your mom is dead?" For Jonathan, the call came from his agency six years earlier, when he was sixteen. He didn't go to a funeral either; the news, once it had filtered its way to Jonathan, had come too late. "It's like, how am I supposed to feel?"

Anthony leaned in, encouraging him. "It must be so many emotions coming at you at once," he said, but Jonathan shook his head. No, that wasn't quite it. Anthony tried again. "Or like, 'Is she really *gone?*'"

That was more like it, and both Jonathan and I nodded. How do you mourn a ghost? How do you let go, really let go, of someone who left you long before? I had been searching, that week, for a model — for some mold of emotion to pour myself into and feel safe. I tried crying for my mom, but I felt false, hysterical; when I'd spent a quarter of a century defending against her memory, the sudden intrusion was alien and sharp. I tried anger but could muster only a thin puff against the lawyer, who'd been too cool and methodical in his delivery. I knew "dead mom" the movie, and "dead mom" the TV show, but I didn't know dead mom in my heart; she hadn't lived there in so long. Or maybe she did, but the vision of her had been so shot through with my guilt, she was almost unrecognizable. For the first time in the strange days since her death, after accepting awkward condolences I didn't deserve, I felt reflected in my confusion by three men nearly half my age.

"You know what's always been told to me by some random person?" Jonathan asked, the razored edge of his haircut making him look more severe than he was. "That you should have thanked your mother for being alive."

"Whaaaaat?" Jay Jay retorted, disdain souring his voice. Jay Jay hated his mother.

Anthony said he was "highly jealous" of all three of us for even remembering our moms; bad memories were better than none. Jonathan looked back at me, still bonded over the discovery that we had missed our mothers' funerals.

"I feel gratitude for her that I'm alive," Jonathan said. "I just don't know how else to feel."

I smiled at him and was quiet again. Like Anthony, I hoped I could reach Jonathan's state one day. My loss was fresher then, but the gratitude escaped me.

13

Experiment

MARY WORKS FOR AN improbable organization with an improbable name. It's not a foster care agency, though it does train and license foster parents. It is not an adoption agency, though it does connect around sixty hard-to-place teenagers with permanent families each year. It's called You Gotta Believe! and what it is, is a kind of bridge: You Gotta Believe! pulls hard-to-place kids from their group homes or RTCs and connects them with adoptive parents their agencies said didn't exist. It calls itself a homelessness prevention program, and according to the founder, Pat O'Brien, it's the first and only organization of its kind in the country.

What Mary and YGB do is find other people like her to adopt the kids the way she's adopted. In a way, YGB has had to create something entirely outside of the system because it's the system that's damaged the kids; it's the system that claimed teenagers would be fine on their own.

I visited You Gotta Believe! on a cold winter morning, stepping off the train to the smell of the ocean and the view of Coney Island's carnival rides, shut down for the season. The headquarters are located a few blocks off the boardwalk, near a Golden Krust, a Mexican deli, and a place called Hair For U. The office was cluttered with file cabinets and file boxes; a box of Raisin Bran perched on the front counter next to a bucket of salt for melting sidewalk ice. The front door advertised the organization's services. "Adopt a Teen!" a poster read, alongside prices for faxing, copying, and enlisting a notary public.

"The whole system is cockamamie," YGB founder Pat O'Brien said by way of introduction. Pat is a gregarious white guy in his forties, with curly hair and a mustache, who spent his early career at a foster agency working to get older kids adopted. "We placed mostly preteens at that agency; the average age was eleven because everybody thought nobody wanted older kids."

These older kids — both then and now — could legally decide at age fourteen that they no longer wanted to find an adoptive family, getting themselves placed on the independent living track and aging out on their own. Because ACS and the Department of Homeless Services are entirely different governmental branches, it's hard to get accurate statistics about the flow from one into the other, but Pat, along with several credible studies, estimates that about 50 percent of the current homeless population were once in foster care. This is why Pat describes YGB, above all else, as homeless prevention.

"The system comes up with all these crazy programs for teenagers — shared parents, bridge parents, lifetime connections, resources, mentors — all this crap that's not going to keep the kids from being homeless when they age out of care. They come up with every cockamamie answer under the sun, except the only answer," Pat said, describing various adolescent programming offered around the country. "And the only answer is to get a kid a family."

"The secret to our approach is to find out who cares about this kid," said Chester Jackson, the associate executive director of YGB. Chester, a tall, broad African American man with an intelligent face and a slight limp, joined Pat when he started the organization in 1995. He explained that YGB staff reach out to group homes and RTCs to identify the teenagers who need and want permanent parents; they contract with every foster agency in New York City and several upstate. Once they have a teenager, Chester said, the YGB staff interview her and then conduct simple detective work to locate one person from her present or past who might want to take on a more prominent role. "We'll say, 'Who visits you? Who's in your life?' We'll talk to the kid's social worker and say, 'Who comes to see her?'"

Pat and Chester have been friends since college, and they tumble and barge into one another's sentences constantly. "We've placed kids with everybody. Professionals from their lives — teachers, therapists, lawyers," Pat said. "And family members! I mean, you terminate a kid's rights, you'd think you've killed the whole family. But it often happens there are loads of family members who were too young to take a kid when he came into care, but are old enough now — including older siblings and cousins and . . ."

"Neighbors!" Chester interrupted. "Even if you're living in foster care, you're living somewhere. Sometimes you live in a lot of somewheres. You're next to people — you may go next door and watch TV every day at the same person's house," Chester said, nodding to Pat.

"And we've placed with those people," Pat interrupted back.

Finding people that the child has loved wouldn't be so hard, I thought, but the next step, getting them to commit, was tougher to picture. I imagined Pat and Chester, both so eager and assured, calling up some kid's former teacher, his bus driver, his older sister, and saying, "Guess what? You're pregnant! With a teenager!"

So they take it in steps. They first explain the teenager's need, and his chances for falling into trouble or homelessness, and then they encourage the potential parent to "take a learning experience," or enroll in the ten-week licensing classes required by the state to become a foster parent. Technically, You Gotta Believe! parents *do* become foster parents, except in the classes that YGB offers, they're encouraged — or mandated, really, if they do house the child — to become "forever parents." Whether they eventually legally adopt or "morally adopt" is up to the kids and the parents. But they're in it for life.

"We don't have all the answers, because family life is hard, but we happen to have the only answer, which is this: You need somebody that'll say, 'I'm that kid's parent,'" Pat said, an old Brooklyn accent flattening his vowels. He offers YGB classes eleven times a week all over the five boroughs, and unlike the standard classes elsewhere where parents have to wait for a start date, they can jump in at any part of the ten-week cycle. Once YGB has identified a potential parent, they want to catch him fast. "All we've got to do is get one. If we hit the jackpot, there's two. But that's all you've got to do."

Pat and Chester and their staff find last-minute families for around sixty kids a year. It's undoubtedly beautiful work, but it's also triage; they're saving the kids teetering at the edge of crisis, and without better system intervention earlier on in their lives, the teenagers will just keep coming. Over time, though, YGB may be expanding awareness about foster care, by expanding the onus of accountability. Rather than continuing the legacy of treating foster kids as other people's children, or as the state's problem to be institutionalized and hidden away, they're connecting deeply with the community. Like the old-time outdoor relief, they're asking the kids, "Who do you know?" and bringing the help to them.

Still, a commitment to lifetime parenthood can be a tough sell, and even after all the sleuthing and mining of contacts, some kids end up without a single prospect. Sometimes YGB teenagers don't know anyone at all who will take them in. For such cases, Chester produces a weekly cable-access television show, where kids can tell their individual stories and ask flat-out for families.

In general, I've always felt uncomfortable with these kinds of public displays: they're a little too close to human auctions, where minors advertise their attributes and hawk their cuteness, their vulnerability, their need. Children aren't products, and they shouldn't be featured on commercials as such. I worry that the clips raise false hopes, but I also know that exhibitionism like the Heart Gallery project, wherein professional portraits of foster kids are displayed in malls or galleries along with their adoption information, has led to some five thousand adoptions. "Wednesday's Child" is a weekly clip of a hard-to-place foster child, featured on the evening news in five major cities. More than 1,500 kids have been adopted through "Wednesday's Child," and forty-two thousand viewers have called up with questions about becoming a parent.

But does this really work? Can the older kids, tired and traumatized by a decade or more in foster care, really jump into adoption with someone they've never met? And can parents promise to adopt a stranger without a trial run? When I talked with Pat and Chester, I worried that the expectations were too high, the damage too deep.

And then I met a couple who were willing to take the risk. Their names were Glenn and Mindy, and they lived in Staten Island. Glenn and Mindy saw a sixteen-year-old girl named Oneida on "Wednesday's Child," and they were intrigued. On the news, Oneida was taking a salsa lesson in a fancy red dress and informing the newscaster that she "wants a family that's hardworking and understanding that will be there and support me and make me smile when I don't have nothing to worry about. That would be the happiest thing in my life, if I was to receive a family."

We could do this, Glenn and Mindy thought when they saw the news. Glenn's biological daughter had just left home for college; her room was empty and Oneida seemed so great, if terribly unlucky. On TV, Oneida's social worker boasted that Oneida "tries to reach the highest goal she can within everything." Oneida, wearing her curly dark hair pinned back with a red flower and big hoop earrings, backed her up. "I want to become a professional dancer, I want to work in movies," she said, grinning. "I want to become a foster parent, a social worker, and a lawyer."

By the time I met Glenn and Mindy, they had completed their classes at You Gotta Believe! and they trusted the program. They believed that teenagers needed "forever families," that no one was too old for adoption. Glenn and Mindy had attended support groups for adoptive parents, had completed their home study and been approved by the city, had swapped survivor stories with other foster kids to better understand their bruises and fears. They were ready to adopt a kid like Oneida. They were ready, in fact, for Oneida. The only thing left was to meet her.

In her regular life, which didn't ever include salsa dancing (that was set up for the television broadcast), Oneida lived at Graham Windham — the same RTC where Jonathan had "rested his head" for five years. In her regular life, Oneida preferred Spanish pop to salsa, and, although she really was a foster kid, she had come to Graham

Windham through the courts: for partying too much, staying out late, and spray-painting a heart onto a bodega wall.

Her primary advocate at Graham Windham was a woman named Doris Laurenceau, whose job title was Director of Family and Permanency Planning Services, which meant that she guided the older kids toward a final, or permanent, goal. Unlike many executives in congregate care, who deem group homes or RTCs the last stop for teenagers, Doris still believed in finding them lifelong families.

Doris thought that Glenn and Mindy would be a good match for Oneida. She hadn't met them in person yet, but she'd read their file, and she reasoned they were fit for a challenge. Oneida had been acting out, but she had a conscience and she could be saved; what she needed was someone to pay attention to her. Glenn and Mindy had family dinners at home every night, and their quiet suburban block could be a welcome respite from the urban distractions that were getting Oneida in trouble. Plus, while Glenn and Mindy were waiting for all the paperwork on Oneida to go through, they had started weekend visits with another foster child, a quiet honor roll student named Nayelly. A smart, bookish sister, Doris thought, could be a good influence.

Doris knew how adoption, even later in life, solidifies one's sense of self and belonging, because she herself was adopted at thirty-eight. By Mary Keane.

In the way that new communities or cultures can seem enormous at first, but tiny once you've gained some traction and familiarity, child welfare in New York City sometimes feels like a small town. I met Pat and Chester at You Gotta Believe! long before I ever met Mary Keane, simply because I had read about their work and was intrigued. Then several friends and colleagues from different circles directed me toward Mary; they'd all heard about this remarkable woman in Yonkers who'd adopted a bunch of kids. When I finally did meet Mary, I found out she was training parents for You Gotta Believe! — and then, over tea one day at her house, in walked Doris Laurenceau.

"I first saw Mary when I was working at Harlem Dowling; my job there was to connect teenagers to adoptive parents," Doris said. This was in 2001, she said, and secretly she had long wished for an adoptive parent of her own. Doris had been a foster child and she was al-

ready in her thirties at the time; she was married, working on a graduate degree, and trying to get pregnant. Maybe it was this last detail
that accentuated the yearning for a maternal lineage, but, Doris said,
when she saw Mary, "I thought to myself, 'That's gonna be her.'"

Mary was running groups for teenagers then, helping to acclimate
them to the idea that they could find families. "I started going everywhere Mary was going; I was stalking her actually," Doris told me,
conspiratorially, with a laugh. Doris's dimples carved half-moons into
her cheeks, and with her pink hoodie and ponytail, she looked like a
girl of twenty-five instead of a woman edging her way to forty. "I'd find
out from the kids where Mary was going to be, and wherever it was,
I'd be there."

"I was really honored," Mary said softly. She morally adopted Doris some years after the stalking, when Doris's own daughter was four.
The legal adoption would come later. "It was a real wake-up call for
me. It never occurred to me that somebody like Doris — married, with
a child — would want somebody."

"The time I needed the most parenting was when I was an adult,"
Doris answered, saying that Mary helped her through a terrible divorce shortly after the moral adoption. Her story spoke to the notion
that a state can't raise a child, because the state deposits that child
squarely into isolation at adulthood. And while that brand-new adult
may well make it on her own for a stretch, at some point she'll need
backup.

Having a mother had changed everything for Doris. When I saw
her again at her office at Graham Windham, she was hoping to carve
a similar path for Oneida.

Glenn and Mindy drove the forty-five miles from Staten Island to
Graham Windham after work one Friday in April of 2009. They were
excited, but both dressed casually, in jeans and black T-shirts, though
Mindy's was studded with rhinestones. Diamond rings glinted from
each of her ring fingers, and her jet-black hair was cut in a shag to her
shoulders. Glenn and Mindy were scheduled to talk with Doris first,
in her office, to discuss Oneida's background and the steps to adoption. Then Oneida would be brought in, to meet them.

"I always tell the kids that *they're* the ones in charge at these meetings, *they're* the ones interviewing the parents," Doris said, after Glenn and Mindy shook her hand and we all settled around a small conference table in her office. "This isn't a pet shop where parents get to pick out a kid. And it's not a guarantee on either side."

Glenn and Mindy smiled and nodded: of course. They said they had seen Oneida on "Wednesday's Child"; they expected to like her, and they were ready to answer any of her questions. Doris relaxed her face and gave one of her characteristic dimpled grins. "You seem like a happy couple," she said.

Despite Doris's introduction, I knew the pressure was on: Oneida was seventeen and scheduled to be released from Graham Windham in a month. After that, Doris wouldn't have any jurisdiction over her anymore, and she could be sent anywhere. Oneida didn't have any other prospects for permanent parents, and without Glenn and Mindy, Oneida would most likely age out of the system on her own. Privately, Doris had told me she had to make this adoption work.

"OK," Doris said with a sigh, "I'm going to tell you everything that's been written in Oneida's file — some of which may be true." Behind her, giant windows revealed the first pink streaks of a sunset, reflecting off three jars of honey on the sill. "She's half Italian, half Cuban and Dominican, with a lot of domestic abuse before the age of five. She has two brothers, both in care, but she was separated from them. The older brother is quite high-functioning. She was first placed in one home, then removed to go into a paraprofessional home, funded through the Office of Mental Health — which is supposed to be for kids going in and out of mental hospitals, because she was labeled depressed. She did well there — "

Suddenly, in the middle of Doris's speech, the office door burst open. There stood Oneida, her eyes wide and expectant, taking in the scene at the table. She grinned and looked down at her hand. She was clutching an umbrella. "Um, is this anyone's umbrella?" she asked quickly. "I thought maybe someone forgot it."

"Oneida!" Doris quickly reprimanded, her tone low and stern. "You know you have to wait outside! We'll ask you in soon."

Oneida popped back out the door, still grinning, and once she closed it, we all laughed. Clearly, she had just wanted to check Glenn and Mindy out. "After that, she had another four or five foster homes," Doris whispered. "And she got into stuff, like partying. She did admit to drinking, and she tried marijuana. She stopped going to school, and she got caught writing on a wall. She also ran away. Maybe I'm minimizing this, but in foster care, two or three days running away is not so bad."

Mindy, who had been nodding along with Doris's story, stepped in. "OK, but you know what? It's all understandable."

Doris looked relieved. "Yes. She's not an angel, but she doesn't deny anything," she said. She told them that Oneida had also forged signatures to get out of work and had once stolen her boyfriend's credit card. "She's a very loving child, and she's excellent at taking her consequences. And if she's connected to you, she won't want to disappoint you."

As Oneida was welcomed back for her official introduction, I felt a terrible anxiety strike my heart. In some ways, Glenn and Mindy were similar to Allyson and Bruce or Mary Keane: they wanted a teenager, they wanted to give her hope and new roots. But they were also very different: they had never fostered before, and they were expecting to love and adopt Oneida, sight unseen. I worried that they were enacting what Francine Cournos at Columbia warned about: jumping into the marriage without the courtship. And yet, I knew YGB was right — a kid like Oneida also needs adoption, needs parents like Glenn and Mindy to say, "I want you, forever."

After her second entrance, Oneida was shyer. She'd abandoned the umbrella and sat quietly at the table, fiddling with a set of pink headphones. She wore jeans, a white sweatshirt, and rectangular glasses festooned with pink and purple geometric designs. She was still smiling, but she glanced around nervously. Doris touched her arm. "What would you like to say?" she asked.

"Ummm, I eat Italian food," Oneida said hopefully. Doris nodded for her to continue. "I like music. My favorite stations are 103.5 and 105.1, the Spanish music, obviously. I like having different types of friends. I like to cook different kinds of food, Spanish food . . ." Oneida trailed off. What can a kid say to people who might, if she played her cards right, want to be her parents?

Glenn smiled at her. He was more soft-spoken than Mindy and had a gentle, reserved demeanor. He was somebody who could be alone for hours a day, as he had delivered mail his entire adult life and was now the postmaster for his region. Mindy was chattier; she worked in sales for a T-shirt manufacturer. "When you cook Spanish food," Glenn asked, "is it spicy?"

"No," Oneida said, uncertain, searching Glenn's face for the correct answer. The she reconsidered. "Well, maybe only the meat."

"Dinner is very important to us," Mindy said earnestly.

"My favorite thing to eat is cheesecake," Oneida answered.

"Well, there are two ways to make it," Mindy said, happily steering the conversation onto baking — a pastime she hoped to share with a daughter. Her accent, like Glenn's, was thick, old-school Brooklyn. "The easy way and the hard way."

This seemed to stump Oneida, so she started chatting about the people who were important to her: her brothers and her boyfriend. Her boyfriend, she said, was a poet, and he drove a car and had parents. Her gaze flicked quickly from Mindy to Glenn and back again, gauging their reactions. "I also like to read," she said. "I'm reading a book right now called *The Dirty Truth*. It's about a murderer and people who sleep with a lot of people. Oh, and in the morning, I just eat cereal."

"Breakfast is very important. Even if it's just a Pop Tart," said Mindy.

"Yeah, and I do my homework. I like to be home on the weekends, and I like to shop," Oneida said, sitting up straighter in her chair.

Mindy's eyes widened in pleasure. "Oh, I *hate* shopping," she said sarcastically. "But I guess I could do it for you."

Oneida grinned; the meeting was going well. Mindy asked her what she was looking for in her life. "A permanent home," she said quickly. "I mean, throughout the years, I've been through some hard times in all the homes. And then I wrote a heart on a wall and got paroled to some Jamaican lady who wouldn't let me eat the same food her own kids ate, and after that there were no more homes for me. Now that I'm getting old, I really don't want to move anymore."

Glenn asked Oneida how she would feel about a sister, and she said she would love to have someone to go shopping with. Oneida asked about house rules, and Glenn told her that honesty was the major directive in the household. "All the rules we have are based on love," Glenn said.

Oneida considered this and squeezed her eyebrows together; love wasn't something she was used to talking about, at least not right away. "I'll probably watch the news with you, every night, while you cook," she said.

Her enthusiasm was catching, as Glenn and Mindy's descriptions grew more concrete and Oneida clung to the idea that she just might go home with them. "Do you like to swim?" Glenn asked. "We live in a development with two Olympic-size pools."

"Cool!" Oneida gushed. "I used to swim a lot. But it was only in the bathtub, and then I got too big. I've never been in a pool."

Pity, or something like it, flickered briefly across Mindy's face. If Oneida caught it, she didn't show it. "Do you like to travel?" Oneida asked.

"Well, I *love* cruises," Mindy said, conspiratorially, leaning in. "I've been on forty-two of them. And we're about to go on my forty-third — to Italy and Greece!"

"Oh," Oneida said. She looked at Doris; this might be a snag in the plans. Parents can't just go off on cruises — or admit it to officials like Doris — with teenagers living in the house. But Doris saved the moment: maybe Oneida could finish out the school year at Graham Windham, she suggested, so Glenn and Mindy could have their vacation, and then she'd make the move to Staten Island. The trick would be getting ACS to approve the cost of an extended stay; if they didn't, they would send Oneida to another foster home and Doris would lose her, when the court order that sent Oneida to the RTC was up in May.

"Or ... maybe I could come visit?" Oneida asked, her voice suddenly small and shy.

"Of *course* we want you to visit!" both Glenn and Mindy said, practically in unison.

Oneida grinned, relieved, and there was an awkward silence. Doris prodded her. "Is there anything else you want to say?"

"Um," Oneida said, looking at Doris for backup, "could I come this weekend?"

Glenn and Mindy exchanged glances; this was happening awfully fast. In the parent training, they tell you to expect a certain process: first you'll meet a child in a neutral setting, then maybe the child will come to visit you at your home. This could lead to an overnight, and then to a weekend visit, and then maybe a longer weekend, and if all goes well, you decide to permanently welcome her into your family. On paper, this gives parents time to adjust (and squeeze in a final cruise) and helps the child smoothly transition from one placement to another. In reality, there often isn't such wiggle room. Kids need to leave unsafe or, as with Oneida, expensive placements when the state says it's time.

Everybody knew adoption was on the line; it's what Glenn and Mindy signed up for. I knew, though, that Mary Keane had adopted her kids when they were ready, after years of building trust. Two of the Green kids had run from adoption when pushed too soon. And Glenn and Mindy were ready right now. I felt as if I was about to witness a grand experiment, or duel. On one side was Oneida, embodying Cournos's idea that trauma blocks attachment, even if she didn't know it. On the other were Glenn and Mindy, with Kecia, chanting, "You've got to rock with a kid, all the way." And everybody wanted to win, together.

Mindy turned her chair toward Glenn and started brainstorming. This weekend wasn't a possibility. There was the barbecue, and the other foster daughter coming to visit; they would need to prepare her. But maybe next Friday — couldn't Glenn leave work early and pick Oneida up from school? Oneida whispered to Doris, "This is like a fantasy. Make them take me."

And then, suddenly, it was decided: Oneida would come the next weekend, for a full three days; Doris would get her excused from school. Glenn and Mindy would take their cruise, and then, after that, Oneida would move in. For good.

14

Touching the Elephant

G LENN AND MINDY HAD TO JUMP so fast with Oneida because foster care and juvenile justice were separate divisions at that time. When Oneida painted the heart on the bodega wall, she was removed from ACS and handed over to the state as a juvenile delinquent. Doris worked for the state and couldn't advocate for Oneida once she completed her sentence — at which point she would be returned to ACS and sent to any number of agencies and any family, rather than to Glenn and Mindy, who wanted her. There are problems with merging foster care and juvenile justice, but one united agency would have benefited someone like Oneida. She could have had one social worker, one judge, one set of files following her through her many transitions and buying her the time to ease into Glenn and Mindy's life slowly. Instead, the trio had to close their eyes to the less savory details (Oneida's history of lying and abuse; Glenn and Mindy's lack of experience). They all wanted a family and believed it could work. They jumped.

Combined criminal and foster services would have helped Tonya over at the Greens' as well. The next time Tonya ran away to her mother's house, she hooked up with an old friend from the Bronx, took a road trip through a few eastern states, and ended up in jail.

When Tonya stood before a criminal court judge in Pennsylvania, she wasn't the Tonya with a thick child welfare file, longtime foster daughter of Bruce and Allyson Green, former star student, and first-time offender. She was a more anonymous adult black female, caught on a ShopRite videotape stealing powdery white toiletries with which a drug dealer could cut cocaine. This Tonya spent one month in a women's penitentiary. Had the judge been privy to a fuller story and to her resources as a ward of New York, Tonya may have been able to avoid this fate altogether.

Then again, Tonya committed her crime across state lines; I don't know that a Pennsylvania court would care that in New York, foster care could handle her. And even now that the system has merged its foster and juvenile justice divisions, it will likely still miss the obvious opportunities to help kids before they stumble into trouble. I wonder, if someone in Tonya's life had caught on to her bed-wetting, her stealing, her fights, as signs of trauma and unmet needs rather than inconveniences and misbehavior, whether she would have faced that judge.

Oneida was also in foster care for many years before she went to Staten Island to be adopted, and she wasn't given enough help. And it was foster care's lack of services that Glenn and Mindy now blame for the entire disaster.

To get to Manhattan's leafiest and least-populated borough without a car, you have to take a ferry. Then there's one subway line, timed with the ferry's landing, which runs tip to tip along Staten Island. If you're a kid, you take a bus to get to a strip mall or the movies. If you want to get to Brooklyn, it takes about two hours.

This was Oneida's first big beef with the place, Glenn told me as he picked me up from the train station in his white Toyota. "Oneida used to call it *carajo*-land," he said, waving his hand toward the white houses with trim lawns tucked along the quiet streets. "She missed the bodegas in Brooklyn."

Mindy understood this stance, at first. She grew up in Bensonhurst in Brooklyn, and her accent still betrayed her roots. The kitchen and living room were festooned with Saint Patrick's Day decorations when I came to visit; green garland chains hung from the ceiling and leprechauns peeped from the cupboards. Mindy said these were a throwback to her childhood. "My mom died when I was ten, and my dad thought that holidays were a way to bring the family together," she explained, but even without the decorations, the 1,500-square-foot house was packed with sentiment. Pictures of the family covered walls and tabletops, but there were none of Oneida. When Mindy pulled out her bulging floral scrapbook so she could trace back the whole arduous demise, she found one, of Oneida curled up on the couch. "Well, she looked cute when she was sleeping," she said hopefully. Glenn shuddered; he wouldn't even look at the photo. "Brings back too many terrible memories," he said.

When Oneida first came to the house, there was a short honeymoon phase, they both told me, finishing each other's sentences. Right at the beginning, they'd splurged on a weekend at Disney World for Oneida, the foster daughter, Nayelly, and the biological daughter, Kristine; Oneida had screamed dramatically and clutched Mindy's hand on the plane, as she'd never flown before. They both admitted that the trip was fun; aside from Oneida wanting to parade herself at the hotel pool, Mindy said, everyone was on good behavior.

When they got home, Glenn said, the agency was frantic: Oneida was classified as "therapeutic" and Glenn and Mindy weren't certified to house a child with therapeutic needs. (Because Oneida had shifted from the state's jurisdiction and back to a city agency, she fell back under her old foster requirements. Doris worked for the state and likely hadn't noticed this stipulation; besides, Doris had landed the much larger prize — a married couple willing to adopt.) The agency argued that Glenn and Mindy had to drop everything for the next three weekends and attend the requisite classes up in the Bronx if they wanted to keep her. So they took the classes.

"That's the way the agencies are. When they need you to do something, they need it done tomorrow. When you need something for the kid, you get nothing," Glenn said, shaking his head. What Glenn and Mindy needed, for the therapeutically classified teenager, was therapy. Within a few weeks of her arrival, Oneida started acting out. At first, she just lied: she'd say she was going to Brooklyn, but she'd end up in the Bronx. Or she'd promise to be home at a certain time and trot in hours later. But then she started disappearing for nights at a time, which later morphed into weeks. Glenn and Mindy would talk to her, ground her, take away her privileges, but they wanted some backup from the agency. They felt that some of this behavior was rooted in Oneida's early traumas and her years in foster care; she was authorized for free therapy, but for the entire summer she lived with them, no one returned Glenn's phone calls to set it up.

"We'd call and they wouldn't call back. When Oneida was in the RTC, she was in therapy all the time. What changed? Just because she's in Staten Island, she doesn't need therapy anymore?" Glenn fumed. He also said they didn't receive an agency check for Oneida's care until August, though she moved in with them in June, and their water and electric bills doubled due to her hour-long showers and her inattention to lights. Arguments in the home escalated; Oneida believed Glenn and Mindy were hoarding her allowance money, and she disappeared for longer and longer stretches. "Even when she was AWOL and she ran away, we'd call the agency and they wouldn't follow up on it. They're useless, totally useless."

The crisis peaked in September, three months after Oneida's arrival. Glenn got a call from someone who knew Oneida, who also made Glenn promise never to reveal his or her identity. Glenn agreed, and the person told Glenn that Oneida wanted out of the house, but she was afraid the agency wouldn't allow it without cause. So Oneida had hatched a plan: she was going to peg Glenn with an accusation of sexual abuse.

"I panicked," Glenn said. "The postmaster is the second most powerful governmental official, and in the little towns like where we are, everybody knows you. If this would have gotten back to my job, I would have been fired, like that." Glenn snapped his fingers. "Once the allegation's been made, even if it's disproved, there are still people who'll believe it. I didn't work twenty-three years to get fired, just because I'm trying to help a kid."

This time, when Glenn called the agency, he got a response. He located a director and said, "When I go home today, I'm packing up all her stuff and leaving it in front of my house. You need to come pick it up, because she's never coming back. We're done with her."

Suddenly, Glenn and Mindy were the terrible stereotype: foster parents who hurl a foster kid's belongings to the curb, in garbage bags.

"We were petrified," Mindy said. "This was our life."

But the agency fought back. Glenn said they told him, "You're not done with her; she's in your house and she's staying there. Otherwise, we will shut down your house as a foster home."

Glenn relented; after all, they had Nayelly, and Nayelly was still a foster child. They couldn't, and wouldn't, lose her. They agreed to have a meeting — with Oneida, with the agency, and with ACS.

Mindy interrupted, her dark eyes blazing: "We had to say we were going to have Oneida removed before they would even think about helping us. And we'd been asking for help all along!"

It was clear at the meeting, both Glenn and Mindy asserted, that Oneida was happy to leave Staten Island. They believe she originally wanted any escape from the residential treatment center, and once Glenn and Mindy had provided that, Oneida could think only of Brooklyn.

"She uses people," Glenn said bitterly.

Mindy nodded, watching her husband carefully. "She uses people, but that's how she's gotten through her life."

At the meeting, despite Glenn's impatience, the agency said Oneida had to stay one more night; then they'd find her another placement.

Oneida stayed, but once everyone was sleeping she used a knife to cut all the cords to the house computer. In the morning she left for Brooklyn.

It took me several months to track down Oneida, so I could get her side of the story. I finally found her online, promoting some dance at a club in the Bronx.

"Ya this is me," Oneida texted when I landed her phone number. "How r u?"

We met on a sunny afternoon in the Bronx, on the corner of 180th and Morris Park, across from the transit police station. She was about half an hour late, giving me plenty of time to peruse the real estate listings tacked onto a sandwich board, offering Section 8 apartments. Little kids bought popsicles from the bodega, and a drug dealer eyed me suspiciously; I was standing there too long.

Oneida looked the same as she had the day of her adoption meeting with Glenn and Mindy some eighteen months before, though she was missing her glasses and squinted a bit to see. Her curly hair was crimped with gel, her bangs crispy straight lines down her forehead. Her puffy upper lip makes her look as if she's been either crying or kissing, though that day it was neither; Oneida had just been relaxing at home — her fifth since she'd left Staten Island.

"Them white people?" Oneida answered, when I asked her what happened with Glenn and Mindy. She made a face as if she had swallowed something bitter, and also as if she was remembering something very long ago. "They was racist."

We were walking toward East Tremont, looking for someplace to eat. McDonald's was out, because Oneida had just been fired from there, for "getting into an altercation with a customer." Oneida waved her hand vaguely down the block. "My biological dad lives not too far from here, just a couple blocks away," she said. I asked if she had seen him. "Not for a long time, maybe a few weeks before the summer. I don't really like seeing him; he lives in this bummy basement apartment. He's a junkie. I mean, I don't mind if people ask me for money, but every time?"

We settled on a Chinese place, with a $6 all-you-can-eat buffet. "I'm a very picky eater," Oneida said, piling her plate with bright red sweet-and-sour pork and cheesecake from the end of the table. She ate only meat and cheese and bread; no rice, no vegetables, no fruits. And cheesecake, when she could get it.

At the beginning, Oneida admitted while chewing thoughtfully on her pork, she liked being a part of the Staten Island family. But shortly after she moved in, Oneida said, Glenn and Mindy became "judgmental." One time her boyfriend stopped by when she wasn't home, and Glenn wouldn't let him in, "not even to use the bathroom!" Oneida was outraged. "And then they were judgmental of my music. The guy was Catholic and the lady was Jewish. If you that way, why take me? I'm Hispanic, you know I'm going to listen to Hispanic music."

The stated issue was one of noise control, but Oneida felt racism was underneath. "I'd only play my music on the computer, and you know that can't get that loud," she explained. "And then one day I came home and they'd put Krazy Glue on the volume!"

Oneida agreed that she took off for Brooklyn a lot, but that was only to visit her best friend, and to get a break from Staten Island, which she described as "too much of a suburb. All you see is bushes and trees." The high school, too, was a difficult adjustment. "The school was huge, like four thousand children, and it was nothing but Chinese and white. I didn't mind being at that school, but it was how the kids looked at me — like I was some ghetto Spanish girl."

Glenn, she told me, was more troubling than Mindy because he had a temper. They had their biggest argument right before their final meeting with the agency. "I wanted to go into my room and he was in there watching TV," Oneida said. Oneida's bedroom was in the basement, where the sixty-four-inch flat-screen TV was mounted to the wall and where Glenn had always watched sports — long before any kids arrived. I saw this room when I visited Staten Island; despite the girly bedspread it still looked like a sports fan's room: team pennants were pegged all over the walls. "I was like, 'Can you get out? I want to get my things for a shower.'"

Glenn told her to wait; he was at an important part of the game. Or she could simply get her clothes and go. Oneida was horrified, and furious. "I said, 'You want to watch me get my bra and panties? Have some type of respect — I'm a female, I sleep here!' I called him a pervert."

Oneida knew from past experience that she had to be extra-vigilant to protect herself. She told me she'd been raped twice, in her teens, by two different men, and she was molested repeatedly as a young child. She never confessed to these early incidents, but she was examined at three different hospitals and the doctors figured it out; she remembers these exams distinctly. Oneida knows these experiences have sometimes made it difficult for her to assess true danger. "Like one night, Glenn stood in my room while I was sleeping because somebody called the house at three in the morning," she said, by way of example. "I was scared. I didn't know what that was about. I didn't know if he was being inappropriate."

So were these incidents the reason that Glenn got a phone call about Oneida's idea of charging him with sexual misconduct? I told her that in Glenn's version of events, she was planning to file an accusation of abuse.

Oneida didn't blink. "Not at all. I guess they just felt like that."

In Oneida's memory, the reason she was removed from Staten Island was that Glenn believed she was going to set fire to the house. It was an apt metaphor, but one I'd never heard from Glenn. In the end it didn't matter much to Oneida what anyone thought she was plotting; all she wanted at that time was out.

Unfortunately for Oneida, she didn't like any of her next placements better. After Staten Island, Oneida was moved to a home where, Oneida claimed, the foster mother hit her children with spatulas and her foster sister stole her sneakers.

Oneida was removed and sent to "a Trinidadian lady who was cool." But she lived in the neighborhood where Oneida had been raped, and Oneida didn't want to leave the house to go to school. "The guys in that neighborhood is all on top of me, on top of me, and the lady is calling me lazy. I kind of messed it up for myself; I got in an altercation," she said. "Horrible."

In the next house, Oneida was alone — too alone. There were no other foster kids, and the mother made Oneida stay home by herself whenever she left. "It was horrible. There was no phone reception there; I had to go to the bathroom and talk through the window, that's how bad the connection was. And there was no cable!"

The next place had kids, but the mom was stingy, Oneida said. She wouldn't give Oneida her allowance money, and she never did the laundry. "She was an elderly lady and all she do is talk about you to the other foster girl. Horrible."

The long string of horrible seemed to have hit pause recently, Oneida said. She liked her new foster family, just a few blocks away from the Chinese restaurant. There was a mom and a dad, and a few foster kids, and the parents had even let Oneida's ex-boyfriend sleep over, on the couch. She had her own room with a queen-size bed, and the family watched movies together, on cable.

Oneida had lived with her latest family for only two weeks, and she knew all about the deceptive promise of a honeymoon period. Still, this short reprieve from upheavals had allowed her to think again about her long-term plans. Oneida was almost eighteen and figured she had about one year of high school left to graduate. She'd attended three different high schools in the past academic year alone, and all of those infrequently, so it was hard to tell where her credits really lined up. She knew she wasn't prepared to take the Regents exams, and the new high school she was thinking of attending didn't even offer a Regents diploma, which was a requisite for college.

"With the diploma that I'll get, I'll be better off with a GED. I can only go to a vocational school, like a cooking school. Or dancing, I love dancing," Oneida said, tapping at her cell phone. "I want to do something professional, where you get up in the morning and wear a suit. Like a lawyer, or a security guard. I want to have high income, but I don't know how to do that with my diploma."

Oneida's real dream, she said, was to move into her own apartment in Bushwick, Brooklyn, near Knickerbocker and DeKalb, where she was born. Ideally, she'd work for the Special Victims Unit. "I want to be a detective, like on *Law and Order*," she added, finally putting down her phone and widening her small brown eyes. "The only thing is it may not be possible because I'm too emotional. I'm emotional when I see dead people, or kids getting raped."

Bruce Green ended up hitting the same psychological wall that Glenn did after Oneida left. While Bruce had once believed he could contain any teenager's chaos in his strict and loving household, Bruce had reached the limits of his faith. Three years after I met Bruce, he and Allyson had accepted their eighth teenager, and they had just called the agency with a ten-day notice to send him back.

"David was on a gay crusade," Bruce said, referring to the boy who had moved in and promptly sparked a crush from their autistic son, Russell. Bruce was standing on the stoop, drinking a beer and sand-ing the door frame, preparing it for a new coat of varnish. Over the past year or so, Bruce had rarely been around when I came over after school let out to see the kids or Allyson; he had taken to working the swing shift as well as most weekends. But a recent knee injury had landed Bruce some comp time, and he was using the spare hours to make repairs around the house. Allyson was down at the carport with Allen and baby Anthony, where the cement had been broken down for some repaving. "We did a ten-day notice on David because he wanted to show out. He was arguing with everybody about being gay — he said we isolated him in the house, said Allyson pushed religion on him."

Rather than working to mold David into the Green ideology, Bruce sent him back; it was easier that way, and besides, Bruce's ideas about foster care had shifted over the past three years. He sanded more slowly and looked at me. "I used to think that any child that came to us, we could help, but . . ." Bruce paused to take a drink from his beer. "We won't be taking any more teenagers. They already have too much damage."

Bruce's tone was sad, with a bitter edge. Allyson was often stressing the ways the system failed the kids, but in Bruce's eyes, the foster parents were a primary casualty. He reminded me of the way he'd suggested that Edwin Gould merely provide photo vouchers for foster families whenever they took in a new child. The agency had loved the idea, he said, but it had been three years, and nothing had come of it.

Still, Bruce said, even without the benefits, and even with all the hard times, he would stick it out with the kids he had left. They may try his patience, they may disobey and run away, but, he said, "Most foster parents would just give up, they'd say, 'You're grown.' But we don't do that — we're family, and we're in it for the long haul."

I asked about Dominique and Bruce flinched. He was squatting to sand the lower part of the door frame. "Dominique was supposed to be a favor," he said, defensive. "She was supposed to be an emergency placement and she stayed seven months."

I reminded him that he was going to adopt her. I was there.

Bruce stood up to look me square in the face. He had a good twelve inches on me. "Yes, we were going to adopt her. But even Dominique, in her most honest moment, will say she pushed. And that was her mistake. She fought with everybody — she fought with Fatimah, she fought with Tonya, she even fought with Charles, and he doesn't fight with anybody." Bruce sighed and wiped his hands on his jeans, which had elaborate crosses stitched into the back pockets. "I used to think I could save any child who walked through my door, but I can't. Dominique just wasn't a fit."

Bruce moved on to varnishing. He worked in silence for a while until Russell suddenly emerged from around the corner.

"Why aren't you downtown?" Bruce and Allyson said, almost in perfect unison. Bruce put down his paintbrush to cross his arms. "What time is it?" Bruce asked.

Russell looked confused. "A little after two?"

"And where should you be?"

Russell turned to leave again. "Downtown."

Both Bruce and Allyson still knew where all the kids should be at every hour of the day, and everyone's schedules were still full of extra classes and tutoring and enrichment programs and counseling. But with the teenagers, Bruce had recently surrendered the strict curfew rules. Everybody was over eighteen, save for Tonya's younger brother, William, who had moved in and was always home by eight anyway. Technically, Bruce knew he couldn't enforce anything anymore.

"They know when they're supposed to be in, that you've got to get to bed for a school night," he said, patiently stroking on varnish. He figured they were old enough now to experience their own consequences. "If you're getting home at midnight, how are you going to do school? If you start failing classes, everything spirals out from there."

And this led us to talking about what had happened to the Green family dream of difficult teenagers settling, and then excelling, within the walls of the house on DeKalb. According to Bruce, it was the Internet that "started everything downhill," with the foster girls variously breaking rules — moving out, running away, getting arrested. He wished he'd never bought the kids their laptops; he traced all the troubles back to his one big splurge at the computer store. "Did they do their homework on there?" he asked me, rhetorically. "No. It was all MySpace, YourSpace, TheySpace, EverybodySpace. As a father, you don't want to *see* the kinds of things these kids look at."

Bruce could control, to some extent, where his kids went and how late they stayed out, as long as he held the keys to the front door. But with the Internet, his authority faded; the outside world permeated his heavily guarded walls, and his kids latched on to the temptations available to them. He had once preached that his kids didn't need friends because the family was enough. With the Internet, the girls could stay up all night, friending hundreds of strangers, creating flimsy, flashy personas, and hatching virtual plans for new and impossible lives.

Fatimah took some personal responsibility for her part in the partial dissolution of the Green family. "Before I got adopted, I felt like I had something to fight for," she said. For as long as she could remember, Fatimah had wanted to break free from the hell of foster care; it's why she did well in school, why she tried to please her foster parents, why she kept herself healthy and fit — as though she were a prize someone would want if only she were perfect enough. "Getting adopted messed up everything. It messed up my train of thought. It messed up my goal. It was like, 'This is it? This is what I got adopted for?' This is not the dream I thought I had."

But Fatimah also said it was the Greens' particular style — their strictness — that made her and the other teenagers want to get out of there. "What made the family fall apart is that everyone was waiting to get to the age to be able to run. I mean, if you cage a bird up it's gonna come out crazy," she said. "Like, for instance, our dog. Before we got the dog, it was caged up for eight months. So now, even when you tell her to come out of the cage, she'll stay in there 'cause that's what she's used to. But when she does come out, she's vicious."

Allyson placed the blame somewhere else. "When they have contact with their birth parents — that's where the problems start," she told me, even though she had once strongly advocated for these connections. She listed a few examples: Fatimah didn't go to school when she lived with her mom in Queens. Tonya had spiraled downhill by first running to her mom's place in the Bronx, and then hooking up with old friends who led her to that shoplifting charge in Pennsylvania. "When they have contact with their birth parents, they start believing they have options. Chanel never behaved that kind of way, because her mother passed when she was five years old."

Just like people discussing the problems in foster care as a whole, everyone at the Greens' was touching a different part of the elephant. And just like their counterparts in the bigger picture, everybody's intentions were perfectly good.

This is why child welfare experts try to fix the myriad problems in child welfare and fail: the problems are rooted in a society that cares little for its children, for its poor, its mentally ill, undereducated, incarcerated, addicted, and isolated. Child welfare is but a thimbleful of water on a raging social fire; the house on DeKalb couldn't begin to contain its flames.

Bruce watched Russell walk away until he turned the corner. He was finished painting and suggested we go inside to heat up the leftover king crab legs from dinner the night before. Bruce knew that the problems he'd experienced stemmed from something much deeper than the Internet, his family dynamics, or even foster care at large. "You know who's responsible for this?" he asked, slathering butter on the crab. "The government."

Bruce went back outside to eat and gestured toward the public elementary school on the corner of their block. It's a brick bunker of a place that had been put on the state's list of failing schools in 2004. Most of the enrolled students came from the Eleanor Roosevelt projects across the street or from nearby homeless shelters, and none of the Green children had ever attended. "Who's teaching our kids? Did they go to the best teaching colleges? Or did they go to some rinky-dink school?" Bruce asked. "And then you've got children having children. Children who went to these schools, who aren't prepared beyond the fifth grade. They're not prepared to have children, so they get their children taken away and the government pays $7,000 a year to someone else to raise that child, and even more to an agency." Bruce paused to watch Anthony trying to climb a plastic chair. He was walking already, and his brother, baby Allen, was almost ready to start kindergarten. "What if they gave that money to the parents directly and didn't take away the child — or to the schools so you wouldn't have this process to begin with? It's a business."

For Bruce, the financial motivations in this business were rooted in historical racism. "What was one of the biggest crimes during slavery?" he asked, wiping his hands on a napkin, not waiting for an answer. "Teaching a slave to read. It pays to keep people stupid."

The pattern looked like this: The government created failing schools, which created failing child-parents whose children were taken away. These children were then failed again in foster care, so they could end up in jail, or else feeding the system with more kids. "Jails are a business too," Bruce said sadly. "You've got women in prison making Victoria's Secret bras. You've got to keep people stupid, so you can put them in jail and get them to do your work."

In 2010, New York's public advocate proposed legislation to track, for the first time, what happens to foster kids once they leave the system. If it passes, the bill will require ACS to coordinate with the Department of Housing and provide public quarterly reports about the kids who receive Medicaid, public housing, food stamps, and welfare within six months of emancipation. It calls for collaboration with the police and Department of Homeless Services to calculate how many end up homeless or in jail. The bill does not require collaboration with local colleges or employment programs to track enrollment, maybe because these figures are too small to matter, or because the main concern is with the youth who continue to drag on public resources. But the bill does not require any direct follow-up with the eight hundred foster kids who leave care each year at all. If the bill passes as it's designed, it will provide only a more precise picture of the worst-case results — indicating the city's expectation from the start.

And still. As Kecia Pittman lamented from prison, the most important thing a family can do for a foster child is "stay." That's what the

Greens were doing—with Tonya, with Fatimah, and when she wants it, with Chanel.

Several months after I met with Fatimah to pick up the art, Fatimah's mom relapsed. Fatimah's sister, whom Fatimah had tried so valiantly to protect, was sent into foster care. So Fatimah reluctantly moved back to the Greens'; she had nowhere else to go.

"The way I see it now, I'm a major breadwinner there," Fatimah told me, proudly jutting out her chin. We were walking around Times Square in the sticky summer heat, searching for some lotion; she was wearing jean shorts and wedge heels, and she worried that her calves looked ashy. "I just go there to sleep. I don't talk to anyone; I don't even eat their food. And they're getting money for me until I'm twenty-one."

Unlike Dominique, Fatimah knew that if she needed it, she'd always have a place to sleep even after her twenty-first birthday—even if she didn't particularly like it. The house on DeKalb, if not a haven, had become a reset button. It was a familiar, steady place where one could still the chaos from the outside world a bit, and then move on.

That's the way Tonya saw it too. When Tonya was released from the jail in Pennsylvania, she called the Greens.

"I only got to make one call from jail, and I got the voice mail," Tonya said. "I didn't know if they'd take me back, but I had no one else to call."

I met Tonya outside of Mercy College on 35th Street where she was taking classes; remarkably, once Tonya had readjusted to life on DeKalb after her release, she finished up her final credits in high school and enrolled in college. The eleven universities that had accepted her the prior year (including the two that had dangled scholarships) had rescinded their offers when she didn't complete high school on time. So Tonya was restricted to a more local, and less prestigious, school.

Like Fatimah, Tonya now viewed the Greens' place as somewhere to rest her head; she said she went there now only to study and to sleep, and she planned to get out as soon as she could. She was waiting for her agency to set her up with Section 8 housing.

"I'll be like my mom," she told me, her eyes sparkling. "My mom's lived in the Bronx for twenty, thirty years and she only pays $150 a month for a two-bedroom; welfare pays the rest. The same thing will happen to me because I'm a foster kid and I'm at the top of the waiting list."

Tonya said she was thankful she was never granted the free SILP apartment that she had once wanted so desperately. In retrospect, she felt such freedom would have provided her with even more poor choices than those she made from the Greens'. "I'm glad I didn't go to SILP because that totally messed Chanel up," Tonya said. "She's twenty-one and she doesn't have a high school diploma. She doesn't have a job. She doesn't have nothing."

I talked with Chanel on the phone early in 2010; she was living in a studio apartment in Red Hook, Brooklyn, and working full-time stocking clothes in the basement of an H&M. She said she moved out of SILP because the place was too hectic; her roommates were always partying and bringing in strangers. She felt safer on her own without any agency supervision. As for the Greens, Chanel would only say, "I don't talk to them anymore." We made a few plans to meet up, but one time she was too hung-over, and once she simply didn't show. Eventually, she stopped returning my calls.

Tonya held up her right hand to show me the chipped nail on her forefinger. "That's from me slamming Chanel's head to the wall," Tonya said, grinning. Apparently, Chanel had been coming by the Greens' every now and then, when she got lonely at her studio apartment. And, according to Tonya, she was "borrowing" clothes. So Tonya beat her up.

I was startled; I remembered Tonya talking about her addiction to fighting, and about how she never felt remorse. But she and Chanel had been so close; her Facebook page was crammed with pictures of the two of them at parties, riding in cars, hamming it up in front of the bathroom mirror.

Not anymore, Tonya said. She hated Chanel. She hated Fatimah too. The sisters may have been floating back into each other's physical orbit, but they were intentionally spinning out of sync. Four thousand square feet wasn't enough space to absorb all the resentment and rage; they looked at one another and saw themselves. The reflection that was once a comfort was now too predictive and frightening.

"Fatimah's not in college," Tonya said with disdain. "She's nineteen and she didn't even finish high school."

She and Fatimah had gotten into an argument some months back, Tonya said, about a lie and a boy, and they hadn't spoken since. Tonya didn't care about Fatimah anymore, and that was it. We had left the college and were strolling around Times Square at night, where Fatimah also liked to hang out. Tonya's bravado seemed thin to me, so I asked her what, if anything, she was afraid of.

"That I'll backslide," she answered, her silver eye shadow glittering from the bright lights overhead. Tourists with backpacks and cameras shoved past us but Tonya stood still. "That I'll stop doing what I have to do. That I'll just decide one day to stop going to school."

Fatimah planned to go back to school, but like Tonya and Chanel and even Dominique, she had downsized her dreams. Part of this was the slow creep of realism that came with growing up, but depression played a role too. Fatimah acknowledged that living with the Greens made returning to school seem more attainable, but living there was also hard: the place represented so many hopes gone wrong. Fatimah had given up on writing her book. She had also decided to abandon the idea of journalism, and her magazine about families all over the world.

"I used to want to be a journalist, but why, what's the point? What's the point now of anything? I just want to get out of here," Fatimah said, gesturing around at the rush-hour taxis and crowded sidewalk. "Maybe I'll move to Philly. Besides, why do something where I can leave my mark on the world? That used to be important to me. But now, if I can just get some kind of job, take care of me, take care of my kid, then die, that's enough."

Only Tonya, who had had her college circumscribed but not her vision, held tight to her original plan of becoming a psychiatrist. But there was a parallel reality living alongside the girl with the Dora the Explorer pillows and the college schedule and the house she could live in even past her graduation from foster care. There was still a girl who lived online, who went by the name of "Chocolate Princess." This Tonya was tough: she posted clip after clip of people beating each other up at parties and in parks, followed by her own LMAOs and biting remarks. I asked Tonya if she'd ever go back to jail, and she wouldn't meet my eyes. "Not right away," she said. "Who knows what the future holds?"

15

Last Call

O NLY DOMINIQUE, THE GREEN girl who had stayed the shortest and severed her ties most acutely, couldn't go back. Dominique believed her biological mother was dead, she had crossed adoption off her list of goals, and she had turned twenty years old in 2010. Dominique had one year left of free meals, a weekly allowance, and a social worker to call upon before she would be set free to her dreams of a Connecticut wedding on the beach with no husband. She had her part-time job at the Walk Shop, which would never cover rent and living expenses in New York City, and she had a few very good friends — mostly kids like her, in similar predicaments. That summer, Dominique had added a new tattoo to her wrist, opposite the butterfly. It read, simply, "Have faith."

I was waiting for Dominique at an iHop in Queens when I heard the sirens. We had planned to have a late breakfast on a hot summer day; Dominique had been craving pancakes. She was still living with the elderly foster mom, and her house was on the last stop on the F line, where apartment buildings give way to single-family homes. The iHop is on a busy boulevard across the street from Trinidad Rotis and Disha Fashion, where you can buy saris and bridal *lenghas*, but inside the pancake chain where Dominique kept me waiting, I could have been in Detroit or Oakland or any city anywhere. All iHops look the same.

Some of the diners had rushed out the front door when the sirens got louder, and since Dominique still hadn't shown up, I followed them outside. A crowd had gathered in the middle of Hillside Avenue, where a silver Toyota was angled in the wrong direction. A woman was lying still in the street, and paramedics were pushing people aside to get to her. A brown moccasin was flung about a hundred feet away. I recognized that moccasin.

"Dominique!?" I shouted, as the paramedics strapped her to the orange board destined for the ambulance. She moaned; she was conscious. I didn't see any blood, but as the medics lifted her carefully aboard, she mumbled about the pain in her arm.

Apparently, the driver of the Toyota had made an illegal left turn across a double yellow line, when she hit Dominique crossing the street. A few pedestrians had seen the accident and were eagerly explaining the details to a cop, who was also trying to extract Dominique's age and address from her at the back of the ambulance. Dominique could only whisper, and her voice was muffled by an oxygen mask. She reached for my hand with her good arm, the one with the faith tattoo.

"I got hit from the side, my hip," she mumbled, the clear plastic mask fogging up with her breath. I squatted next to her and repeated her words for the cop. "I fell against the car, then on the ground, on my arm. My arm really hurts."

Nobody asked who I was, but the medics assumed I was along for the ride, as one gently pressed me back into a seat in the ambulance and snapped a seat belt across my chest. The doors slammed shut and the sirens were surprisingly quiet from inside the cabin. I smiled at Dominique, who suddenly let out a loud scream and yanked the oxygen mask from her face. She saw the scissors before I did.

"We have to do this, ma'am," the paramedic said, calmly snipping the seam to Dominique's jean shorts. "We're just looking to see if you're hurt."

If Dominique hadn't been strapped down, she would have jumped right off the gurney. Another medic had replaced the mask to cover her mouth and nose, but Dominique's eyes were bulging and wild.

"It's OK, they're not going to hurt you," I murmured, squeezing her hand as Dominique thrashed back and forth.

The medic with the scissors told her to stay calm as he sliced her T-shirt and cut through the center of her bra. My fingers buckled in Dominique's panicked grip, but she was quiet as both men palpated her belly, listened to her heart, and checked her skin for abrasions. "That was a $40 bra," she finally whispered when it was over.

I had scooped up Dominique's cell phone, which had also been thrown to the far side of the street. After Dominique had been rushed through the back of Jamaica Hospital, I flipped through her contact list to call her foster mom.

I reached her on the third ring and told her, as evenly as I could and with a preface that Dominique was basically fine, that there had been an accident. Dominique had been hit by a car.

"Call the agency! Call the agency!" shouted the woman at the other end. This was not the answer I expected, so I explained the incident more thoroughly. I said the car had been going slowly, Dominique was conscious, and so on.

"Call the agency!"

"OK," I answered. "But she'll need someone here with her. They cut her clothes and — "

"I can't come there!" the foster mom interrupted. "I'm in Manhattan. Call the agency."

My stomach knotted and dropped as the subtext of her words hit me full on. She didn't care to know what had happened to Dominique. She just wanted to pass on the responsibility.

I spoke slowly, realizing I was going to have to start issuing commands. "We're at the emergency room of Jamaica Hospital in Queens. Dominique is going to need some clothes to leave here, so — "

Again, the woman interrupted. "I'm all the way in Manhattan. Call the agency. They should have some clothes."

I said I would give her my number so she could call to find out how Dominique was.

"I don't have anything to write it down with. Call the agency." And she hung up.

Sadness folded through my body and I slumped in my chair alongside all the other tired people in the waiting room. After Dominique's fifteen-year tenure in foster care, this is what it could offer her: a final stop with a "grandmotherly type" who wouldn't come to the hospital.

I called her caseworker. I'd called her before, several times actually, whenever Dominique had fallen off my radar or changed her phone number or lost her phone (which was fairly often), to find out where Dominique was living and how she was faring. I had gotten only the caseworker's voice mail, and she had never once returned my calls. This time, though, perhaps because there had been an accident, she called back in ten minutes.

But the caseworker couldn't come to the hospital either; she was working in Harlem and she didn't have time. She'd send a colleague who was in the neighborhood and who could bring Dominique some clothes. I knew Dominique wouldn't be happy in a gown that flapped open in the back, and the caseworker agreed; her colleague could arrive in ten minutes.

I waited four hours. I couldn't in good conscience leave Dominique alone, sad and scared in the ambulance drop-off area, where she lay sequestered in a bed next to eight other patients, one of whom was visibly pregnant with bandages wrapped around both wrists. It was crowded and chaotic in that room, with patients groaning in pain or yelling for water; every time I tried to get information about Dominique's case, someone in scrubs would tell me he wasn't her doctor and no, he didn't know who was. All Dominique and I could gather was the obvious physical evidence: she had been x-rayed and catheterized, and she had an IV dripping fluids into her arm. We figured nothing was broken or she would have been set up with a cast by now, but we couldn't tell for sure.

"Oh, her?" said a doctor, when I had finally commandeered some attention from an exhausted-looking man at a computer terminal. "She's been admitted. We're just waiting for a room to open up."

Dominique wasn't having it; she tried to yank the IV from her arm as soon as I brokered the news. "I'm signing myself out!" she shouted. "They can't make me stay!"

A nurse shuffled up to her bed and explained that Dominique couldn't leave. She'd had a head trauma and needed to be monitored for the night. Then he walked away.

"I hate hospitals," Dominique moaned. "The last time I was in one, they said I attacked the doctor! I didn't attack the doctor! I just can't be having people examining me."

I asked her if it would be possible to sleep over if she had someone stay with her, to make her feel safer. Even as I said it, though, I felt the falseness of my words: Dominique didn't have anybody like that in her life.

"I don't like people to pity me," she said, her voice now small and miserable. She agreed at least to wait until she could talk to her doctor, whoever he was, to determine the risks in leaving. I wondered where the agency social worker was, and why I was doing her job. And despite Dominique's wishes to avoid "pity," I went outside to make a phone call. To Fatimah.

"Oh my God, oh my God, is she OK?" Fatimah gasped when I told her where we were. Even though they didn't see each other so much anymore, Fatimah still considered Dominique her sister. They had lived together at the Greens' for seven months, but more than that, they shared a kind of unspoken understanding about growing yourself up in the free fall of foster care.

"She's fine," I said. "But can you come to Jamaica Hospital? I'm with her now, but I don't know if anyone from the agency is going to show up. And she needs clothes, and she doesn't want to stay the night; maybe you could talk to her?"

And there was the irony: with all of the people paid to care for Dominique, hired expressly to provide her clothing and family and tools to navigate bureaucracies like hospitals, I was reduced to calling another foster kid for help.

"Of course!" Fatimah gushed. She said she'd be right there. But Dominique was a lot bigger than she was; maybe she could buy something for her on the way. Fatimah had a job at a high school cafeteria;

she wasn't enrolled in classes, but she had a paycheck, and she could buy Dominique some clothes.

And then, finally, the social worker showed. Without any clothes.

"Did you call her foster mom? Can't she bring them?" the social worker asked me, patting down her hair. She couldn't explain why it had taken her four hours to arrive at the hospital, but she wanted to know if I could drive Dominique home.

"I don't have a car," I said. "I came in the ambulance." I explained that Dominique wanted to sign herself out, and that the social worker would need to locate the doctor, as I hadn't yet found him.

But the social worker, who was probably just a few years older than Dominique, was entirely focused on transportation. "Where's your car then?" she asked.

I ignored her. I tried to get her to follow me past all the rushing nurses and people on cell phones and into the room where Dominique was waiting.

"I prefer to do things professional," she said, glancing around at the patients on gurneys lined against the walls. "I'll wait in the waiting room until a doctor calls me."

I stared at her. We were in Jamaica Hospital, famous for its overcrowding; the emergency room was built to hold sixty thousand patients a year, but it had admitted more than double that the year before. No doctor was going to call her.

"Couldn't you stay and sign the release papers?" the social worker asked when I explained again that Dominique would need help getting someone to pay attention to her in the chaos of the emergency patient room. "I can't sign anything for her."

I spoke as if the social worker were a very young child: "Dominique is an adult," I said. "She can sign her own name. She needs someone to advocate for her, because she is hooked up to an IV, in bed. Advocacy is your job."

The social worker looked bewildered, but when I said I had to leave, she followed me when I went to say goodbye to Dominique. I found her sitting up in bed, texting messages into her phone.

"I'm leaving," Dominique said happily, as I leaned down to give her a hug, gingerly avoiding the IV drip. "I already posted it to Facebook. And they're gonna give me some scrubs to leave in."

The social worker waved to Dominique from a few yards away and then trotted off to wait in the waiting room, presumably for someone to call her name. I felt bad going, but I had to teach a class, and anyway, an hour later, when I logged on to my computer, Dominique was back on Facebook, saying she was home and mad as hell. Did anyone know a lawyer? She was going to sue that lady in the Toyota.

Epilogue

OVER THE SEVERAL YEARS I spent writing this book, a few lines
from a few people kept rising above all the noise of research and interviews to guide my thinking and final theories. One was Kecia's "You
gotta rock with a kid, all the way," as that simple dictum consistently
proved key to a foster child's ultimate internal survival. Kids who had
someone who would "just stay," whether they be biological parents
who had support shored up beneath them or foster or adoptive parents who would go the distance, fared the best. If Kecia's prescription
were the central goal in child welfare policy — rather than, say, child
safety or parental reunification — I think we'd start shifting toward a
healthier system in general.

The other line came from Doreen. She was discussing her daughter, but it could be (and has been) applied to extended families, the
child welfare system, civil rights, and civil wars — anything where human beings trot out their personal traumas and try to make change.
Doreen said, "History keeps playing itself." Over the five years of this
book, kids replayed their parents' patterns; agencies repeated their
mistakes of the past. We do what we know, usually, not what we think,
and we're all, as Arelis once put it, "the self-destruct buttons of ourselves."

Lei, the foster kid who aged out of care into college and then went
to teach in Taiwan, also repeated a part of her history, by returning to
New York to work in child welfare. I met with her this past summer,
my very last interview, behind the 42nd Street library. It was the day
of the National Puerto Rican parade, and all around us families waved

flags, slurped up flavored ices, or leaned against one another on the library steps.

"In my own foster care experience, I had so many different workers, because the turnover rate is so high, but now that I'm in the field I know why: the low pay, the high stress. Over time, you get burned out, and you feel really disappointed," Lei said about her new perspective as a giver rather than receiver. She looked different from four years prior: her hair was cut in a shaggy bob, and her face had softened. Gone was the "mmm-hmmm" tic that punctuated the end of most of her sentences, and she seemed tired — probably because she was working full-time in preventive services for an agency that contracted with ACS and going to graduate school on the weekends. She earned $41,000 to case-manage thirteen high-risk families, and she was "disappointed" because she had to spend more time writing reports than meeting with her clients, and, she said, she had to "conform" to the bureaucracy around her. "There's a timeline for every case we have, and a number of contacts we have to make per week. The statistics are all about money — so you know a family needs more help but you have to close the case because you've met the expectations."

Still, preventive services, I think, are the hopeful future of child welfare, especially as states shift toward the Florida-esque waiver options. In 2011, President Obama signed an act that allowed all states to apply for flat-sum waivers from the government. With flat sums, kids don't have to be in foster homes to garner income for the agencies, so money is generally spent on preventive services to avoid the more costly removals. And agencies can spend waiver money as they choose (as opposed to the per diem pay structure where they have to justify each move with time-consuming paperwork), so ideally, people like Lei will be able to spend the time they should on the needier cases.

By the end of 2012, nine states had been approved for waivers, though more could still sign up. In New York City, ACS is currently piloting a foster care program with five of its agencies, wherein they're allocating more money to hire more workers to provide deeper, more meaningful foster parent support and to make sure their kids are out of care within the ASFA timeline. They're "front-loading the system," as Francine Cournos would say. And if it works, Commissioner Richter told me, it would be like operating under a waiver system — wherein the pilot program has the freedom to allocate funding up front where the kids need it, and before they've tumbled down a roster of more restrictive and expensive placements. In fact, he told me he'd like to use the experience with the five agencies and expand it to the entire foster care system in New York — by applying for a waiver for the whole city. Later, the state did apply for the waiver and is now awaiting federal review; this is undoubtedly a positive trajectory.

Lei said she didn't know that ACS had merged with juvenile justice, even though the merger happened long before we spoke. Mostly, she spent her days battling bureaucrats who did the same old things in the same old ways: "history playing itself." So Lei worked extra hours for the families she cared about. In one of her recent cases, a teenage boy hadn't attended school for three years; he was physically too large for the frustrated mom to force anywhere. Lei called the police, hospitals, the courts, the Board of Education, even her congresspeople, and everybody told her the boy didn't fall under their jurisdiction; he hadn't committed a crime. Eventually, after nearly a hundred phone calls, Lei forced a residential school to accept him, the Board of Education to foot the bill, and ACS to pick him up and deliver him to the locked campus.

I don't know if that boy will feel abandoned, as Kecia did, to a residential school, or if he'll feel that someone rocked with him all the way to an education; perhaps, right now, this is the best we can do. I do know that mother needed outside help, and she got it from an agency that contracted with ACS. Persuading families to trust child welfare will take tremendous effort, and perhaps several more generations. Lei lamented the grim reputation ACS still held with most of her clients.

"When an ACS worker investigates a case, they knock on the door like they're the real police, and that's still a big problem for a lot of my clients. The agency is always talking about cultural competence, but how dare you go into a home, check this, check that, when all sorts of families — Indian, Chinese — are not very open, not very American in that way," Lei said. She waved her hands up toward the fancier apartments surrounding the library. "I say this because ACS rarely investigates the upper class. They know those people have lawyers."

Still, I think there's some hope on this front too, as in the past few years, groups like the Child Welfare Organizing Project in New York have changed the very business of child removals, making sure biological parents are involved in deciding where their kids go, and that they have more peer support as they work with the system rather than against it. There's more room for allegiance and trust, but any partnership is promising.

And everywhere, the foster care numbers are down, which means everywhere, more kids are staying home to begin with. When I started this book five years ago, there were 488,285 children in care nationwide; when I was done, there were 400,540. All the problems — the racial disparity, the institutionalizations, the aging out into nothingness — are ongoing and likely will be for decades, if history keeps playing. And the poverty aspect of foster care is particularly troubling, as the one shining truth in my research was this: the poorer you are, the more likely you are to get entangled with child welfare. Between 2000 and 2008, the number of children living in poverty in America increased by 2.5 million, or 21 percent. And that was before the recession. In New York City, more than a quarter of all kids lived at or below the poverty line in 2008.

So that's the bad news. Poverty is everywhere. And we have a broken system, made by fallible people with fallible families (stare at my tree; stare at yours). As Arelis said, we may have better and more creative ways to shove the puzzle pieces together, but the game was shattered so long ago, it's never going to integrate perfectly. There are fault lines; tap them and they'll break again.

And still. Poverty is a wide, wide road with many on-ramps for improvement. That's where I feel some courage and optimism for child welfare — because we don't have to fix the system directly to make things better for our kids. Work on one small aspect and we'll be working on the whole. Better school lunches, better libraries, after-school care, neighborhood resources — anything that touches social reform touches foster care too.

I wrote this book to be more descriptive than prescriptive, placing

the *why* above the *what next*. There are countless academics and or-
ganizers and families with countless good ideas. Even politicians are
getting in on it; in 2012, Congress launched its first-ever "listening
tour" for its Congressional Caucus on Foster Youth, and listening is a
good place to start. As for Lei, though, she's getting out. She'll stay in
her job as long as it takes to get her master's degree in social work, and
then she'll move on to higher ground — maybe, she thinks, doing policy for the UN. "This is my steppingstone; I need some 'staybility,'" she
told me, and she pronounced it that way — *stay-bility*. She watched
her case-managing peers, and she saw a depressing trajectory. "People
who have been in social work for a long time, they lose their passion.
I mean, where's their empathy? I don't want to lose my faith in humanity."

Still, if I believe that everything around us touches child welfare —
and I do — then Lei's future work, whatever it is, will ripple out. Looking around at all the families clutching their Puerto Rican flags and
heading home, Lei said, "I want to get old and say to myself, 'You have
treated people well. That's all.'"

Notes

Preface

page

xi *daughter, Alicia:* Name has been changed.

more than 400,000 kids: When I began reporting for this book (September 2007), there were 488,285 children in care nationwide; by September 2011, there were 400,540. *The AFCARS Report,* No. 19 (Washington, DC: U.S. Department of Health and Human Services, Administration for Children and Families, Administration on Children, Youth and Families, Children's Bureau, estimates as of July 2012). http://www.acf.hhs.gov/pro grams/cb/resource/afcars-report-19.

veterans of war: Based on a study of 659 former foster kids conducted by Harvard Medical School, reported in an article by Dave Reynolds, "Foster Kids Experience Far More Trouble as Adults, Study Shows," *The New Standard,* April 8, 2005. http://newstandardnews.net/content/index.cfm /items/1655.

than they are at home: The Center for the Support of Families, a consulting firm for social service agencies, released a study indicating that 12 percent of the children in Oklahoma's Department of Human Services had substantiated cases of maltreatment while in care, based on a statistically representative sample. *Foster Care Case Review of the Oklahoma Department of Human Services* (Silver Spring, MD: Center for the Support of Families, Inc., February 17, 2011). An Indiana study showed that children in group homes experienced ten times the rate of physical abuse and twenty-eight times the rate of sexual abuse of kids in the general population. A study of kids in Oregon and Washington State foster homes showed one-third being abused by an adult in the home. Both studies were reported in an issue paper entitled "Foster Care vs. Family Preservation: The Track Record on Safety and Well-Being" (Alexandria, VA: National Coalition for Child Protection Reform, updated January 3, 2011). http://www.nccpr.org/reports/01SAFETY.pdf.

xii *two years on average nationwide:* The average length of stay in foster care for children in the United States is 25.3 months, as of September 30, 2010, according to *The AFCARS Report, No. 18* (Washington, DC: U.S. Department of Health and Human Services, Administration for Children and Families, Administration on Children, Youth and Families, Children's Bu-

reau, June 2011). http://www.acf.hhs.gov/programs/cb/resource/afcars-re
port-18.

three years in New York: The average length of stay for foster children in
New York as of 2008 was 36.7 months. Reported in "Child Welfare in New
York" (Washington, DC: Children's Defense Fund, January 2010), citing
data from U.S. Congress, House of Representatives, Committee on Ways
and Means, *Background Materials and Data on the Programs Within the
Jurisdiction of the Committee on Ways and Means* (2008), Tables 11–62
and 11–72, calculations by CDF. http://www.childrensdefense.org/child-re-
search-data-publications/data/state-data-repository/cwf/2010/child-wel-
fare-financing-new-york-2010.pdf.

$15 to $20 billion a year: The actual figure is difficult to calculate, as child
welfare is funded through a combination of federal, state, and local sources.
In 2005, the Urban Institute completed the fifth in a series called *The Cost
of Protecting Valuable Children: Understanding State Variation in Child
Welfare Financing,* by Cynthia Andrews Scarcella, Roseana Bess, Erica
Hecht Zielewski, and Rob Geen (May 2006), available at http://www.ur-
ban.org/UploadedPDF/311314_vulnerable_children.pdf. Based on an
analysis of forty-seven states, the authors found that, in 2004, states spent
$23.3 billion in federal, state, and local money on foster care. Although this
was the last study of its kind, and foster care enrollment figures have gone
down overall since 2004, this same study claimed that federal spending
accounted for 49 percent of total foster care spending, state spending for
39 percent, and local spending for 12 percent, and these percentages have
likely remained relatively stable. The budget estimate for the lion's share of
the federal portion of foster care funding (the federal government also provides capped grants and other monies) for 2012 was $7,256,000,000, ac-
cording to the Fiscal Year 2012 Budget for the U.S. Government's Department of Health and Human Services, page 91, available at https://www.acf
.hhs.gov/sites/default/files/olab/fy_2012_bibpdf.pdf. We can assume that
the total figure for 2012 is somewhere between $15 billion and upwards of
$20 billion.

xiv *upwards of $100 billion:* Ching-Tung Wang, PhD, and John Holton, PhD,
Total Estimated Cost of Child Abuse and Neglect in the United States, an
Economic Impact Study published by Prevent Child Abuse America, and
Time for Reform: Investing in Prevention, Keeping Children Safe at Home,
by Kids Are Waiting (KAW), a project of the Pew Charitable Trusts, in September 2007 found that, in 2007, the costs associated with child abuse
and neglect were $103.8 billion. The study is available on the Pew Char-
itable Trusts website at http://www.pewtrusts.org/news_room_detail.
aspx?id=34676.

xv *I said to Frankie:* Name has been changed.

xvi *serious emotional problems:* From the "Facts About Foster Care" page of
the watchdog and advocacy organization Children's Rights, based in New
York City, citing the American Academy of Pediatrics' "Testimony of Lau-
rel K. Leslie, MD, MPH, FAAP, House Ways and Means Subcommittee on
Income Security and Family Support Hearing on the Utilization of Psycho-

tropic Medication for Children in Foster Care," May 8, 2008. http://www
.childrensrights.org/issues-resources/foster-care/facts-about-foster-care/.
by their twenty-first birthdays: Twenty-two percent of foster care alumni
are homeless for a day or more after exiting foster care, compared to 2.6
to 6.8 percent of eighteen- to twenty-four-year-olds in the general population in any given year. Casey Family Programs fact sheet "Foster Care by the
Numbers." http://www.casey.org/Newsroom/MediaKit/pdf/FosterCareBy-
TheNumbers.pdf.
No state met more than two of the seven criteria: Robert Pear, "U.S. Finds
Fault in All 50 States' Child Welfare Programs, and Penalties May Follow,"
The New York Times, April 26, 2004.

1. King Solomon's Baby

4 *so they can share:* Kings 3:16–28, New International Version.
6 *without a warrant:* Technically, in New York, parents have the right to re-
fuse entry to ACS investigators, though it's not always in their best interests to do so. According to the Child Welfare Organizing Project (CWOP),
ACS could decide to file a neglect or abuse case in family court, or request
a warrant for the parents to come to court. They could also simply return
with the police, who can enter the home without permission or court order.
Child Welfare Organizing Project, *The Survival Guide to the NYC Child
Welfare System: A Workbook for Parents by Parents,* http://www.cwop.org/
documents/survivalguide2007english.pdf; and Mike Arsham, executive director of the Child Welfare Organizing Project, e-mail correspondence, July
2012.
this law is often ignored: Arsham, e-mail correspondence, July 2012.
even if they're related: Data on state licensure requirements is compiled by
the National Resource Center for Family-Centered Practice and Permanency Planning at the Hunter College School of Social Work. http://www
.hunter.cuny.edu/socwork/nrcfcpp/downloads/Foster_Home_Licensing
.pdf.
one of the roughly thirty foster care agencies: As of early 2012, ACS had
contracts with thirty-two foster care agencies. A list of current agencies can
be found on the ACS website: http://www.nyc.gov/html/acs/html/home/
home.shtml.
9 *That was Russell:* Name has been changed.
11 *fifty family court cases every day:* According to a spokesperson from the
Citizens' Committee for Children of New York, 64,035 petitions were filed
in family court in 2008. There are forty-seven judges to hear all of these
cases, meaning that each judge hears about fifty-one cases per day. A lawyer
with ACS, who spoke with me on the condition of anonymity, said that in
her experience, judges heard this many cases daily.
to live in ten or twenty different houses: Reducing the number of placements is a clear goal in child welfare, and thankfully, as kids spend less
time in care we may start seeing a shift in the number of moves these kids
make. In New York in 2010, 56 percent of the kids who had been in care for

twenty-four months or longer had experienced three or more placements —
a 3 percent drop from 2007. From "Child Welfare Outcomes Report Data,"
2010, a report that is published annually by the U.S. Department of Health
and Human Services to meet the requirements of section 203(a) of the
Adoption and Safe Families Act of 1997 (ASFA). http://cwoutcomes.acf.
hhs.gov/data/tables/six_one_more_than_24?years[]=2007&years[]=
2008&years[]=2009&years[]=2010&viz=table&states[]=33&state=&
region=.

17 *Oliver's mom, Caitlin:* Caitlin's name, as well as the names of her boyfriend
and his family members, has been changed.

2. *Eye of the Beholder*

18 *three-quarters of the maltreatment cases in this country:* The U.S. Department of Health and Human Services, Administration for Children and
Families, Administration on Children, Youth and Families, Children's Bureau, "Child Maltreatment 2010," reported that there were 695,000 kids
who experienced substantiated abuse or neglect in fiscal year 2010. Of
these, 78.3 percent suffered neglect; 17.6 percent suffered physical abuse;
9.2 percent suffered sexual abuse. http://www.acf.hhs.gov/programs/cb/
pubs/cm10/cm10.pdf#page=9.

Still, one-third of New York's foster children have spent three years or
more in foster care, according to *The Long Road/One Year Home Symposium:
Proceedings* (New York: Children's Rights, November 2011), and in 2006,
ABC Primetime published a brief wherein they claimed, "It is not uncommon to hear of children who have been in 20 or 30 different homes." "Facts
on Foster Care in America," *ABC Primetime,* May 30, 2006. http://abcnews
.go.com/Primetime/FosterCare/story?id=2017991&page=1#.T_2iuGjD
Pww.

19 *with this as its minimum definition:* The child abuse and neglect definition was obtained from the "Definitions of Child Abuse and Neglect State
Statutes Series," Child Welfare Information Gateway, 2007. http://www.
childwelfare.gov/systemwide/laws_policies/statutes/define.cfm.

20 *assistant attorney-in-charge of the Juvenile Rights Practice:* When I met
him, Rudy Estrada was the LGBTQ coordinator at New York's ACS, creating training models for working with queer kids, recruiting foster and
adoptive parents for them, and developing policies to protect them from
further discrimination. Before this job, he was actually suing ACS and state
welfare administrations like it, in his job as a staff attorney for Lambda Legal's Foster Care Project in Chicago.

22 *The agency had also hired more detectives and consultants:* Ronald Richter,
personal interview, June 14, 2012.
*benchmark figures for children's adoptions and reunifications with biologi-
cal parents have gone up:* A lawsuit was filed in 1989 (*LaShawn v. A. Gray,*
C.A. No. 89–1754, U.S. District Court for the District of Columbia) against
DC's child welfare, seeking whole-scale reform. The case was appealed, but

in 1993, a modified eighty-four-page final order was handed down, which mandated, among many other things, that all persons hired as social workers must have a master's degree in social work. See *LaShawn A. v. Dixon, Modified Final Order* (November 18, 1993), 47, retrieved from http://www. childrensrights.org. The system was reorganized as a Cabinet-level agency within the District government, and there were many internal changes, so it's difficult to tell what influenced what precisely, but still, according to a major independent audit conducted in 2009, benchmark figures were still not as high as expected. See *An Assessment of the District of Columbia's Child Welfare System (as of January 31, 2009)* (Washington, DC: Center for the Study of Social Policy, April 30, 2009). Also, according to Richard Barth, PhD, professor and dean of the School of Social Work at the University of Maryland in Baltimore, there are many other counties that require a master's degree in social work — as well as more than twenty states where the MSWs getting trained spend two years specifically learning about child welfare work.

23 *"causeth contempt and irreverence":* Stephen O'Connor, *Orphan Trains: The Story of Charles Loring Brace and the Children He Saved and Failed* (New York: Houghton Mifflin Company, 2001), 10.

indentured servants to richer families: Local governments removed children via "poor laws" based on a British system of the same name. Jillian Jimenez, "The History of Child Protection in the African American Community: Implications for Current Child Welfare Practices," *Children and Youth Services Review* 28, no. 8 (August 2006): 888–905.

almshouses or even jails: See Mimi Abramowitz, *Regulating the Lives of Women: Social Welfare Policy from Colonial Times to the Present* (Boston: South End Press, 1988), chapter 5. This was happening particularly in New York, according to O'Connor, *Orphan Trains*, 37.

"quite untaught": O'Connor, *Orphan Trains*, 103.

religious example for the world: For a more thorough discussion of this idea, see chapter 1 in Elizabeth Pleck's *Domestic Tyranny: The Making of American Social Policy Against Family Violence from Colonial Times to the Present* (New York: Oxford University Press, 1987).

24 *the girl's* foster *mother:* "The Catalyst: 1870–1874," on the New York Society for the Prevention of Cruelty to Children website: http://www.nyspcc.org.

250 child protection associations nationwide: Nina Bernstein, *The Lost Children of Wilder: The Epic Struggle to Change Foster Care* (New York: Vintage, 2001), 8.

flogging as punishment: Pleck, *Domestic Tyranny*, 10.

hitting urban centers at the time: There had been lurid reports of violent crimes and murders in crime gazettes after 1874. Ibid., 79.

control the children of immigrants: Historian Elizabeth Pleck writes about many reasons for the rise of SPCCs. Because of all of the violence and crime reported in the papers, some people argued for drastic measures to stop the children of immigrants, primarily, from becoming criminals. Most SPCC directors didn't talk about the family directly, or even the prevention of cruelty, really, but rather a kind of faulty moral character that emerged in society too. A wealthy urban elite was fearful of the social disorder and disease and poverty they saw in the cities, and they blamed the immigrant, Catholic, and poor inhabitants. They wanted to stop the kids of these families from becoming thieves and drunks. Ibid., 70, 76, 79.

remove a child from an unsafe home: States reaffirmed an old English law, called *parens patriae*, which establishes the state as the ultimate parent for children. The law had been in use since the mid-nineteenth century, but only in cases of property inheritance. Suddenly it became a firm legal principle justifying a social worker's right to remove a child from an unsafe home — without police and without a warrant. It's still in use today. Jimenez, "The History of Child Protection in the African American Community," 892.

on the books: John E. B. Myers, "A Short History of Child Protection in America," *Family Law Quarterly* 42 (2008–9): 456.

more than a million in 1980: Ibid.

25 *two or three a month: Don't Turn Back: Reform Has Made New York's Children Safer,* an analysis of trends in New York City child welfare (Alexandria, VA: National Coalition for Child Protection Reform, released January 2006; updated, January 2009). http://www.nccpr.org/reports/dontturnback.pdf.

Her murder was nationally publicized: Elisa Izquierdo was featured on the cover of *Time* magazine; the article was David Van Biema, Sharon Epperson, and Elaine Rivera, "Elisa Izquierdo: Abandoned to Her Fate," *Time,* December 11, 1995. Her story was also featured on *Dateline* in August 1996.

"removing the child from harm's way": The Honorable Rudolph W. Giuliani, Mayor of the City of New York, and Nicholas Scoppetta, Commissioner, *Protecting the Children of New York: A Plan of Action for the Administration for Children's Services* (New York: Administration for Children's Services, December 19, 1996).

ACS removals had increased by 50 percent: Don't Turn Back: Reform Has Made New York's Children Safer.

26 *no running water:* These three examples come from Rachel L. Swarns, "In a Policy Shift, More Parents Are Arrested for Child Neglect," *The New York Times,* Section A, "Metropolitan Desk," October 25, 1997, 1.

from twenty-four in 1996 to thirty-six in 1998: Don't Turn Back: Reform Has Made New York's Children Safer.

monitored by an outside panel of experts: Marisol v. Giuliani, Settlement Agreement, United States District Court, Southern District of New York, 95 CV 10533 (RJW), December 1, 1998. http://www.childrensrights.org/wp-content/uploads/2008/06/1998-12-2_ny_marisol_city_settlement.pdf.

"yank 'em out" philosophy: Nina Bernstein, "Effort to Fix Child Welfare Draws Praise," *The New York Times,* December 8, 2000. http://www.nytimes.com/2000/12/08/nyregion/effort-to-fix-child-welfare-draws-praise.html?scp=390&sq=&st=nyt&pagewanted=1.

case could be determined in family court: Ibid.

reduce time spent in care: Ibid.

removals dropped further: Since the reforms began after the height of Foster Care Panic in 1998, reabuse — or parents reabusing their kids after being given preventive help — also fell 30 percent by 2005.

27 *eight hundred new workers were hired:* Todd Venezia and Tim Perone, "ACS at Fault in 10 Kid Deaths — Probe Bares 'Tragic' Carelessness, Pattern of 'Lying' and Covering Up," *New York Post,* August 10, 2007.

files on neglect rose by 163 percent: Sewell Chan, "Rise in Child Abuse Reports Has Family Court Reeling," *The New York Times Abstracts,* The New York Times Company, January 12, 2007.

children die from abuse or neglect every single day: The advocacy organization Children's Rights claims that four children die per day in the United States from abuse or neglect. Madelyn Freundlich, Sarah Gerstenzang, Pamela Diaz, and Erika London, *Continuing Danger: A Report on Child Fatalities in New York City* (New York: Children's Rights, February 2003). http://www.childrensrights.org/wp-content/uploads/2008/06/continuing_danger_february_2003.pdf.

convicted of murder in May 2012: Associated Press, "Mother Guilty of Murder in Death of 4-Year-Old," *The New York Times,* New York Edition, May 10, 2012.

a kernel of corn in her belly: Mirela Iverac, "Girl, 4, Had Just a Kernel of Corn in Her Stomach at Time of Death: ME," WNBC News Blog, May 3, 2012. http://www.wnyc.org/blogs/wnyc-news-blog/2012/may/03/medical-examiner-take-stand-trial-4-year-olds-death/.

"evidence of alleged systemic failures" at the agency: N. R. Kleinfield and Mosi Secret, "A Bleak Life, Cut Short at 4, Harrowing from the Start," *The New York Times,* New York Edition, May 9, 2011.

criminally negligent homicide: When this book went to press, the caseworker and supervisor were awaiting trial.

supporting the families with intensive home-based therapies: Ronald Richter spoke about this at a forum at the New School in New York City entitled "The Ties That Bind: Reimagining Juvenile Justice and Child Welfare for Teens, Families and Communities," held on February 2, 2012.

medically fragile children like Marchella: A Planning Group was formed by ACS and the public advocate in November 2010 following the death of Marchella Pierce. The Planning Group investigated the work of ACS as well as services available to medically fragile children and recommended that $11.7 million for preventive services and $2.6 million for homemaking services be fully recognized and stabilized in future budgets, to provide care for at-risk and medically fragile children. The mayor agreed that these services should be funded. From an ACS press release, "ACS and Public Advocate Bill DeBlasio Release Children's Services Group Report on Death of Marchella Pierce," March 31, 2011. Retrieved from the ACS website: http://www.nyc.gov/html/acs/html/home/home.shtml.

28 *law later that summer:* Governor Cuomo signed a bill on August 20, 2012, that would make assaulting a social worker a felony — affording caseworkers the same protection as transit workers and hotel employees. David Sims, "Cuomo Enacts Bill to Give Social-Service Assaults Felony Status,"

The Chief Leader, August 27, 2012. http://thechiefleader.com/news/news_
of_the_week/cuomo-enacts-bill-to-give-social-service-assaults-felony-sta-
tus/article_38215e34-f04f-11e1-91e6-0019bb30f31a.html.

He blamed the death on ignorance and dysfunction: See Associated Press,
"Mother Guilty of Murder in Death of 4-Year-Old"; Orin Yaniv and Rich
Schapiro, "Mother Found Guilty in Marchella Pierce's Death," *New York
Daily News,* May 9, 2012, http://www.nydailynews.com/new-york/prose-
cutor-describes-brooklyn-mom-trial-4-year-old-starvation-death-heart-
less-article-1.1075182; Jose Martinez, "Jury Finds 'Monster' Mom Guilty in
Daughter's Starving Death," *New York Post,* May 9, 2012, http://www.ny-
post.com/p/news/local/brooklyn/make_monster_mom_pay_for_daugh-
ter_BssjFrOlIF84vkWzFGRuTJ; and Mirela Iverac, "Mom Found Guilty
in Daughter's Death," WNYC News Blog, May 9, 2012, http://www.wnyc.
org/blogs/wnyc-news-blog/2012/may/09/summations-begin-trial-mom-
accused-murdering-toddler/.

29 *and 10 percent sexual abuse:* U.S. Department of Health and Human Services, Administration for Children and Families, Administration on Children, Youth and Families, Children's Bureau, "Child Maltreatment 2010."
http://archive.acf.hhs.gov/programs/cb/pubx/cm10/cm10.pdf.

leave the baby with an older sibling: The National Coalition for Child Protection Reform (NCCPR) is a good example of an organization that advocates for fewer removals and family preservation, in part because far too
many investigations and removals are based on family poverty. See the NC-
CPR issue paper 5, "Who Is in 'The System' and Why" at the NCCPR website: http://www.nccpr.org/reports/05SYSTEM.pdf.

*children do better with their (even marginal) birth parents than with foster
parents:* The most reliable data on this comes from Joseph Doyle at MIT,
who used the removal tendency of investigators as an instrumental variable
to identify causal effects of foster care placement on a range of outcomes for
school-age children and youth. Doyle looked at roughly sixty-five thousand
children between the ages of five and fifteen in the state of Illinois whose
families had been investigated for abuse. All of these children were right on
the margins of being removed — and a rotational assignment process effectively randomized their families to their investigators. Doyle's results suggest that children assigned to investigators with higher removal rates are
more likely to be placed in foster care, and they have higher delinquency
rates, teen birth rates, and lower earnings. Large marginal treatment effect estimates suggest caution in the interpretation, but the results suggest that children on the margin of placement tend to have better outcomes
when they remain at home, especially older children. Joseph J. Doyle, PhD,
"Child Protection and Child Outcomes: Measuring the Effects of Foster
Care," *American Economic Review* 97, no. 5 (December 2007): 1583–1610.

35 *This is called a "secure attachment":* This is an oversimplified description
of an enormous and dynamic theory. When young children's attachment
is disrupted, for example, they develop what's known as "avoidant attachment," "resistant attachment," or "disorganized attachment." For a good article on various attachment responses to foster care placement see Mary

Dozier, Deane Dozier, and Melissa Manni, "Attachment and Biobehavioral Catch-Up: The ABC's of Helping Infants in Foster Care Cope with Early Adversity," *Zero to Three* 22, no. 5 (April/May 2002): 7–13.

36 *scientific papers on foster care's child-parent dynamics:* Attachment theory is referenced in the abstracts of nearly a thousand articles retrieved in the Social Science Citation database of the Institute for Scientific Analysis since 1996, and 1,600 times in the American Psychological Association's PsycInfo database since 1998, according to Richard P. Barth, Thomas M. Crea, Karen John, June Thoburn, and David Quinton, "Beyond Attachment Theory and Therapy: Towards Sensitive and Evidence-Based Interventions with Foster and Adoptive Families in Distress," *Child and Family Social Work* 10, no. 4 (2005): 257–68.

37 *really rooting for the kid:* Douglas F. Goldsmith, David Oppenheim, and Janine Wanlass, "Separation and Reunification: Using Attachment Theory and Research to Inform Decisions Affecting the Placements of Children in Foster Care," *Juvenile and Family Court Journal* 55, no. 2 (Spring 2004): 1–13. Some experts, like Barbara Rittner, PhD, a dean and director of the PhD program at the University of Buffalo SUNY School of Social Work, and Rick Barth, PhD, professor and dean at the University of Maryland School of Social Work, have argued for understanding children's behavior in broader or different constructs, such as in the context of trauma or a tremendous loss of resources. See Barbara Rittner, Melissa Affronti, Rebekah Crofford, Margaret Coombes, and Marsha Schwam-Harris, "Understanding Responses to Foster Care: Theoretical Approaches," *Journal of Human Behavior in the Social Environment* 21, no. 4: 363–82; and Barth et al., "Beyond Attachment Theory and Therapy."

3. Timing Is Anything

40 *mentor the biological parents of their kids:* This program was called the Model Approach to Partnerships in Parenting, or MAPP, and it's described in Rudolph W. Giuliani, Mayor, and Nicholas Scoppetta, Commissioner, *A Renewed Plan of Action for the Administration for Children's Services* (New York: Administration for Children's Services, July 2001). http://www.nyc.gov/html/acs/downloads/pdf/pub_reform_plan_2001.pdf.

this program didn't have a lot of traction: In the 2009 Children's Rights report, *The Long Road Home*, the authors reported that, based on their research into the cases of 153 children in foster care whose permanency goals were designated as Return to Parent (RTP) or Adoption for two years or more, foster care agencies did not "regularly take steps to facilitate relationships between parents and resource [foster] parents — and that they typically had to take their own initiative to reach out to one another. Additionally, while nearly three-fourths of the caseworkers interviewed said they had received training on how to facilitate these relationships, 27 percent had not received any such training. Contacts between parents and resource parents were rarely documented in the case files of the children in the study sample, and little documentation existed regarding the nature of the relationships between the two." *The Long Road Home: A Study of Children Stranded in New York City Foster Care* (New York: Children's Rights, November 2009), 8.

43 *number of adoptions from foster care growing from 25,693 in 1995 to 52,468 in 2004:* Richard P. Barth, "Adoption from Foster Care: A Chronicle of the Years After ASFA," in *Intentions and Results: A Look Back at the Adoption and Safe Families Act,* a paper series produced by the Center for the Study of Social Policy and the Urban Institute (December 9, 2009), 65. http://www.urban.org/url.cfm?ID=1001351.
but only fifty thousand adoptions: Ibid.
will be adopted eventually: Ibid.

44 *reportedly affected by substance abuse:* Nancy Young and Sid Gardener, "ASFA Twelve Years Later: The Issue of Substance Abuse," in *Intentions and Results: A Look Back at the Adoption and Safe Families Act,* a paper series produced by the Center for the Study of Social Policy and the Urban Institute (December 9, 2009), 94. http://www.urban.org/url.cfm?ID=1001351.
documented substance abuse among investigated parents: This comes from a study based on the National Survey of Child and Adolescent Well-Being (NASCAW) cited in Young and Gardener, "ASFA Twelve Years Later."
asking instead for more research: Ibid.
meant to accomplish from the start: Dorothy Roberts, *Shattered Bonds: The Color of Child Welfare* (New York: Basic Civitas Books, 2002), 111.

45 *preventive and family reunification programs:* New York State passed its own law, analogous to AACWA, called the New York State Child Welfare Reform Act of 1979. According to Mike Arsham, executive director of the Child Welfare Organizing Project (CWOP) in New York, New York once led the nation — but even by 1980, funding for foster care continued to outpace funding for prevention by about a ten-to-one ratio (Arsham, e-mail correspondence, June 2012).
build their skills and their bonds: Elizabeth Bartholet, *Nobody's Children: Abuse and Neglect, Foster Drift and the Adoption Alternative* (Boston: Beacon Press, 1999), 42.
the number of New York's foster children almost doubled: Douglas J. Besharov, "Crack Children in Foster Care: Re-examining the Balance Between Children's Rights and Parent's Rights," *Children Today* 19, no. 4 (July/August 1990): 51, citing *Children of Substance Abusing/Alcoholic Parents Referred to the Public Child Welfare System: Summaries of Key Statistical Data Obtained from States,* final report submitted to the American Enterprise Institute (Washington, DC: American Public Welfare Association, February 1990).

46 *annually to fifty-four thousand within five years:* Roberts, *Shattered Bonds,* 105.
$6,000 for each "special needs" adoption: Ibid., 110.
agencies that successfully reunify families: For instance, see Lynne Miller, "'You Have to Get It Together': ASFA's Impact on Parents and Families," in

Intentions and Results: A Look Back at the Adoption and Safe Families Act, a paper series produced by the Center for the Study of Social Policy and the Urban Institute (December 9, 2009).

providing further motivation for parental progress: Variations of this idea have been presented many times, notably by Richard Wexler, author of *Wounded Innocents: The Real Victims of the War Against Child Abuse* (Amherst, NY: Prometheus Books, 1995), 263.

Shirley Wilder case in New York: A famous, and sadly typical, case of the time was that of Shirley Wilder, an eleven-year-old African American child in New York City in 1971. Because of inadequate housing options for black children (because the agencies that contracted with the state were religious and not public, they were exempt from antidiscrimination laws and could choose, for instance, to serve only Catholic or Jewish children), she was placed in a turn-of-the-century detention center in the South Bronx. When it rained, the kids had to wade through several inches of dirty water to get their meals. At this home, Shirley was sexually assaulted by the older girls, and she ran away. When the authorities caught her, she was considered harder to place because of her wariness and tendency to run, and while they waited for a suitable home to open up, they placed her in a boys' jail, because they had nowhere else to put her. By the end of her tenure in foster care, Shirley was pregnant and her baby was put into foster care at birth. This story comes from Nina Bernstein, *The Lost Children of Wilder: The Epic Struggle to Change Foster Care* (New York: Vintage, 2001).

Wilder's case was famous because the lawyer, Marcia Lowry, filed a class-action suit on her behalf in 1973. She claimed that the public oversight of religious foster care services was a constitutional violation of the First Amendment, and since these charities discriminated based on religion and race, they also violated the Fourteenth Amendment. Lowry finally demanded that the city stop placing children in "injuriously inadequate programs" (Bernstein, 44–45). The case took twenty-six years to resolve, with the numerous appeals and the city requesting more time for implementation. The core focus of the case grew from one of prejudice (as the city can no longer discriminate on the basis of race or religion) to one of poor services overall — and a call to restructure the entire system. Ultimately, the judge terminated the Wilder case in favor of another of Lowry's lawsuits that she had filed against the city, along with another agency, after the death of Elisa Izquierdo and the creation of the newly titled ACS. Finally, Lowry settled; a panel of independent national experts would come in, investigate ACS, and make requirements for systemic change. See Sarah Hultman Dunn, "The *Marisol A. v. Giuliani* Settlement: 'Innovative Resolution' or 'All-Out Disaster'?" *The Columbia Journal of Law and Social Problems* (Summer 2002): 275–90. For the whole story of the shift from the Wilder case to the *Marisol A. v. Giuliani* case, read Bernstein, *The Lost Children of Wilder.*

51 *take months or even years:* In New York, for instance, as of February 2011, of the children in care for at least fifteen of the previous twenty-two months,

the time between filing a termination of parental rights petition and actually becoming free for adoption exceeded two years for 36 percent. Of all legally freed children in care for at least fifteen of the prior twenty-two months, the time between placement and freeing was *four or more years* for 44 percent, and *seven or more years* for 13 percent. *The Long Road/One Year Home Symposium: Proceedings* (New York: Children's Rights, November 2011), 9–11.

"death penalty of child welfare": Mike Arsham, e-mail correspondence, June 2012.

"parenting is more about bonding than blood": Bartholet, *Nobody's Children,* 243.

55 *one-third being abused by an adult in the home:* National Coalition for Child Protection Reform, "Foster Care vs. Family Preservation: The Track Record on Safety and Well-Being," Issue Paper 1, updated January 3, 2011. http://www.nccpr.org/reports/01SAFETY.pdf.

57 *if you gave them the right help:* This is not an actual statistic, but rather a theory Arelis is positing based on her own anecdotal experience. It's difficult to obtain real data on the types of biological parents she's referring to because they can be under the influence of so many factors — mental illness, substance use, domestic violence, and so on — and then the types of services they're offered range so dramatically too.

4. Drugs in the System

58 *daughter, Shameka:* Name has been changed.

59 *others put the figure much higher: Targeted Grants to Increase the Well-Being of, and to Improve the Permanency Outcomes for, Children Affected by Methamphetamine or Other Substance Abuse: First Annual Report to Congress* (Washington, DC: U.S. Department of Health and Human Services, Administration for Children and Families, Administration on Children, Youth and Families, Children's Bureau, current through July 2012). http://www.acf.hhs.gov/programs/cb/pubs/targeted_grants/targeted_grants.pdf.

61 *baby is born "positive tox," or drug-exposed:* Child Welfare Information Gateway, a division of the Administration for Children and Families, *Parental Drug Use as Child Abuse,* State Statutes Series (Washington, DC: U.S. Department of Health and Human Services, 2006). http://www.childwelfare.gov/systemwide/laws_policies/statutes/drugexposed.cfm.

(meaning a fetus can be abused in utero): Ibid.

or while still pregnant: Tara Husley, "Prenatal Drug Use: The Ethics of Testing and Incarcerating Pregnant Women," *Newborn and Infant Nursing Reviews* 5, no. 2 (June 2005): 93–96.

up to ten times more often than white women: This statistic comes from an oft-cited study conducted in Florida: Ira J. Chasnoff, Harvey J. Landress, and Mark E. Barrett, "The Prevalence of Illicit-Drug or Alcohol Use During

Pregnancy and Discrepancies in Mandatory Reporting in Pinellas County, Florida," *New England Journal of Medicine* 322 (1990): 1202–6.

studies show that drug use: Minorities and Drugs: Facts and Figures, a survey (Washington, DC: The National Office of Drug Control Policy, 2007).

but only 38 percent of the foster care kids: Fred Wulczyn and Bridgette Lery, *Racial Disparity in Foster Care Admissions* (Chicago: Chapin Hall Center for Children at the University of Chicago, 2007), 9.

62 *record or risk of removal:* Robert B. Hill, "Institutional Racism in Child Welfare," in *Child Welfare Revisited: An Africentric Perspective,* ed. Joyce Everett, Sandra P. Chipungu, and Bogart R. Leashore (New Brunswick, NJ: Rutgers University Press, 2004), 62.

delinquent behavior or status offenses: Ibid., 63.

in white families as "accidents": Dorothy Roberts, *Shattered Bonds: The Color of Child Welfare* (New York: Basic Civitas Books, 2002), 5.

the system's legacy of institutionalized racism: This theory of the three types of factors is commonly discussed. It's summarized in Robert B. Hill, *Synthesis of Research on Disproportionality in Child Welfare: An Update* (Casey-CSSP Alliance for Racial Equity in the Child Welfare System, October 2006). http://www.cssp.org/reform/child-welfare/other-resources/synthesis-of-research-on-disproportionality-robert-hill.pdf.

63 *distribution in low-income families:* Hill, "Institutional Racism in Child Welfare," 57–76.

strong risk factor for all forms of maltreatment: Andrea J. Sedlak and Dana Schultz, "Race Differences in the Risk of Maltreatment in the General Child Population," in *Race Matters in Child Welfare: The Overrepresentation of African American Children in the System,* ed. Dennette Derezotes, John Poertner, and Mark F. Testa (Washington, DC: CWLA Press, 2005), 47. In one large, longitudinal study on poverty in child welfare, the authors looked for class bias as a reason for the overrepresentation of poor kids in child welfare and determined "that the overrepresentation of poor children is driven largely by the presence of increased risk among the poor children that come to the attention of child welfare rather than high levels of systemic class bias." Melissa Jonson-Reid, Brett Drake, and Patricia L. Kohl, "Is the Overrepresentation of the Poor in Child Welfare Caseloads Due to Bias or Need?" *Children and Youth Services Review* 31 (2009): 422–27.

across any ethnic or racial lines: Sedlak and Schultz, "Race Differences in the Risk of Maltreatment in the General Child Population," 47.

73 percent higher rate of black maltreatment over white: E. Bartholet, F. Wulczyn, R. P. Barth, and C. Lederman, *Race and Child Welfare* (Chicago: Chapin Hall Center for Children at the University of Chicago, 2011), 3.

direct help toward the families that need it: The issue brief is Bartholet et al., cited in the preceding note.

64 *one of the most dangerous substances for a fetus:* For instance, a baby with fetal alcohol syndrome can have skeletal, heart, or brain malformations or be born permanently mentally retarded. For more information, see "Fetal Alcohol Spectrum Disorders; Fetal Alcohol Syndrome," facts from the

American Pregnancy Association, http://www.americanpregnancy.org/pregnancycomplications/fetalalcohol.html.

exposure to cocaine and a decrease in functioning: Deborah Frank, MD, Marilyn Augustyn, MD, Wanda Grant Knight, MD, et al., "Growth, Development, and Behavior in Early Childhood Following Prenatal Cocaine Exposure: A Systematic Review," *Journal of the American Medical Association* 285, no. 12 (March 28, 2001): 1613. The National Institute of Child Health and Human Development (NICHD) and the National Institute on Drug Abuse launched the largest study of cocaine-exposed newborns and have been comparing these children to nonexposed kids living in comparable conditions for the past fifteen years. (See the Maternal Lifestyle Study at the government clinical trials website at http://clinicaltrials.gov/ct2/show/NCT00059540.)

They have found an IQ differential of four points, which emerges by age seven, but other than that, there are no substantial differences, according to Barry Lester, MD, founder and director of the Brown University Center for the Study of Children at Risk, Women & Infants Hospital and Brown University Medical School. Lester, who is a principal investigator for the NICHD study, spoke at a New York University conference called "Drugs, Pregnancy and Parenting: What the Experts Have to Say," held at NYU School of Law on February 11, 2009, and provided these figures.

thousands of these babies are now in their late teens: Barry M. Lester is founder and director of the Center for the Study of Children at Risk, Women & Infants Hospital and Brown University Medical School. Approximately 1,400 children were enrolled at birth in Detroit, Miami, Memphis, and Providence, and as of early 2012, the kids were around sixteen years old. From the Brown Center for the Study of Children at Risk.

no substantial differences had emerged: Lester provided these figures.

kids started showing poor inhibitory control: Lester and colleagues published an article indicating that by five years of age, the meth-exposed infants in the study showed some attention deficit/hyperactivity and emotional reactivity, and the kids who had been exposed to heavy use showed attention problems and withdrawn behavior. Linda L. LaGasse, Chris Derauf, Lynne M. Smith, et al., "Prenatal Methamphetamine Exposure and Childhood Behavior Problems at 3 and 5 Years of Age," *Pediatrics* 29, no. 4 (April 2012): 681–88. Also see Cathleen Otero, MSW, MPA, Sharon Boles, PhD, Nancy K. Young, PhD, and Kim Dennis, MPA, *Methamphetamine Addiction, Treatment and Outcomes: Implications for Child Welfare Workers,* draft prepared for the Substance Abuse and Mental Health Services Administration Center for Substance Abuse Treatment (Irvine, CA: National Center on Substance Abuse and Child Welfare, April 2006), 7.

65 *"not adequate parents either":* Lester, telephone interview, May 2012.

wrong up to 70 percent of the time: Troy Anderson, "False Positives Are Common in Drug Tests on New Moms," *Los Angeles Daily News,* July 28, 2008.

66 *drug laws were designed to prevent:* "Maternal Decision Making, Ethics, and the Law: ACOG Committee Opinion Number 321," *Obstetrics & Gynecology* 106 (2005): 1127–37.

methamphetamines around children as a particular felony: Parental Drug Use as Child Abuse: Summary of State Laws (Washington, DC: Child Welfare Information Gateway, a division of the Administration for Children and Families, U.S. Department of Health and Human Services, current through May 2009). http://www.childwelfare.gov/systemwide/laws_policies/statutes/drugexposed.cfm. Crystal meth isn't yet a major concern in New York City, but it has had an enormous impact on child welfare in other places, and from one perspective these tighter laws make sense. Meth users appear to be more psychologically disturbed and can be more out of control than other types of substance abusers. Chronic meth use can lead to intense paranoia, hallucinations, and violence. Because meth addicts, in general, are more likely to use the drug continuously throughout the day at evenly spaced intervals rather than concentrated at night like cocaine users, kids are exposed to their high parents more frequently and for longer periods of time. See Otero et al., "Methamphetamine Addiction, Treatment and Outcomes: Implications for Child Welfare Workers." Meth is unique, too, in that people can concoct it right at home. Still, despite the media attention that meth labs have garnered, only a few thousand children were taken into custody for living in meth labs over a three-year period, as opposed to 1.2 million kids overall (Otero et al.) — though exposure to meth production is very dangerous. There are explosions, toxic chemicals, and the associated risks of violence from trafficking or selling to people who are also high on the drug.

parents who don't receive treatment: Beth L. Green, Anna Rockhill, and Carrie Furrer, "Does Substance Abuse Treatment Make a Difference for Child Welfare Case Outcomes? A Statewide Longitudinal Analysis," *Children and Youth Services Review* 29, no. 4 (April 2007): 460–73.

complete treatment at a higher rate: Wendy B. Kissin, Dace S. Svikis, Glen D. Morgan, and Nancy A. Haug, "Characterizing Pregnant Drug-Dependent Women in Treatment and Their Children," *Journal of Substance Abuse Treatment* 21, no. 1 (July 2001): 27–34.

68 *less stable funding grounds than direct foster care:* Stephen Ceasar, "Mayor's Budget Would Cut Help to Families in Trouble," *The New York Times*, June 9, 2010.

69 *several thousand cases that come through Brooklyn's family court each year:* According to a spokesperson from the Citizens' Committee for Children of New York, there were 64,035 petitions filed in family court in 2008. There are forty-seven judges to hear all of these cases (seventeen of them in Brooklyn family court), meaning that each judge hears about fifty-one cases per day.

crimes committed against their children: For a better understanding of this issue, see Diane R. Martell, *Criminal Justice and the Placement of Abused Children* (New York: LFB Scholarly Publishing, 2005).

a crime against the state: Ibid., 24.

70 *can lead to brutal cross-examinations:* Ibid., 27.

71 *The mother, Lupe:* Name has been changed.

5. Catch as Catch Can

75 *Nationwide, there's a shortfall:* Marisa Kendall, "Shortage of Foster Parents Seen as U.S. Trend," *USA Today,* September 22, 2010. http://www.usa-today.com/news/nation/2010-09-23-fostercare23_ST_N.htm. For a more detailed description of the low retention rates for foster parents, see Kathryn W. Rhodes, John G. Orme, Mary Ellen Cox, and Cheryl Buehler, "Foster Family Resources, Psychosocial Functioning, and Retention," *Social Work Research* 27, no. 3 (2007): 135–50.

twice as many foster kids as they do available parents: In 2010, Pennsylvania had twenty thousand kids in care and only nine thousand homes; Oklahoma tallied 8,865 children and 4,669 homes, according to Marisa Kendall's article "Shortage of Foster Parents Seen as U.S. Trend."

undergo a criminal background check: For more information about each state's rules, see the National Foster Parent Association website: http://www.nfpainc.org. There is a FAQ page on becoming a foster parent, as well as contact information for each state.

$568 for a sixteen-year-old kid: Hitting the M.A.R.C.: Establishing Foster Care Minimum Adequate Rates for Children (Children's Rights, National Foster Parent Association, and the University of Maryland School of Social Work, October 2007).

estimated real cost of $790: Ibid.

close to or below the poverty line: There are startlingly few studies about foster parent demographics; most are quite old, and others are fairly small samples. A 1978 report showed foster families to be living at $4,000 above the poverty line; a 1990 report on Connecticut showed that more than half of the foster families lived on less than $20,000 per year, in one of the wealthiest states in the nation. Almost half of the single foster mothers (about a third of the foster parent population) lived on an annual income of less than $10,000. William Epstein, *Children Who Could Have Been: The Legacy of Child Welfare in Wealthy America* (Madison: University of Wisconsin Press, 1999), 57–58. Also see Joan Shireman, *Critical Issues in Child Welfare* (New York: Columbia University Press, 2003), 229; and Richard P. Barth, Rebecca Green, Mary Bruce Webb, Ariana Wall, Claire Gibbons, and Carlton Craig, "Characteristics of Out-of-Home Caregiving Environments Provided Under Child Welfare Services," *Child Welfare* 87, no. 3 (2008): 31.

79 *twenty hours annually depending on your state:* Federal law requires that prospective foster parents be "prepared adequately with the appropriate knowledge and skills to provide for the needs of the child," but each state requires different mandatory training hours — ranging from zero in Hawaii

to twenty hours per year in Texas and Ohio. Individual agencies within each state may offer or require extra classes. Sarah Gerstenzang, "Foster Parent Training in America," *Fostering Families Today*, July/August 2009, 28. Agencies that contract with ACS must provide eight to ten hours of foster parent training. From "Become a Foster or Adoptive Parent," New York City Administration for Children's Services. http://www.nyc.gov/html/acs/html/become_parent/become_parent.shtml.

85 *delivered directly to the family home:* Michael B. Katz, *In the Shadow of the Poorhouse: A Social History of Welfare in America* (New York: Basic Books, 1996, Tenth Anniversary Edition, Kindle Edition), Loc. 139–46.

thus creating the first foster homes: Jillian Jimenez, "The History of Child Protection in the African American Community: Implications for Current Child Welfare Practices," *Children and Youth Services Review* 28, no. 8 (August 2006).

Colored Orphans Asylum in New York as early as 1836: John Francis Richmond, *New York and Its Institutions, 1609–1871: A Library of Information, Pertaining to the Great Metropolis, Past and Present* (E. B. Treat, 1872), 302–3.

execute a son for misbehaving: Elizabeth Bartholet, *Nobody's Children: Abuse and Neglect, Foster Drift and the Adoption Alternative* (Boston: Beacon Press, 1999), 33.

86 *even work in factories:* Stephen O'Connor, *Orphan Trains: The Story of Charles Loring Brace and the Children He Saved and Failed* (New York: Houghton Mifflin Company, 2001), 36.

neglected their daughters' decency: Nina Bernstein, *The Lost Children of Wilder: The Epic Struggle to Change Foster Care* (New York: Vintage, 2001), 87, citing Linda Gordon's *Heroes of Their Own Lives* (New York: Viking, 1988).

remove children from their homes at will: Ibid.

(usually in religious-run institutions or orphanages) once removed: Ibid.

post–World War I: Ibid., 88.

87 *a mix of the two:* Dorothy Roberts, *Shattered Bonds: The Color of Child Welfare* (New York: Basic Civitas Books, 2002), 7.

first established in Illinois: Alexia Pappas, "Welfare Reform: Child Welfare or the Rhetoric of Responsibility?" *Duke Law Journal* 45, no. 6 (April 1996, Twenty-Seventh Annual Administrative Law Issue): 1301–28.

character evaluations from neighbors and clergy: Susan Tinsley Gooden, "Contemporary Approaches to Enduring Challenges: Using Performance Measures to Promote Racial Equality Under TANF," in *Race and the Politics of Welfare Reform*, ed. Sanford F. Schram, Joe Soss, and Richard C. Fording (Ann Arbor: University of Michigan Press, 2003), 255.

"mothers' aid law": Pappas, "Welfare Reform: Child Welfare or the Rhetoric of Responsibility?"

"other racial extraction": Gooden, "Contemporary Approaches to Enduring Challenges."

by and large for white children: Robert B. Hill, "Institutional Racism in

Child Welfare," in *Child Welfare Revisited: An Africentric Perspective*, ed. Joyce Everett, Sandra P. Chipungu, and Bogart R. Leashore (New Brunswick, NJ: Rutgers University Press, 2004), 57–76.

"moral character, etc. — as it [saw] fit": Pappas, "Welfare Reform: Child Welfare or the Rhetoric of Responsibility?"

88 *during cotton-picking season:* Susan Tinsley Gooden, "Examining the Implementation of Welfare Reform by Race: Do Blacks, Hispanics and Whites Report Similar Experiences with Welfare Agencies?" *The Review of Black Political Economy* 32, no. 2 (December 2004): 27–53.

another for whites: Ibid.

were effectively dismantled: Ibid.

welfare queen with too many kids: Ibid.

89 *poor enough to receive welfare:* "Brief History of Federal Child Welfare Financing Legislation" (Washington, DC: Child Welfare League of America, July 2003). http://www.cwla.org/advocacy/financinghistory.htm.

Of all children served in 2009 who had been in foster care for at least twenty-four months, only 30.5 percent had two or fewer placements, according to *Child Welfare Outcomes: Report to Congress*, a report created by the U.S. Department of Health and Human Services to meet the requirements of section 203(a) of the Adoption and Safe Families Act of 1997 (ASFA). This data comes from chapter 5, Table V-2, "2009 Outcomes 6 and 7, Achieving Stable and Appropriate Placement Settings." http://www.acf.hhs.gov/programs/cb/pubs/cwo06-09/cwo06-09.pdf.

93 *more thoroughly funded and supported, foster care:* All the information in this section comes from the study by Ronald C. Kessler et al., "Effects of Enhanced Foster Care on the Long-Term Physical and Mental Health of Foster Care Alumni," *Archives of General Psychiatry* 65, no. 6 (June 2008): 625–33.

6. Surge Control

98 *been in care for a little over two years:* Adoption and Foster Care Analysis and Reporting System (AFCARS), *Preliminary FY 2011 Data (October 1, 2009 Through September 30, 2010), Estimates as of July 2012* (Washington, DC: U.S. Department of Health and Human Services, Administration for Children and Families, Administration on Children, Youth and Families, Children's Bureau, No. 19, 2012). http://www.acf.hhs.gov/sites/default/files/cb/afcarsreport19.pdf.

though this has come down some: Ten years earlier, in 2001, the average length of a foster care stay was 32.5 months. *The AFCARS Report, Final Estimates for FY 1998 Through FY 2002 (12)* (Washington, DC: U.S. Department of Health and Human Services, Administration for Children and Families, Administration on Children, Youth and Families, Children's Bureau, October 2006). http://archive.acf.hhs.gov/programs/cb/stats_research/afcars/tar/report12.pdf.

three or more years: The Long Road/One Year Home Symposium: Proceedings (New York: Children's Rights, November 2011).

nearly five and a half years: This investigation was launched by Children's Rights and was published in *The Long Road Home: A Study of Children Stranded in New York City Foster Care, Executive Summary* (New York: Children's Rights, November 2009), 7. Also, most of New York's foster kids are from the city, and the state ranked fortieth in the nation for speed in getting them home in 2009. For timeliness to adoption, it ranked forty-fourth, according to the same study.

28 percent of the general population: "Foster Care by the Numbers," a fact sheet produced by Casey Family Programs. http://www.casey.org/Newsroom/MediaKit/pdf/FosterCareByTheNumbers.pdf.

99 *supposed programs it never ran:* Benjamin Weiser, "City Slow to Act as Hope for Foster Children Fails," *The New York Times,* November 6, 2007.

101 *7 percent of children between one and five:* Fred H. Wulczyn, Lijun Chen, and Kristen Brunner Hislop, *Foster Care Dynamics, 2000–2005: A Report from the Multistate Foster Care Data Archive* (Chicago: Chapin Hall Center for Children at the University of Chicago, December 2007).

102 *foster kids nationwide are fifteen or older:* Data is for the period ending September 30, 2011, and is taken from *Adoption and Foster Care Analysis and Reporting System (AFCARS) Preliminary FY 2011 Data (October 1, 2009 Through September 30, 2010),* estimates as of July 2012.

$8,000 per year: Mark E. Courtney, Amy Dworsky, JoAnn S. Lee, Melissa Rapp, *Midwest Evaluation of the Adult Functioning of Former Foster Youth: Outcomes at Ages 23 and 24* (Chicago: Chapin Hall at the University of Chicago, 2011).

were once in foster care: From "Facts on Foster Care in America" *ABC Primetime,* May 30, 2006. http://abcnews.go.com/Primetime/FosterCare/story?id=2017991&page=1#.T_2iuGjDPww.

103 *rather than cumulative or comprehensive:* J. G. Orme and C. Buehler, "Foster Family Characteristics and Behavioral and Emotional Problems of Foster Children: A Narrative Review," *Family Relations* 50, no. 1 (2001): 315.

104 *provide stimulating environments for their kids:* Richard P. Barth, Rebecca Green, Mary Bruce Webb, Ariana Wall, Claire Gibbons, and Carlton Craig, "Characteristics of Out-of-Home Caregiving Environments Provided Under Child Welfare Services," *Child Welfare* 87, no. 3 (2008): 5–39.

105 *group home facility than in a family home:* Different studies cite different figures, as costs can vary widely depending upon whether the foster care is enhanced, or on what type of congregate care is offered. One report claimed that group home or residential care can cost between three and seven times more than family foster care: Madelyn Freundlich, *Time Running Out: Teens in Foster Care* (Children's Rights, Juvenile Rights Division of the Legal Aid Society and Lawyers for Children, November 2003), 133. Another report said the monthly cost could be six to ten times higher for institutional care, or two to three times higher if the family is providing treatment foster care: Richard P. Barth, *Institutions vs. Foster Homes: The Em-*

pirical Base for a Century of Action (Chapel Hill, NC: Jordan Institute for Families, June 17, 2002), ii.

106 *disproportionate number of minority children in care:* Ramona Denby and Nolan Rindfleisch, "African Americans' Foster Parenting Experiences: Research Findings and Implications for Policy and Practice," *Children and Youth Services Review* 18, no. 6 (1996): 523–55.

7. *Chutes and Ladders and Chutes*

118 *or the birth of a new sibling:* See, for instance, Howard J. Bennett, MD, "Nocturnal Enuresis: Bedwetting in the Older Child" (Charleston, SC: The National Association for Continence), http://www.nafc.org/online-store/consumer-leaflets-and-pamphlets/for-parents-and-children/nocturnal-enuresis-bedwetting-in-the-older-child-3/; and "Secondary Nocturnal Enuresis," an information page published by the National Kidney Foundation at http://www.kidney.org/patients/bw/BWbedwetSecondary.cfm.

122 *the child, back in control:* Good descriptions of this phenomenon abound in Bruce Perry and Maia Szalavitz's *The Boy Who Was Raised as a Dog and Other Stories from a Child Psychiatrist's Notebook: What Traumatized Children Can Teach Us About Loss, Love, and Healing* (New York: Basic Books, 2006). A succinct description is on page 55.

123 *"Hey, Clarence":* Name has been changed.

125 *punitive diagnostic centers for months and months:* In the eighties, kids were known to stay in diagnostic centers for years, as bureaucratic i's and t's were dotted and crossed, and better beds elsewhere were slow to open up, according to Michael Oreskes and Sara Rimer, "Youths Languish in Diagnostic Centers," *The New York Times*, March 27, 1987. http://www.nytimes.com/1987/03/27/nyregion/youths-languish-in-diagnostic-centers.html?pagewanted=all.

they may land in a hospital: In May of 2010, the Legal Aid Society launched a lawsuit against the city of New York for detaining children in psychiatric hospitals, in locked quarters, after doctors had recommended their release. The suit also claimed that ACS and its agencies had been using psychiatric hospitals as detention centers, sending children there for disciplinary reasons like breaking curfew or running away. A. G. Sulzberger, "Foster Children Mistreated, Suit Against City Claims," *The New York Times*, Late Edition, May 13, 2010, "Metropolitan Desk."

kids in out-of-home care live in RTCs: "Office of Juvenile Justice and Delinquency Prevention Model Programs Guide: Residential Treatment Centers" (Washington, DC: U.S. Department of Justice). http://www.ojjdp.gov/mpg/progTypesResidentialTreatment.aspx.

had a history of psychiatric hospitalization: This study looked at sixteen RTCs and found, interestingly, that all three groups had nearly the same rate of substance abuse. Nan Dale, Amy J. L. Baker, Emily Anastasio, and Jim Purcell, "Characteristics of Children in Residential Treatment in New York State," *Child Welfare* 86, no. 1 (January/February 2007): 16.

126 *behavior on the wall:* Jorge Fitz-Gibbon, Leah Rae, and Shawn Cohen, "Throwaway Kids: Part of a Journal News Special Report on Residential Treatment Centers: Mental Health Care Lacking for Traumatized Kids," *The [White Plains, NY] Journal News,* October 28, 2002.
serious emotional disturbances: Ibid.
psychological or otherwise: Charting a New Course: A Blueprint for Transforming Juvenile Justice in New York State: A Report of Governor David Paterson's Task Force on Transforming Juvenile Justice (New York State, December 2009), 29.

127 *first two years at Holy Cross:* The data in this paragraph covers 1998 through May of 2000.

128 *"high levels of vandalism":* Alan G. Hevesi, Comptroller, *A Report by the New York State Office of the State Comptroller: Office of Children and Family Services: Contract C-500158: Pius XII Youth and Family Services, Inc. 2001-R-5* (Albany, NY, 2003), 16.
references had been checked: In the comptroller's report, auditors found that when residents filed a claim of abuse or neglect, it took the state an average of 183 days to launch an investigation — exceeding the requirement by more than four months. Ibid., 8.
conducted site visits at both facilities: Ibid., 1, 15.
"corrective action plan" to improve safety: They also temporarily closed intake and removed twenty children, to reduce pressure on staff. Ibid., 16.
they'd get some response: Ibid., 18.
shuttered the Chester facility of its own accord: Ibid., 1.

129 *special ed is all they get:* In a 2003 study of RTCs across New York, the advocacy groups Lawyers for Children, Children's Rights, and Legal Aid found that most RTCs in New York offered only special-ed schools. Madelyn Freundlich, *Time Running Out: Teens in Foster Care* (Children's Rights, Juvenile Rights Division of the Legal Aid Society, Lawyers for Children, 2003), 128. http://www.childrensrights.org/wp-content/uploads/2008/06/time_running_out_teens_in_foster_care_nov_2003 .pdf.

130 *a dozen kids staged a riot in 2009:* Melissa Holmes, "Riot at Randolph Children's Home," WIVB.com, Channel 4, June 2, 2009. http://www.wivb. com/dpp/news/local/Riot_at_Randolph_Childrens_Home_20090601.

131 *cost taxpayers an estimated $210,000 per year: Charting a New Course: A Blueprint for Transforming Juvenile Justice in New York State: A Report of Governor David Paterson's Task Force on Transforming Juvenile Justice,* 10.
half of what was paid out to Graham Windham: David Satcher, Surgeon General, "Therapeutic Foster Care," in *Mental Health: A Report of the Surgeon General* (Rockville, MD: U.S. Department of Health and Human Services, Substance Abuse and Mental Health Services Administration, Center for Mental Health Services, National Institutes of Health, National Institute of Mental Health, 1999).
those in residential treatment centers: Ibid.

died at the hands of two adult aides at the Tryon School for Boys: Jennifer Gonnerman, "The Lost Boys of Tryon," *New York* magazine, January 24, 2010.

shoulder separations and displacements: Letter from Loretta King, Acting Assistant Attorney General, U.S. Department of Justice, Civil Rights Division, to David Paterson, Governor of New York, Re: Investigation of the Lansing Residential Center, Louis Gossett, Jr. Residential Center, Tryon Residential Center, and Tryon Girls Center, August 14, 2009. http://www.justice.gov/crt/about/spl/documents/NY_juvenile_facilities_find let_08-14-2009.pdf.

132 *"choice of absolute last resort":* Charting a New Course: A Blueprint for Transforming Juvenile Justice in New York State: A Report of Governor David Paterson's Task Force on Transforming Juvenile Justice, 11.

"be replaced with a service-based, family-like model": Freundlich, *Time Running Out: Teens in Foster Care.*

with close to six hundred beds: Administration for Children's Services, "Administration for Children's Services Unveils Major Initiative to Strengthen New York City's Child Welfare System," press release (New York: Administration for Children's Services, February 3, 2005). At the time of this press release, ACS had already closed 473 beds and had plans to close 121 more within the next six months.

by April of 2011: Julie Bosman, "City Cuts Ties to Catholic Agency That Provides Foster Care," *The New York Times,* May 4, 2010.

133 *the most serious or violent offenders:* Julie Bosman, "City Signals Intent to Put Fewer Teenagers in Jail," *The New York Times,* January 21, 2010. Also see "Children's Services and Juvenile Justice to Integrate Operations," press release (New York: Administration for Children's Services, 2010). http://www.nyc.gov/html/acs/html/about/news_djj.shtml.

from one of punishment to one of support: For more information about the creation of the OCFS, see John A. Johnson, "Organizational Merger and Cultural Change for Better Outcomes: The First Five Years of the Office of Children and Family Services," *Child Welfare* 83, no. 2 (March/April, 2004): 129–42.

abused or neglected children were more likely to be arrested: The Child Welfare League of America's Juvenile Justice Division claimed in 2002 that abused or neglected children are more likely than other children to be arrested at a rate of 27 percent to 17 percent. Cited in *Children's Services Practice Notes* 12, no. 4 (August 2007). http://www.practicenotes.org/vol12_no4.htm.

8. Arrested in Development

137 *a study on a single state (Illinois):* This Illinois study was conducted by the National Association of Social Workers and was cited in Dorothy Roberts's book *Shattered Bonds: The Color of Child Welfare* (New York: Basic Civitas

Books, 2002), 205, as well as by Beth Azar, "Foster Care Has Bleak History," *APA Monitor,* November 1995.

though reputable sources: For instance, see Mike Wereschagin and Reid R. Frazier, "Foster Children Face the World at 18," *Pittsburgh Tribune-Review,* November 28, 2005. The Freddie Mac Foundation makes this claim too, in "Foundation Sponsored Groundbreaking Documentary Sheds Light on America's Foster Care Systems," press release (McLean, VA: Freddie Mac Foundation, 2004).

the state's adult inmates came from child welfare: This comes from California Assemblymember Bonnie Lowenthal, representing California District 54, promoting bill AB 719 in September 2009, which would grant food stamps to foster kids who had aged out for one year after their eighteenth birthday. See "Bonnie Lowenthal's Foster Youth Bill Heads to Governor," press release (Sacramento, CA, September 9, 2009), http://asmdc.org/members/a54/news-room/press-releases/item/2567-bonnie-lowenthal's-foster-youth-bill-heads-to-governor; and "'Aged-Out' Foster Youth at Terrible Risk," *San Francisco Chronicle,* September 2, 2009, http://www.sfgate.com/opinion/article/Aged-out-foster-youth-at-terrible-risk-3287718.php.

state's criminal justice system were former foster kids: Fred Bayles and Sharon Cohen, "Chaos Often the Only Parent for Abused or Neglected Children. Families: Drug Addiction, Poverty and Teen-Age Pregnancy Overwhelm State Protective Services. And Failures Can Be Fatal," *Associated Press,* April 30, 1995, run in the *Los Angeles Times.* http://articles.latimes.com/1995-04-30/news/mn-60640_1_drug-addiction.

a careful 25 percent: ABC News, "Facts on Foster Care in America: A Grim Picture for Many Kids, but There Are Reasons for Hope," May 30, 2006. http://abcnews.go.com/print?id=2017991.

138 *family, the Taylors:* Name has been changed.

139 *up to the mother to initiate:* Michelle Chen, "A Tangle of Problems Links Prison, Foster Care," *Gotham Gazette,* April 13, 2009.

more than fifty miles away from their children: Only 17.4 percent of state inmates and 7.5 percent of federal inmates live less than fifty miles from their children; 20.7 percent of state and 8.5 percent of federal inmates live fifty to one hundred miles away; and 51.2 percent of state and 40.7 percent of federal inmates live up to five hundred miles away. And 10.7% of state and 43.3 percent of federal inmates live more than five hundred miles away from their kids, according to 1997 data collected by the Bureau of Justice Statistics policy analyst Christopher J. Mumola, *Incarcerated Parents and their Children,* Bureau of Justice Statistics Special Report (Washington, DC: U.S. Department of Justice, Office of Justice Programs, August 2000), 5.

family's hearings in family court: Julie Kowitz Margolies and Tamar Kraft-Stolar, *When "Free" Means Losing Your Mother* (New York: Women in Prison Project of the Correctional Association of New York, February 2006), 10–12.

between an order and an appearance are endless: Ibid.

140 *termination proceedings for incarcerated parents more than doubled:* Keach Hagey, "Dodging ASFA's Hammer," *Child Welfare Watch* 15 (Winter 2008): 24.

learn critical mothering skills: A good discussion about the efficacy of prison nurseries can be found in Chandra Krinag Villanueva, *Mothers, Infants and Imprisonment: A National Look at Prison Nurseries and Community-Based Alternatives* (New York: Women's Prison Association, May 2009). http://www.scribd.com/doc/80686032/Mothers-Infants-and-Imprisonment-Prison-Nurseries-Community-Based-Alternatives-2009.

watching the clock tick by on ASFA's deadline: In 2010, New York State Governor Patterson signed into law the Adoption and Safe Families Act (ASFA) Expanded Discretion Bill, which gives individual caseworkers some leeway with regard to ASFA deadlines. They can decide, on a case-by-case basis, whether to refrain from filing a parental termination petition if a parent is currently incarcerated or attending a residential drug treatment program. Again, though, under original ASFA law, caseworkers always had discretion to defer filing if it was in the best interests of the child. See Correctional Association of New York, "A Fair Chance for Families Separated by Prison," June 16, 2010. http://www.correctionalassociation.org/news/a-fair-chance-for-families-separated-by-prison.

141 *aggression, isolation, and depression:* A few of these studies are discussed in Eric Eckholm, "In Prisoners' Wake, a Tide of Troubled Kids," *The New York Times,* July 4, 2009.

nature or degree of these effects: For more information on what's been said about incarceration's effects on kids — and its limitations — see Jeremy Travis, Elizabeth M. Cincotta, and Amy L. Solomon, *Families Left Behind: The Hidden Costs of Incarceration and Reentry* (Washington, DC: Urban Institute, Justice Policy Center, October 2003, revised June 2005).

she named Sharisha: Name has been changed.

142 *learning disorders per se:* Deborah A. Frank, Marilyn Augustyn, Warida Grant Knight, Tripler Pell, and Barry Zuckerman, "Growth, Development, and Behavior in Early Childhood Following Prenatal Cocaine Exposure: A Systematic Review," *Journal of the American Medical Association* 285, no. 12 (March 28, 2001): 1613. In the article the authors claim that developmental toxic effects that may have previously been associated with cocaine exposure are correlated to other risk factors, including alcohol, tobacco, and marijuana.

150 *top foster care agency in New York in 2004:* "Children's Services Commissioner John B. Mattingly Releases 2004 Performance Evaluation Scores for Foster Boarding Home Providers," press release #050620 (New York: Administration for Children's Services, June 20, 2005). http://www.nyc.gov/html/acs/html/pr/pr05_06_20.shtml.

No agency received straight As: Fred Scaglione, "Get Your Scorecard Here!" *New York Nonprofit Press* 9, issue 3 (March 2010): 9. In August 2012, ACS Commissioner Richter wrote an open letter to agency directors, explaining that the Scorecard system would be altered once again, to a quarterly model, with fewer questions, among other changes. The letter is available on the ACS website: http://www.nyc.gov/html/acs/downloads/providers_ newsletter/aug16/commissioner_richter_letter.pdf.

151 *twice as likely to be placed in care:* Patricia L. Kohl, Melissa Jonson-Reid, and Brett Drake, "Maternal Mental Illness and the Safety and Stability of Maltreated Children," *Child Abuse & Neglect* 35 (2011): 309–18.

152 *some form of public assistance in 2008:* Brooklyn Community District 3, retrieved from http://www.nyc.gov/html/dcp/pdf/lucds/bk3profile.pdf. The report gives figures for 2005 and 2011, when 45.9 percent and 44.5 percent of all residents received income support, respectively.

153 *he'd shown tremendous progress:* This therapist wanted to protect her client's confidentiality so she chose to remain anonymous. Interview conducted in May 2012.

154 *trafficking of minors for sex work is on the rise:* Kristin M. Finklea, Adrienne L. Fernandes Alcantara, and Alison Siskin, *Sex Trafficking of Children in the United States: Overview and Issues for Congress* (Washington, DC: Congressional Research Service, June 21, 2011).

pimps target girls in homeless shelters or group homes: Heather Clawson and Lisa Goldblatt Grace, "Finding a Path to Recovery: Residential Facilities for Minor Victims of Domestic Sex Trafficking," prepared for the Office of the Assistant Secretary for Planning and Evaluation, U.S. Department of Health and Human Services, September 2007. http://aspe.hhs.gov/hsp/07/HumanTrafficking/ResFac/ib.htm.

often have no training about these types of predators: Finklea et al., *Sex Trafficking of Children in the United States*, 2.

who in New York are often gang leaders: Karen Zraick, "8 Charged in Brooklyn in Sex-Trafficking Case," *The New York Times*, June 3, 2010, A28.

many experts claim that's too low: Clyde Haberman, "The Sexually Exploited Ask for Change: Help, Not Jail," *The New York Times*, June 12, 2007. http://select.nytimes.com/2007/06/12/nyregion/12nyc.html?fta=y.

who sexually exploit women and girls: Zraick, "8 Charged in Brooklyn in Sex-Trafficking Case."

155 *whose story was fairly typical:* The foster girl I know has a story very similar to the one described in Zraick, "8 Charged in Brooklyn in Sex-Trafficking Case."

ran from the foster care system entirely: This is an unfortunate but all-too-common end result because there are only about four treatment facilities in the country for minor victims of domestic sex trafficking. Clawson and Goldblatt Grace, "Finding a Path to Recovery."

9. Taking Agency

163 *more than thirty agencies contracting with ACS: Family Foster Care Awarded Slots by Borough, Contract Term Begins July 1, 2011* (New

York: Administration for Children's Services, September 27, 2010. http://www.nyc.gov/html/acs/downloads/pdf/contracts/Family%20Foster%20Care%20Awarded%20Slots%20by%20Borough.pdf.

164 *of around $140 million a year:* Richard Wexler, "Child Welfare Waivers: The Stakes for Families," *Journal of Family Strengths* 11, no. 1 (2011). This figure rises 3 percent a year for inflation. *Department of Children and Families Family Safety Child and Family Services Annual Progress and Services Report* (Florida State: Florida Department of Children and Families, June 2011), 41.

165 *least experienced removed 18 percent:* Alan Abramowitz, talk given at a New York University conference called "Drugs, Pregnancy and Parenting: What the Experts Have to Say," held at NYU School of Law, February 11, 2009.

166 *will fall off the map:* For a good overview of the issues raised by privatization in child welfare, see *Literature Review on the Privatization of Child Welfare Services,* a report written as part of the Quality Improvement Center on the Privatization of Child Welfare Services on behalf of the Children's Bureau, U.S. Department of Health and Human Services (Planning and Learning Technologies, Inc., and the University of Kentucky, August 25, 2006). Also helpful is *An Analysis of the Kansas and Florida Privatization Initiatives* (Seattle, WA: Casey Family Programs, April 2010).

on a smaller scale, in select counties: Title IV-E Waiver Demonstrations: Overview of Evaluation Requirements and Considerations, Webinar (Children's Bureau, Administration for Children and Families, Administration on Children, Youth and Families, James Bell Associates, June 6, 2012). http://www.acf.hhs.gov/sites/default/files/cb/waiver_demo.pdf.

it's nothing new: An Analysis of the Kansas and Florida Privatization Initiatives, 5.

167 *in terms of government involvement: Privatization of Child Welfare Services: Challenges and Successes Executive Summary* (New York: Children's Rights, 2003). http://www.childrensrights.org/wp-content/uploads/2008/06/privatization_of_child_welfare_services_exec_sum.pdf.

or more business-oriented services: The federal Administration for Children and Families has launched a major five-year study to look at the effectiveness and efficiency of this general shift toward privatization in several states. The study was launched in 2005 with the University of Kentucky. The Children's Bureau funded the University of Kentucky and Planning and Learning Technologies to create the National Quality Improvement Center on the Privatization of Child Welfare Services (QIC PCW) in 2005. The purpose of this five-year project is to build knowledge and inform decision making regarding public/private partnership in child welfare service delivery. http://www.uky.edu/SocialWork/qicpcw/index.htm.

advocates the waiver system: See *Ensuring Safe, Nurturing, and Permanent Families for Children: The Need to Expand Title IV-E Waivers: Second in a Series of Four Reports on Improving Child Welfare* (Seattle, WA: Casey Family Programs, May 2010). http://www.casey.org/Resources/Publications/pdf/NeedForWaivers.pdf.

seems to be doing well with its choices: A good story about Florida's overhaul is Erik Eckholm, "Florida Shifts Child-Welfare System's Focus to Saving Families," *The New York Times,* July 25, 2009. For a later overview, see *Summary of the Title IV-E Child Welfare Waiver Demonstrations* (Arlington, VA: James Bell Associates for Children's Bureau on Children, Youth and Families, U.S. Department of Health and Human Services, March 2012), 1.

head of child welfare at the national level: George Sheldon was appointed acting assistant secretary for the Administration for Children and Families under the U.S. Department of Health and Human Services in May 2011. Prior to joining ACF, Sheldon served as the secretary of the Florida Department of Children and Families (DCF).

lasting through 2016: President Obama signed the Child and Family Services Improvement and Innovation Act (Public Law 112-34) into law on September 30, 2011. For more information, see http://www.acf.hhs.gov/programs/cb/laws_policies/policy/im/2011/im1106.pdf.

for another five-year waiver: Florida's application letter to the federal Administration for Children and Families has been widely circulated and can be found on Florida's Department of Children and Families website at http://www.dcf.state.fl.us/initiatives/preservingfamilies/docs/Letter%20 Requesting%20Extension%20of%20IV-E%20Waiver%20from%20Secretary%20Sheldon%20to%20David%20Hansell%20of%20Administration%20for%20Children%20and%20Families.pdf.

23 percent in nearly three years: Ensuring Safe, Nurturing, and Permanent Families for Children.

claimed the data wasn't contextualized: See, for instance, Daniel Heimpel, "Responsibility Lost," *Huffington Post,* November 16, 2010. http://www.huffingtonpost.com/daniel-heimpel/responsibility-lost_b_781910.html.

unnecessary removals from other, safer homes: A good analysis of this can be found in Richard Wexler, *Foster-Care Panic in Los Angeles* (Alexandria, VA: National Coalition for Child Protection Reform, released April 2010, updated February 2011). http://www.nccpr.org/reports/LA2010.pdf.

director to another job: Garrett Therolf, "Ploehn Removed as Head of L.A. County Child Welfare Agency," *Los Angeles Times,* December 14, 2010. http://articles.latimes.com/2010/dec/14/local/la-me-dcfs-chief-20101214.

168 *experiment needed to go on longer to really tell: Synthesis of Findings: Title IV-E Flexible Funding Child Welfare Waiver Demonstrations* (Washington, DC: U.S. Department of Health and Human Services, Administration for Children and Families, 2011), 36–37.

recruiting and training qualified staff: "Program Instruction, Procedures for Adoption Incentive Payments" (Washington, DC: U.S. Department of Health and Human Services, Administration for Children and Families, Log No.: ACYF-CB-PI-99-04, March 5, 1999). http://www.acf.hhs.gov/programs/cb/laws_policies/policy/pi/1999/pi9904.htm.

left their computers sitting on their desks: Garrett Therolf, "Deaths of 2 Children Are Tied to Lapses in L.A. County's Welfare System," *Los Angeles*

Times, July 18, 2011. http://articles.latimes.com/2011/jul/18/local/la-me-child-fatalities-20110718.

10. Homespun

169 *any race and over the age of ten:* "New York State Subsidy Profile," FAQ page published by the North American Council on Adoptable Children, updated June 2008. http://www.nacac.org/adoptionsubsidy/stateprofiles/newyork.html.
plus a $62 monthly clothing allowance: Ibid. http://www.nacac.org/adoptionsubsidy/stateprofiles/newyork.html.

183 *little sister, Kimberly:* Name has been changed.

185 *age out on her own: Preparing Youth for Adulthood* (New York: Administration for Children's Services, June 2006), 3. This document claims that 80 percent of the kids who age out of ACS do so primarily without adults to rely upon.

11. Fantasy Islands

191 *over six thousand adolescents under ACS supervision:* In 2009, ACS reported that approximately 8,500 adolescents were in care, representing 46 percent of the foster care population. This data refers to material published August 14, 2009, and numbers are current as of March 2009. *Outcome 6: Increase Permanency for Adolescents, Citywide* (New York: Administration for Children's Services, August 14, 2009).

By 2012, the total foster care numbers had gone down, to roughly fourteen thousand, according to *NYC Administration for Children's Services Monthly Flash* (New York: Administration for Children's Services, June 2012), http://www.nyc.gov/html/acs/downloads/pdf/stats_monthly_flash.pdf. Presuming that adolescents are still 46 percent or so of this total, we would arrive at roughly 6,400 adolescents.

as soon as they reach legal age: According to the Administration for Children's Services, "In September 1999, ACS adopted a set of Permanency Principles that articulated its philosophy toward serving families and children. These principles are tools that offer the agency a framework for directing policy, formulating practice guidelines and protocols, and developing staff training" (http://www.nyc.gov/html/acs/downloads/pdf/outcomes/out6_citywide.pdf). In August 2009, ACS released data, in a performance report called *Outcome 6,* in reference to these permanency principles. *Outcome 6* specifically "provides measures of the foster care system's success at moving adolescents (children 12 years and older) into permanent homes on a timely basis." This data refers to material published August 14, 2009, and numbers are current as of March 2009. *Outcome 6: Increase Permanency for Adolescents, Citywide.*

had shifted their goal to independent living: Outcome 6: Increase Permanency for Adolescents, Citywide.

192 *"must rely primarily on themselves": Preparing Youth for Adulthood* (New York: Administration for Children's Services, June 2006), 3. The authors state, "Every year, approximately 1,200 of New York's foster youth over the age of 18 leave the foster care system, but only 20% of them are leaving their families to be adopted. The remaining 80% must rely primarily on themselves." http://www.nyc.gov/html/acs/downloads/pdf/youth_for_adulthood.pdf.

discharged directly from group homes or institutions: Outcome 6: Increase Permanency for Adolescents, Citywide.

supervised living arrangement for kids in their late teens: In 2008, forty-five states responded to a survey about young people transitioning out of care. Eighty percent of these states had some sort of supervised independent living option. Amy Dworsky and Judy Havlicek, *Review of State Policies and Programs to Support Young People Transitioning Out of Foster Care* (Chapin Hall at the University of Chicago, submitted to the Washington State Institute for Public Policy, Olympia, WA, December 2008), 9.

199 *as they aged out of the system:* Kendra Hurley, "NYC Closes Transitional Housing for Foster Teens," *Child Welfare Watch* (January 14, 2011). http://blogs.newschool.edu/child-welfare-nyc/2011/01/nyc-closes-transitional-housing-for-foster-teens/. In a personal interview with Commissioner Richter in June 2012, he confirmed that ACS was no longer funding the SILP apartments.

200 *named David:* Name has been changed.

203 *providing them with housing, training, and health care:* "Frequently Asked Questions About the Foster Care Independence Act of 1999 and the John H. Chafee Foster Care Independence Program" (National Foster Care Awareness Project, February 2000), published on the website of the National Resource Center for Youth Development (a service of the Children's Bureau): http://www.nrcyd.ou.edu/publication-db/documents/chafee-faq1.pdf.

how well, or even if, the programs were working: See Wilhelmina A. Leigh, Danielle Huff, Ernestine F. Jones, and Anita Marshall, *Aging Out of the Foster Care System to Adulthood: Findings, Challenges, and Recommendations* (Washington, DC: Joint Center for Political and Economic Studies, Health Policy Institute, December 2007). Also, a 2006 article in *Children and Youth Services Review* provided a review of the literature on Independent Living Programs and found that "the effectiveness of ILPs remains unknown" as "reviewers were unable to find any randomized controlled trial evaluating ILPs." Paul Montgomery, Charles Donkoh, and Kristen Underhill, "Independent Living Programs for Young People Leaving the Care System: The State of the Evidence," *Children and Youth Services Review* 28, no. 12 (December 2006): 1435.

national report later that year: The Administration for Children and Families (ACF) within the U.S. Department of Health and Human Services published this Final Rule on February 26, 2008. ACF created a National Youth in Transition Database at this time and required that all states engage in two data collection activities. The ACF website states that these two activities are "to collect information on each youth who receives independent living services paid for or provided by the State agency that administers the CFCIP. Second, States are to collect demographic and outcome information on certain youth in foster care whom the State will follow over time to collect additional outcome information. This information will allow ACF to track which independent living services States provide and assess the collective outcomes of youth." The services, according to ACF, are as follows: "The regulation requires that States report to ACF the independent living services and supports they provide to all youth in eleven broad categories: independent living needs assessment; academic support; post-secondary educational support; career preparation; employment programs or vocational training; budget and financial management; housing education and home management training; health education and risk prevention; family support and healthy marriage education; mentoring; and supervised independent living. States will also report financial assistance they provide, including assistance for education, room and board and other aid." ACF describes the outcomes as follows: "States will survey youth regarding six outcomes: financial self-sufficiency, experience with homelessness, educational attainment, positive connections with adults, high-risk behavior, and access to health insurance." "About NYTD," on the U.S. Department of Health and Human Services Administration for Child and Family Services website: http://www.acf.hhs.gov/programs/cb/systems/nytd/about_nytd. htm.

how many of their kids had aged out in the past year: The study was conducted by Chapin Hall, a research and policy center at the University of Chicago, wherein authors contacted the independent living services coordinators in all fifty states as well as Washington, DC. They received a response rate of 88.2 percent (or forty-five states), and of these respondents, thirty-five did not or could not report the number of youths seventeen or older who were even currently in foster care and replied "do not know." Thirty-one percent didn't know how many kids had aged out. Amy Dworsky and Judy Havlicek, *Review of State Policies and Programs to Support Young People Transitioning Out of Foster Care* (Chicago: Chapin Hall at the University of Chicago, submitted to the Washington State Institute for Public Policy, Olympia, WA, December 2008), 4–5.

who had graduated from college: M. Courtney, A. Dworsky, J. Lee, and M. Raap, *Midwest Evaluation of the Adult Functioning of Former Foster Youth: Outcomes at Age 23 and 24* (Chicago: Chapin Hall at the University of Chicago, 2009), 95.

not prepare them for adulthood: Mary Elizabeth Collins and Cassandra Clay, "Influencing Policy for Youth Transitioning from Care: Defining Problems, Crafting Solutions, and Assessing Politics," *Children and Youth Services Review* 31, no. 7 (July 2009): 743.

204 *at states' discretion, until they turned twenty-one:* This act is called the

Fostering Connections to Success and Increasing Adoptions Act (H.R. 6893/P.L. 110-351). Among other things, the act also allows kinship guardians to receive subsidized guardian payments — thus increasing the chances that children will be placed with relatives.

12. There's Something About Mary

209 *subway travel to and from the classes can take several hours:* William Scarborough (Chair), *The Needs of Youth Aging Out of Foster Care*, testimony before the New York State Assembly Standing Committee on Children and Families, Subcommittee on Foster Care (New York: The Legal Aid Society, December 14, 2007), 6.

priority status on the waiting list for public housing: "Housing Support Services," New York Administration for Children's Services website: http://www.nyc.gov/html/acs/html/support_families/housing.shtml.

Applications are frequently lost or misprocessed: Scarborough, *The Needs of Youth Aging Out of Foster Care*, 9–10.

210 *that's when the checks were cut:* The New York Education and Training Voucher (ETV) Program is a federally funded, state-administered program designed to help youth who are in foster care. Students may receive up to $5,000 a year for qualified school-related expenses. The official website, for the 2010–11 school year, read: "Funding for the 10–11 academic year will not be available until after November 1, 2010. Funding is limited and available on a first-come, first-served basis to eligible students."

where they can go on to get a GED, say, or a mentor referral: Preparing Youth for Adulthood (New York: Administration for Children's Services, June 2006). http://www.nyc.gov/html/acs/downloads/pdf/youth_for_adulthood.pdf.

211 *Kids don't realize their coverage has been terminated until they receive bills in the mail:* Also, Legal Aid threatened a class-action lawsuit against ACS and the Department of Health if they didn't improve. Scarborough, *The Needs of Youth Aging Out of Foster Care*.

13. Experiment

223 *estimates that about 50 percent of the current homeless population were once in foster care:* The Coalition for the Homeless in its 1989 *Blueprint for Solving New York's Homeless Crisis, New York City: A Report to Mayor David Dinkins*, claimed that 60 percent of the homeless in New York City municipal shelters had some history of foster care (101). In a study called *Runaway and Homeless Youth in New York City: A Report to the Ittleson Foundation, NYC* (New York: New York State Psychiatric Institute and Columbia University College of Physicians and Surgeons, Division of Child Psychiatry, 1984), David Shaffer and Carol Caton found that 50 percent of

the young people came to shelters from a group home, foster home, or other foster institution. Nationally, according to the Child Welfare League of America, 58 percent of all young adults who access federally funded youth shelters had previously been part of the foster care system in 1997 (Child Welfare League of America's data page, "The Links Between Child Welfare and Homelessness," http://www.cwla.org/programs/housing/homeless-nesslinks.htm#note13). In California, the Department of Social Services estimated in 2004 that 65 percent of the kids who age out of foster care face homelessness and up to 50 percent end up sleeping on the streets. See Ken Fagan, "Saving Foster Kids from the Streets," *San Francisco Chronicle*, April 11, 2004.

225 *has led to some five thousand adoptions:* The Heart Gallery was launched in New Mexico in 2001 and is now nationwide. Matthew Straeb, "A Message from Our President," *Heart Gallery of America Newsletter*, Inaugural Edition, January 2010. http://www.heartgalleryofamerica.org/Newsletter/2010_Jan.htm.

forty-two thousand viewers have called up with questions about becoming a parent: "Freddie Mac Foundation's Wednesday's Child: Finding Adoptive Homes for Children," retrieved from the Freddie Mac Foundation website: http://www.freddiemacfoundation.org/ourwork/founwedn.html.

14. Touching the Elephant

246 *put on the state's list of failing schools in 2004:* From insideschools.org, a division of the nonprofit Advocates for the Children of New York, which provides individual case assistance to families and children who need educational services. Insideschools.org provides independent monitoring of New York City's public schools.

247 *"You've got women in prison making Victoria's Secret bras":* It was widely reported that inmates in South Carolina were subcontracted to sew Victoria's Secret garments in the 1990s, and several other corporations, including Nintendo, Starbucks, Microsoft, and Eddie Bauer, have also been known to utilize prison labor, wherein they get to pay workers well below minimum wage. See, for example, Beth Schwartzapfel, "Your Valentine, Made in Prison," *Prison Legal News*, February 12, 2009, https://www.prisonlegalnews.org/(S(v5lg5m45z4zku255xtp5ndmf))/displayNews.aspx?newsid=216&AspxAutoDetectCookieSupport=1; and Caroline Winter, "What Do Prisoners Make for Victoria's Secret?" *Mother Jones*, July/August 2008, http://motherjones.com/politics/2008/07/what-do-prisoners-make-victorias-secret.

what happens to foster kids once they leave the system: Julie Bosman, "City Is Urged to Evaluate Foster Care," *The New York Times*, April 15, 2010. The author of this article wrote that ACS would review the proposed bill, and as of this publication, the bill had yet to pass. It was referred to the Committee on General Welfare at a City Council meeting in April 2010 (from the New

York City Council Meeting Minutes, City Hall, New York, April 14, 2010) and then didn't seem to appear again.

15. Last Call

257 *it had admitted more than double that the year before:* Mark Levine, "Saint Vincent's Is the Lehman Brothers of Hospitals," *New York* magazine, October 25, 2010. http://nymag.com/news/features/68991/.

Epilogue

260 *allowed all states to apply for flat-sum waivers from the government:* President Obama signed the Child and Family Services Improvement and Innovation Act (Public Law 112-34) into law on September 30, 2011. Read the full text of the bill at http://www.gpo.gov/fdsys/pkg/BILLS-112hr2883rds/pdf/BILLS-112hr2883rds.pdf.

though more could still sign up: Child Welfare Title IV-E Waiver Demonstration Projects 2012–2014 Overview (Washington, D.C., National Conference of State Legislatures). http://www.ncsl.org/issues-research/human-services/child-welfare-title-ive-waiver-2012-thru-2014.aspx.

261 *is now awaiting federal review:* E-mail correspondence with ACS press office, November 2012.

262 *when I was done, there were 400,540:* The first figure is from September 30, fiscal year 2007, and the second from September 30, fiscal year 2011. *The AFCARS Report, No. 19* (Washington, DC: U.S. Department of Health and Human Services, Administration for Children and Families, Administration on Children, Youth and Families, Children's Bureau, estimates as of July 2012). http://www.acf.hhs.gov/programs/cb/resource/afcars-report-19.

increased by 2.5 million, or 21 percent: Saki Knafo, "Bloomberg Budget: Slashed Children's Services Contribute to National Crisis, Advocates Say," *Huffington Post,* May 3, 2012. http://www.huffingtonpost.com/2012/05/03/bloomberg-budget-cuts-child-care-after-school-programs_n_1475333.html.

at or below the poverty line in 2008: The federal poverty level was $17,600 for a family of three in 2008. *Keeping Track of New York City's Children: 2010,* 9th ed. (New York: Citizens' Committee for Children of New York, 2010).

263 *Congressional Caucus on Foster Youth:* The caucus is cochaired by Representative Karen Bass (D-CA), Representative Tom Marino (R-PA), Representative Jim McDermott (D-WA), and Representative Michele Bachmann (R-MN). They went to Los Angeles on the first stop of their listening tour and were headed to south Florida and two cities in other states. From Karen Bass's Congressional Caucus on Foster Youth website: http://fosteryouth-caucus-karenbass.house.gov/.

Acknowledgments

So many kind, wise, and generous people contributed to this book; thank you, as Kecia would say, for rocking with me all the way.

My deepest gratitude goes to all the people on these pages: thank you for sharing these years of your lives, and for offering that most precious commodity — trust — even when it had been stolen before. Thank you, Fatimah, for the title. I hope you change your mind one day and write your book.

Many books helped me frame my thinking about foster care. Some of the most important were *The Lost Children of Wilder* by Nina Bernstein for its context and history of ACS, and Stephen O'Connor's *Orphan Trains* for an even earlier look at New York City's systemic removals of children. Jennifer Toth's *Orphans of the Living* was a helpful narrative exploration of the ways foster kids' rage and trauma compound over time. *Shattered Bonds* by Dorothy Roberts provided extra clarity on historical and current racism in the system, and Elizabeth Pleck's *Domestic Tyranny: The Making of American Social Policy Against Family Violence from Colonial Times to the Present* provided exactly what its title promised.

Several people granted interviews or provided critical information for this book and yet weren't directly quoted in its pages. Thank you to Velma Roberts, who sat with me for many hours in her Bronx kitchen and in her kids' school, sharing her family's story — living proof that foster and biological parents can work together. Thank you to Mary Chancie, who also brought me home to meet her adult children and to share with me the importance of adopting the kids who have already aged out. Mary and Velma, you give us all faith. Thank you to Lieutenant Pat Montagano at Safe Horizon's Manhattan Advocacy Center, who explained to me the legal issues around child abuse and parent prosecution while we stood in a cell; and to Anna Owusu for talking extensively with me about preventive services. Thank you to Emily Banach for explaining hospital investigations. Thank you to Nora McCarthy at *Rise* magazine for your nuanced, humanitarian perspective on parents' needs, and thank you to Stephanie Schwartz for explaining some of the legal details of family court. Thank you to Susan Grundberg for your early explanations of child welfare and its troubles, and for your take on teenagers in care. Thank you, Fall Willeboordse and Rabiya Tuma. Thank you, Madeleine George, for connecting me with Bayview, and for being a friend. Thank you to the press offices at ACS and OCFS for responding to my endless queries, and to the librarians at Columbia University, especially Jennifer Wertkin at Columbia Law Library. Columbia University also provided me with a graduate student fellow, Kyle Valenta, whose research and thoughtful criticism were very helpful.

I'm deeply grateful to the friends, colleagues, and child welfare experts who read various incarnations of the manuscript and provided vital feedback. Mike Arsham and Rick Barth each read a full draft in near-final form; thank you for your careful and conscientious critiques. Meehan Crist read a full early draft and helped me change direction. Wesley Brown, Richard Perry, Charlotte Carter, Carol Paik, Jennie Yabroff, and Kelly McMasters all read multiple chapters and sections and, with love and furious red pens, pushed this book further than I could have on my own. Thank you all so much.

Far and above, though, the best editor a writer could wish for is Andrea Schulz. Andrea, you have the unparalleled ability to recognize a book amid my wild clutter of ideas and false starts and abundant digressions. From the beginning, you've seen this book and helped me find its beating heart. Thank you also to Nicole Angeloro, Lisa Glover, Barbara Wood, and the entire brilliant team at Houghton Mifflin Harcourt. Thank you, Amy Williams, for leading me long ago to Andrea and for being agent par excellence.

I'm enormously grateful to the Corporation of Yaddo for twice providing me the incalculable gift of time and space to write. Thank you also to the Point Foundation for your early support and to the Lambda Literary Foundation for supporting me and other queer writers.

For five long years, my family of friends has been with me as I built and unbuilt and rebuilt this book. Thank you for bearing with me. Especially Teresa Dinaburg Dias, Lisa Hanauer, Gemma Baumer, Batyah Shtrum, Sharon Krum, Mark Hollander, Ellis Avery, Sharon Marcus, Alison Smith, Cindy Tolan, Rachel Sedor, Kit Rachlin, Remy Steiner, Trista Sordillo, Heart Montalbano, and Dorla McIntosh. And Robin Goldman, Aunt Mary, Sophie, and Sami. Thank you also to Claire Hertz, who saved me more than once.

And then to my immediate family: to my daughter, Christina, who survived foster care and taught me to be a parent, thank you for staying so true. And Lo, my beloved Lo: nobody knows better than you the sacrifice of shacking up with a book in progress. Thank you for your patience, your encouragement, and your unshakable faith in me and my work, and for sailing us through it all. I love you.

Index